SURA'S

TOU

TAMIL NADU

(The Wonderland of Towering Temples)

SURA MAPS

An imprint of Sura Books (Pvt) Ltd.

(An ISO 9001: 2000 Certified Company)

Chennai • Tirunelveli • Ernakulam
Palakkad • Thiruvananthapuram • Bengalooru

Price : ₹ 80.00

©PUBLISHERS

TOURIST GUIDE TO TAMILNADU

This Edition : December, 2011
Size : 1/8 Demy
Pages : 168
Code No. : K 1

Price : ₹80.00
ISBN : 81-7478-177-3

SURA MAPS

[An imprint of Sura Books (Pvt) Ltd.]

Head Office: 1620, 'J' Block, 16th Main Road, Anna Nagar,
Chennai - 600 040. Phones: 044-26162173, 26161099.

Branches :
- KAP Complex, I Floor, 20, Trivandrum Road,
  Tirunelveli - 627 002. Phone : 0462-4200557

- XXXII/2328, New Kalavath Road,
  Opp. to BSNL, Near Chennoth Glass, Palarivattom,
  Ernakulam - 682 025. Phones: 0484-3205797, 2535636

- Shop No. 7, Municipal Complex, Robinson Road,
  Palakkad - 678 001. Phone : 0491-2504270

- TC 28/2816, Sriniketan, Kuthiravattam Road, Chirakulam,
  Thiruvananthapuram - 695 001. Phone: 0471-4063864

- 3638/A, IVth Cross, Opp. to Malleswaram Railway Station,
  Gayathri Nagar, Back gate of Subramaniya Nagar,
  Bengalooru - 560 021. Phone: 080-23324950

Printed at G.T. Krishna Press, Chennai - 600 102 and Published by
V.V.K.Subburaj for Sura Maps [An imprint of Sura Books (Pvt) Ltd.]
1620, 'J' Block, 16th Main Road, Anna Nagar, Chennai - 600 040.
Phones: 26162173, 26161099. Fax: (91) 44-26162173.
e-mail: enquiry@surabooks.com; website: www.surabooks.com

12 11 2000

Contents

Tamil Nadu

General Information

Capital	:	Chennai
Districts	:	32
Language	:	Tamil
Area	:	1,30,058 Sq.km.
Population	:	6,24,05,679 (2001 census)
Density (People in Sq.Km.)	:	480 (2001)
Literacy	:	80.33%
Temperature	:	26° C to 43° C
Airports	:	Chennai, Coimbatore, Trichy, Madurai
Municipal Corporations	:	10
Municipalities	:	152
Town Panchayats	:	611
Village Panchayats	:	12,618
Sex Ratio (Male:Female)	:	100 : 98
Lok Sabha Seats	:	39
Rajya Sabha Seats	:	18
Legislative Assembly Seats	:	234

Tamil Nadu, a place of peace and serenity in the far south of the Indian sub-continent with its feet washed by the Indian Ocean, is a paradise for tourists. People, who come here, go back with an everlasting memory cherished forever of the land and its people. It is a land of magnificent temples that remain intact exposing the marvel and glory of the Dravidian culture, art, architecture and spiritual values. Not only temples but churches and mosques too declare the inborn secularism of the land. Numerous festivals and fairs, throughout the year add colour and mirth wherever you go. The ancient glory and modern hub of life mingle amazingly well, giving joy and soothing comforts. Long, sandy and sunny beaches abound to brace your health and enhance your happiness.

It is also a land of sanctuaries for birds and animals, forests, mountains, hill stations, natural sceneries and waterfalls - enough to forget everything and be immersed in enchanting beauty. Modern amusement theme parks have come up in various places to provide heart-throbbing and thrilling experience to young and old. The people are traditionally hospitable - the very meaning of a newcomer is 'guest' in the Tamil language - and friendly making you feel at home wherever you go. Comfortable and efficient public transport systems, air, road and rail links are available in almost all places. Good hotels, restaurants, lodges and guest-houses are available in all tourist centres affordable to your purse. From time immemorial, Tamil Nadu has been attracting travellers from abroad and the various accounts they have left are credible documents prized by the historians of this land. Tamil Nadu with such a hoary past in entertaining visitors and tourists welcomes you wholeheartedly. The moment you enter the land you enter a tourist paradise.

HISTORY

Tamil Nadu is considerably older than North India. North India and the Himalayan ranges appeared on the globe quite recently in terms of geological time scales. Even before that, Tamil Nadu existed as part of the continent that linked Africa and Australia together. It was called 'Lemuria' or 'Kumarik Kandam'. So, the origin of the first man should have taken place somewhere in this continent, and later, the race should have migrated to various parts of the world. The Tamils or the Dravidians are therefore one of the earliest races of the world. Prehistoric tools and weapons and burial sites have been discovered in various parts of Tamil Nadu.

THE SANGAM AGE

The earliest known period of organised life and history of the Tamils belong to the 'Sangam age'. Though the exact dates are disputed, it is pre-Aryan, non-Aryan and roughly goes back to 4000 B.C. The first, second and third Sangams flourished during this period and the Tamil poets of these 'Sangams' or Academies produced numerous literary works. Though most of them have been lost, a few anthologies are available in printed form. They throw considerable light on the everyday life of the people of those times and also reveal their culture, polity and social set-up. The country was ruled by three kingdoms called the Pandyas, Cheras and Cholas.

Rock-cut cave temples of Five Pandava Rathas of Pallava period carved in single granite boulder belonging to the 7th century AD are still a tourist attraction.

The 8th century Shore Temple built by Pallavas of Kanchipuram withstands even today the fury of sea tides and erratic weather conditions and not to say of miscreants. The temple has a Dravidian style Vimana of 60 ft. high. In the Sanctum, Vishnu - the preserver, is seen reclining on the ground.

The carvings represent Arjuna's penance praying to be blessed by Lord Siva to gain strength and vigour to win over his enemies. Some are of the opinion that it is Bagirath's penance to bring the celestial Ganges to the earth. However, the scenes in the rock are a superb poetry in sculpture which no visitor can miss.

The Chera Kingdom is the modern Kerala state. The Pandyas ruled the south and the Cholas the north. The Sangam Age is supposed to be the Golden Age of Tamils.

Gangaikondacholapuram Temple built by the Chola emperor Rajendra (1012-1044 AD) is a Siva temple. The rulers of many kingdoms near the Ganges (Ganga in Tamil) were won over by him. They were made to bring Ganga waters to be emptied into a huge tank near the temple. Hence the name 'Gangaikondacholapuram.'

Darasuram Temple built by Raja Raja II (1146-72 AD) was dedicated to Iravatheeswara. The reliefs sculptured in the basement walls depict the 63 Saivaite saints and the episodes in their lives.

Brahadeeswara Temple, Thanjavur represents the perfect example of Dravidian art and architecture. Begun in 1003 AD and completed in 1010 AD by Raja Raja Chola, the great King of Tanjore, the gopuram rises to a height of 208 ft. with 14 tiers. Though the temple is full of Saivaite iconography, there are Vaishnavaite and Buddhist themes also.

POST-SANGAM AGE

After the Sangam age, there is a dark period and the land comes under the domination of an alien race called the 'Kalabras'. There was chaos and confusion and instability with the result we get little evidence of the happenings of this period. This period was followed by the Pallavas who ruled the country for over two centuries (600 AD to 800 AD). Though the Pallavas were also alien, there was stability, peace prevailed and a lot of constructive works followed. Kanchipuram was their headquarters and the Pallavas were patrons of art, architecture and literature. The advent of rock temples by the Pallavas is a break-through in the construction of temples which were hitherto been built with wood, bricks and mud. Even today, these rock-cut temples can be seen in their pristine beauty in various places.

The Pallava period was followed by the later Cholas. They ruled the

Gingee Fort was bastion of Chola Kings during 9th century AD. Later Vijayanagara Kings fortified and made it impregnable. This fort is built on 7 hills – the most important being Krishnagiri, Chandragiri and Rajagiri.

Ekambareswara Temple, Kanchipuram, is the largest Siva Temple spread over 9 acres. Its huge gopuram (192 ft. high) and its massive walls were constructed by Krishnadeva Raya in 1509.

Ten giant gopuram towers beckon the faithful to worship at the Meenakshi Temple in Madurai, one of Hinduism's busiest centres. Madurai is considered the heart of Tamil country. Goddess Meenakshi is the presiding deity with her consort Lord Sundareswarar. Lord Nataraja dances in Velliambalam, the dance hall here, in a different style, raising his right leg up instead of left.

Mariamman Teppakulam, Vandiyur, Madurai, was built by Thirumalai Naicker. The tank is a natural evolution when earth was digged out to make bricks to construct Thirumalai Naicker Mahal. The tank is almost a square with 1000 ft. long and 950 ft. wide.

Thirumalai Naicker Mahal, Madurai, constructed in Indo-Saracenic style was the palace of Thirumalai Naicker. Its gigantic granite pillars cased in mortar and imposing arches are of engineering marvel and fine example of the architectural style of Naicker dynasty.

country from 9th century A.D. to 13th century A.D. They gave a clean administration and people were free from worries. They were great conquerors and builders of great temples. Art, architecture, literature and spiritualism flourished during the Chola reign. The art of metal casting and bronze icons were a speciality of this period. The amazing product is the icon of the cosmic dancer 'Nataraja' - the presiding deity of Chidambaram Temple.

The Cholas were overthrown by the later Pandyas for a brief period in the early 14th century. During this period, the Khiljis invaded the south and the Pandya capital was sacked and a sultanate was formed which was destroyed by the rise of the

Hindu Vijayanagar empire. The Vijayanagar empire prevented the spread of the Muslim rule south of river Thungabadra and thus was able to preserve temples and deities from being razed by the iconoclastic frenzy of the Mohammedans.

The Vijayanagar kings and their governors renovated most of the temples damaged by the earlier Muslim invaders. The main feature of their temple works was the erecting of 'Raja Gopuram' or the tall temple towers at the threshold of the temples. As a result of their supremacy, the Nayak dynasty adorned the thrones

Kailashnatha Temple, Kanchipuram, was built by Rajasimha Pallava in the late 7th century AD. The front was added by Mahendra Varma Pallavan later on. It is a fine piece of early Dravidian architecture and we can say, the only piece of the original Pallava temple architecture.

of Madurai, Thanjavur and Tiruchi. Their contribution to temple architecture was considerable and a valuable addition to those already done by the Pallavas, Cholas and the Pandyas. The Nayaks continued long after the fall of the Vijayanagar empire. The rise of the Marathas had its impact on Tamil Nadu and there was Maratha rule for a brief period in Thanjavur and its neighbourhood. After this, Tamil Nadu was under the muslim rule of the Nawab of Arcot. The advent of the Europeans and their struggle for supremacy resulted in the founding of the British empire. The

first presidency established by them was Madras i.e. Tamil Nadu. The British rule ended with India attaining its freedom on 15th August 1947.

During the Pallava period Buddhism, Jainism, Vaishnavism and Saivism had ardent following. Then came Islam and Christianity. Thus, a secular seed of tolerance was sown in

The Arunachaleswarar Temple of Tiruvannamalai is dedicated to Jothi lingam (God incarnate of fire). The temple was constructed and extended by the Cholas, Vijayanagar Kings, Hoysalas and the Nayaks. The underground lingam where sage Ramana Maharishi did penance is a great attraction.

Tamil Nadu and places of worships of all of them flourished. Today, one can find monuments and temples of all sorts throughout Tamil Nadu.

TEMPLES AND DEITIES

There are over 30,000 temples in Tamil Nadu. "Don't live in a place where there is no temple" is the motto of the people of Tamil Nadu. Therefore, you cannot find a hamlet, a village, a town or a city here without a temple. Each place and temple has its own presiding deities. Almost all the temples have similar features - the gopuram or the Portal Tower from all four directions, the vimanam or the Tower over the sanctum sanctorum, spacious halls and corridors. Besides a place of worship, the temple also serves as a community centre. All activities like education, fine arts, functions, marriages, festivals, etc. were performed, and they served

Swamimalai is also an abode of Lord Muruga. Lying 6 kms west of Kumbakonam, the temple has 60 steps to represent the cycle of Sixty Tamil Years. Another abode of Lord Muruga at Tiruttani in Thiruvallur district has 365 steps to represent the days in a year. Swamimalai is the ideal place for craftsmen who shape the metal of bronze into idols.

The Srirangam temple situated on an island formed between Cauvery and Kollidam rivers is the abode of Lord Ranganatha (Vishnu) who is reclining on Adhisesha (Serpent) majestically. The sanctum is surrounded by 7 large enclosures and 21 majestic gopurams. Almost all the Kings who ruled Tamilnadu, spent lavishly to enrich the grandeur of the shrine.

as hospital, dharmasala, storehouse and during emergencies and wars it also served as a bastion. The Marathas practically utilised the temples at Thiruvannamalai and Chidambaram as their barracks for a prolonged period.

The main deity of the Tamils is Lord Muruga who is called 'Seyon' in Tamil literature and is the God of hills. The God of forests is called 'Mayon' or Vishnu, Siva is worshipped in the form of 'Lingam'. 'Kottravai' or 'Kali' is the Goddess of 'Palai' or arid lands. Indra is the God of fertile lands and Varuna is the God of rain. Only these deities were worshipped in the Sangam period. Vinayaga or 'Pillaiyar' who is the most worshipped God nowadays, is a later addition brought to Tamil Nadu by Mahendra Varman, the Pallava king, from Badami. There are no temples at present for Indra and Varuna. Besides, there are umpteen number of lesser deities and local 'devathas'. Arupadai Veedu of Lord Muruga - Thiruttani, Swamimalai, Palani, Thiruparamkundram, Pazhamudirsolai and Thiruchendur and the Pancha Bootha Sthalam or the five exclusive centres of worship of Lord Siva, representing the five elements of Lord Siva, Chidambaram (sky), Thiruvanaik- kaval (water), Thiruvannamalai (fire), Kanchipuram (earth) and Kalahasti (air) now in Andhra Pradesh, are famous pilgrimage centres of the Saivaites. The Vaishnavaites have 108 sacred abodes of Vishnu most of which are located in various places like Kanchipuram, Madurai, Srirangam etc. The consorts of Vishnu, Sridevi and Bhoodevi, Lakshmi and the consorts of Siva, Parvathi, Kamatchi, Abhirami, Meenakshi also have separate temples in various places. The temples of Kali are varied like Durgai Amman, Mariamman, Angalamman etc. They are found all over Tamil Nadu.

Besides these Hindu deities, churches of Virgin Mary, Shrine Velankanni, St. Antony have large following in Tamil Nadu. People of all religions and sects visit them.

Muslim durgahs at Nagore, Chennai, Madurai etc., are also worshipped and visited by people of all sects and religions. Wherever and whenever there are festivals in these places of worship, people throng without any distinction of their native religion or faith - a unique feature in Tamil Nadu manifesting the religious tolerance of the Tamils.

GEOGRAPHICAL FEATURES

Tamil Nadu is located in the Northern hemisphere in the torrid zone between 8° and 13° N. latitude and between 78° and 80° E. longitude. It is bounded by the states of Karnataka and Andhra Pradesh in the north and Kerala in the west. The southern tip is in the Indian Ocean and the long eastern coast is

Udagamandalam (Ooty) lake is an artificial one created by Sullivans. Boating is the privilege of all with a fee but fishing can be done only with the permission obtained from Assistant Director of Fisheries.

High in Tamil Nadu's Nilgiri Hills (Blue Hills), women pluck tea leaves from cultivated bushes on a tea plantation. Nilgiri-grown tea is considered to be one of the world's finest. One must visit Kodanadu viewpoint to have breathtaking view of the river Moyar.

Udagamandalam (Ooty) is connected to Mettupalayam by narrow gauge rail track of 89 kms. Though the train mainly carries railway employees, the tourist must travel atleast once to have the panoramic view of Ooty hills and feel the richness of fauna and flora.

lapped by the Bay of Bengal. Point Calimere forms the easternmost tip and the Mudumalai wildlife sanctuary is the westernmost tip. The northern extreme touches lake Pulicat. The southernmost tip is Cape Comorin or Kanyakumari.

Tamil Nadu, the 11th largest state in India has a population over 6 crores and occupies an area of 130,058 sq. kms. The union territory of Pondicherry is a tiny pocket within the boundaries of Tamil Nadu near Cuddalore district; Karaikal, a little away from Pondicherry is near Nagapattinam district.

The ancient Tamils divided the land into 5 major physiographic parts as follows: Kurinji - mountainous region, Mullai - forest region, Marudham - the fertile plains, Neidhal - the coastal region and Palai - the arid region.

The Western ghats and the Eastern ghats meet in the Nilgris of Tamil Nadu. The hill stations of Tamil Nadu, Ooty, Kodaikanal, Kothagiri and Yercaud are situated in this region. Though the Eastern ghats is broken and appears to be a residual mountain, the Western ghats stretches along almost as an unbroken chain except for a 25 km gap at Palakkadu and a still

Mudumalai Sanctuary, is the most important in South India. It borders with Bandipur National Park in Karnataka and Wyanad sanctuary in Kerala. The nights of April are lit by millions of glow-worms which look like a dream world of illuminated paradise.

lesser gap in Shencottah. These gaps are the entry points to the state of Kerala.

Unlike the Eastern ghats, the Western ghats receive abundant rain and are full of evergreen forests and the valleys of Cumbum and Pollachi besides having picturesque sceneries contain tea, coffee and spice plantations. The upper reaches of the Eastern ghats are called the Shervaroys famous for their fruit gardens and coffee plantations. Yercaud is situated in this region.

Tamil Nadu has a rich variety of flora and fauna. Indira Gandhi wildlife sanctuary in Anaimalai and Mudumalai wildlife sanctuary are situated in the Eastern ghats. Elephants, tigers, bisons and a variety of monkeys and deer roam about freely in them. Over 3000 plant species are also found there. The most important of them is the Kurinji plant which blooms once in 12 years. The name Kurinji to the hilly region is derived from this flower. Various medicinal herbs are also found in Palani hills and Courtallam. Palmyrah groves are abundant in Tirunelveli district which is the major source of a plethora of cottage industries. Rubber plantations abound in Kanyakumari district and sandal trees are grown in Javvadu hills of the eastern ghats near Vellore.

The rivers of Tamil Nadu are not perennial and one could only see a sandy dry river bed in summer. The Cauvery is the longest and most important river originating in Coorg in the state of Karnataka. Its water is utilised for cultivation in the deltaic region of Thanjavur and Nagapattinam districts. The other rivers are the Palar, Pennar, Vaigai, Tamiraparani which are flooded during the rainy season.

The only arid region or Palai is found in Tirunelveli district. It is called *Theri* by the natives. Tamil Nadu has a long coastal line, about 912 km which is named coromandal coast or *cholamandalak karai* in the northern half and the southern coast is the pearl fisheries coast. Mylapore, Poompuhar, Mamallapuram and Kayalpattinam were the ancient seaports along the coromandal coast. Maritime trade flourished between these ports and the ports of Rome, Greece and the East Indies. Mangrove forests found at Pichavaram near Chidambaram, Pulicat lake and Vedanthangal are important bird sanctuaries.

CLIMATE

As Tamil Nadu falls in the torrid zone, the climate is tropical and there is little difference between the summer and winter. April, May and June are the hottest months during which time the mercury may soar above 40° C. Near coastal regions, the climate is warm and humid and one cannot avoid perspiring. But, sea breeze sets in in the afternoon making the evenings and nights cooler. A mild winter falls between December and February, the most ideal time to visit Tamil Nadu. The weather is then pleasantly cool with no perspiration. The rainy season is marked by the onset of the north-east monsoon between mid-September and mid-December. Cyclonic storms occur during this time due to bay depression.

CLOTHING

Summer garments and cottons are ideal throughout the year if you do not visit hill stations where mild woollen clothes may be needed during summer and heavy woollen clothes during winter. Raincoats and umbrellas will come in handy during the monsoon i.e. mid-September to mid-December.

FOREIGN TOURISTS

Customs - A green channel is available for tourists without any dutiable or contraband articles. High value articles have to be entered on tourist baggage i.e. export form.

Passport, visa: Citizens of all nations barring Nepal and Bhutan and South Africans of Indian origin require valid passports and visas.

INDIAN CURRENCY

The hundred paise worth rupee is the Indian currency. The deno-mination of coins comes in 25 and 50 paise and 1, 2 and 5 rupees. Currency notes are available in denominations of 5,10,20, 50,100 and 500 rupees.

Foreign currency notes and traveller's cheques brought by the tourists should be entered in the currency declaration form issued to tourists on arrival by airport officials.

FESTIVALS OF TAMIL NADU

Tamil Nadu is a land of festivals. Umpteen festivals are observed throughout the year and no fortnight ever passes without a festival. Most of them are associated with religion and temples. People celebrate them with gay and enthusiasm. A brief narration of a few festivals are given so that

tourists can enjoy them realizing their significance. The tourism department too arranges festivals periodically so that the visiting guests may enjoy them and understand the cultural and spiritual values embedded in them.

January

Pongal

This is the most important of all festivals to the people of Tamil Nadu. It is often called as **"Tamilar Thirunal"** or the Prosperity Day of the Tamils. It comes in the middle of January. It celebrates the arrival of fresh harvest and everyone appears in new garments with a beaming smile greeting each other on this day. New earthen pot is put on a hearth in a central place in a open corridor and newly harvested rice and milk are cooked. As the milk boils over, people shout in chorus **"Pongalo Pongal! Pongalo Pongal!!"**. Tamil Nadu Government has declared 1st 'Thai' as the Tamil New Year day and a legislation to this effect was enacted on 01.02.2008. Therefore, the people of Tamil Nadu now celebrate Pongal and Tamil New Year day on 1st 'Thai' with redoubled joy. Pongal literally means boiling. The preceding day of Pongal is called **'Bhogi'**. It means Bogam or enjoyment and was originally devoted to Indra who is the Bogi or supreme enjoyer. Nowadays, old unwanted things are heaped on the middle of the road and a bonfire is made. Children beat hand drums and go round the roads beating the drums and shouting 'Bhogi Bhogi!'.

It is a three-day festival. The second day is called **Mattu Pongal**. Bullocks and cows are taken care of on this day and they are worshipped and given nourishing food called **'Sarkarai Pongal'**. **Poet-Saint Thiruvalluvar Day** is also celebrated on the 15th of January. The third day is called 'Kanru Pongal' or Calf Pongal. On that day the calves are fed. It is also called **'Kanum Pongal!'**. 'Kanum' means seeing and people visit elders or relatives and friends and seek their blessings.

Jalli Kattu (Manjuvirattu)

On the second day of the Pongal i.e. on Mattu Pongal day, Jalli Kattu or Manjuvirattu takes place in almost all villages. Youths come forward to tame the bull as they come ferociously rushing on them. It is a traditional, spine-chilling fight. The winner gets the prize money tied on the horns. Alanganallur near Madurai is famous for this sport.

Republic Day

The Republic Day falls on 26th January. It is a national festival. Spectacular march past, cultural and gay pageantry mark the celebrations in the state capital and the capitals of the districts.

Trade Fair - Chennai

During January, Trade Fair is conducted at Island Grounds in Chennai by the Tamil Nadu Tourism Development Corporation. All government departments and public sector enterprises take part in it. Every day folk dances and dramas are conducted. It presents a bird's eye view of Tamil Nadu. All the places of tourist interest and a wealth of information about the progress of Tamil Nadu besides cultural shows and food fairs form part of the fair. The fair lasts for nearly 3 months.

Dance Festivals - Mamallapuram

This festival conducted by the Department of Tourism is generally held at Mamallapuram where monolithic rock sculptures of the Pallava kings are built on the shore. The dances are held on an open-air stage near these sculptures. A spectacular dance festival in a beautiful surrounding that brings everlasting joy to the onlookers. Bharatha Natyam - the classical dance of Tamil Nadu, Kuchipudi - similar dance of Andhra Pradesh, Kathakali of Kerala and Odissi the dance of Orissa are performed by renowned artistes. Folk dances also form part of the festivals. Mamallapuram is just 58 km. south of Chennai, capital of Tamil Nadu.

February, March & April

Sivarathri

A festival observed in all Siva temples and Saivaite families. Special poojas and chanting of 'Siva Siva' are done throughout the night. Devotees observe fasting and remain awake throughout the night. Special abhishekam or holy anointing and ablution of Lingams are done from midnight.

Chitthirai Festival: Brahmothsavam or Chitthirai festival is the chief festival celebrated in all temples for 10 days. Every day 'urchavar' or the processional deity is carried in procession on different *vahanas* like horse, bull, swan, lion, sun, moon etc. The one at Madurai is indeed spectacular with Lord Vishnu landing on a golden horse for His sister Meenakshi's marriage. One major festival day of the 10 days is the 'Arubathumoovar Festival' day on which day all 63 Saivaite saints are taken in procession along with Lord Siva. The one at Kapaliswarar temple, Chennai, is very famous. The 63 bronze idols of the 'Nayanmars' or Saivaite saints are taken in procession - a magnificent sight. Lakhs of people throng during these festivals.

Sri Rama Navami

It is celebrated in all Vishnu temples and at homes. It is the birthday of Rama, one of the Avatars of Vishnu. The Ramayanam is recited on this day.

Good Friday

The holy day of the Christians is observed throughout Tamil Nadu. Churches all over Tamil Nadu would conduct special masses on this day.

May, June & July

Summer Festival

The summer festival is celebrated in hill stations like Ooty, Kodaikanal, Yercaud etc. It is mainly a tourist festival. It is called 'Kodai Vizha'. Boat races, flower and fruit shows, are arranged. Cultural programmes are conducted. Trekking in hill stations are also done - a unique thrilling experience. There are competitions of flower arrangements, Rangoli and vegetable and fruit carving - an enticing feast to the eyes.

August, September

Adi Perukku

It is the eighteenth day of the Tamil month *Adi*, on which most of the rivers will be in spate after rains. People go to the river banks and worship the river goddess and float their offerings on river. They also carry different varieties of cooked rice and eat them on the banks and spend their time merrily.

Independence Day

15th August is the day on which India won Independence. It is a national festival. The National Flag is hoisted every year on this day. Processions and meetings are held. Flag hoisting ceremony at Fort St. George, Chennai and cultural pageantry mark the occasion. It is a public holiday and public buildings are illuminated colourfully on this day.

Krishna Jayanthi

It is the birthday of Lord Krishna. It is celebrated in all Vaishnavite Temples and at homes. People prepare different delicacies and offer them to Lord Krishna. Balls of butter are also offered.

Vinayaka Chathurthi

The birthday of Lord Vinayaka or the elephant-headed god. It is celebrated in all homes as well as in all Saivite temples and temples of Lord Vinayaka. The one celebrated at Pillaiyarpatti shrine of Lord Vinayaka is very famous. A gigantic *'Modhaga'* or *'Kolukkattai'* using about 80 kilos of rice, jaggery, coconut and dhall is prepared. It is baked for 3 days and offered to the deity. Lakhs of people from all over Tamil Nadu throng there on that day. Pillaiyarpatti is near Karaikudi about 500 km. from Chennai.

In all cities and district headquarters, giant Vinayaka statues ranging from 10 feet height to 32 feet are erected in public places. On the last day which varies from the 3rd day to the 10th day, big processions are held and the image is immersed in the sea, lake or nearby rivers. The procession will be colourful with various folk dances, nadhaswaram etc. performed enroute. In houses, clay image of Vinayaka is worshipped and immersed into wells, tanks or ponds the next day. The image is invariably adorned with a colourful umbrella called *'Pillaiyar Kudai'*.

September & October

Navarathri

Festival of nine nights: 'Navam' means nine and 'rathri' means night. It is the festival of Goddesses Durga, Lakshmi and Saraswathi. The first 3 days are devoted to Durga or Parvathi, the goddess of valour. The next 3 days are devoted to Lakshmi or goddess of wealth and the last 3 days are devoted to Saraswathi, the goddess of learning. On the ninth day, a pooja for

Saraswathi is performed in a traditional way by piling up books in an orderly way. This day is called 'Ayudha Pooja' - on this day all the machines, tools, instruments and vehicles are cleaned and arranged in order and worshipped. The vehicles are adorned with flowers and plantain saplings. This festival is also known as **Dussehra**. It is also called Durga Pooja. The next day is called 'Vijayadasami' or the day of victory.

During this period, most of the Hindus celebrate Kolu festival and even in temples Durga or the main female deity is specially decorated in various ways and kept in the main hall for worship. In the houses, dolls are arranged on steps numbering 3, 5, 7, 9 or 11 and the hall is decorated with festoons. Dolls of different deities and ordinary life scenes and of a secular nature are also erected. Every day visitors are invited and *Prasadam* is also given. The origin of this festival is traced to the Vijayanagar period. Doll exhibitions and sales are also arranged during this time. Especially the ones at Khadi Bhavan and Kuralagam in Chennai are feast to the eyes. People throng in large number to these places to see and enjoy them and also to purchase the dolls, the prices of which range from Re.1/- to Rs.5,000/-. The Ramakrishna Mutt at Mylapore celebrates the Durga Pooja during these ten days, as it celebrates the festivals of all religions and faiths, and on the final day a big image of Kali is taken in procession and immersed in the sea. These ten gay days are full of visitors, visitings and feasts. Children wear fancy dresses. The temples overflow with devotees.

Shrine Velankanni Festival

The renowned church of Shrine Velankanni near Nagapattinam has wondrous legends. The 16th century ship-wrecked Portuguese sailors had built this shrine in gratitude for saving and guiding them to the shore during a severe cyclone. Thousands of people visit the place during the festival, clad in orange robes to the sacred location where the ship landed. The Virgin Mary Church is the *'Courdes of the East'* and is believed to have miraculous power of healing. This festival attracts peoples of all religions: Hindus, Muslims and of course Christians - it is rather a secular gathering.

Kanthuri Festival

This too could be said to be of a secular nature since people of all faiths flock to the shrine of saint Quadirwali believed to be doing good to all. One of the descendants of the saint is chosen as the spiritual leader or 'peer' and honoured with offerings. The tenth day is most important. On that day, the tomb of the saint is anointed with sandal paste and later it is distributed to one and all. This holy paste is believed to possess healing powers as it is considered a remedy for all ills. The festival is celebrated at Nagore durgah near Nagapattinam.

Mahamagam Festival

This festival comes once in 12 years. This period is called 'Mamangam' in Tamil. This occurs once in 12 years when planet Jupiter enters the constellation of Leo. It is believed that all the holy rivers of India bathe in the sacred tank here at Kumbakonam on this holy day to wash away their sins - accrued from the devotees who bathe in them. The Mahamagam tank is situated in the temple city of Kumbakonam. The legend has it that a few drops of divine nectar from the 'Kumba' (pot of nectar) has fallen into this tank. Lakhs of people take a holy bath on this day. The unique feature is that residents of the whole city become hosts to the visitors. Lord Siva called *Adhi Kumbeswara* is worshipped here. Kumbakonam derives its name from this 'Kumba' or pot.

October - November - December

Deepavali

This is the most important festival that brings joy to both the rich and the poor. This is also called *'Naraka Chathurdasi'*, on which day the fearsome giant Narakasura was killed by Lord Krishna. According to his last wishes his death day is celebrated with festivity. People take oil bath in the early hours of the day, called *"Ganga Snanam"* or holy dip in the Ganges, wear new clothes, fire crackers and eat sweets. The following new moon day is observed as "Kethara Gowri Viratham" and ladies observe this for the longevity of their husbands. In North India, it is observed as *Ramlila* on which day great fireworks are a feast to the eyes; they mark the defeat of Ravan by Sri Rama. It is said that it is a day of triumph of the good over the evil. In the North, lamps are also lit in a row in the houses. 'Deepam' means lamp and 'Avali' means row. On this day, sweets are prepared and distributed. People greet each other with a traditional question *"Ganga Snanam Aachcha?"* which means 'Have you finished your holy Ganges bath". People visit temples in large numbers on this day.

Vaikunta Ekadasi

This festival is a Vaishnavite festival and it is believed that the gates of Paradise are thrown open on that day. In all Vishnu temples, a decorative gate is erected called *'Vaikuntha Vasal'* or the threshold of paradise. Thousands of people come to pass through the threshold of paradise. Bhajans are held and the day is a fasting day. During the night most people stay awake and end their fast with a feast the next morning. The Srirangam temple on the island of Srirangam near Tiruchirappalli and the Parthasarathi temple built by the Pallavas at Triplicane in the city of Chennai attract lakhs of people. It is an interesting sight to see Bhajan groups called 'Bhajanai Koshti' singing the names of Lord Vishnu in high pitch and dancing in a trance around the temple.

Arudra Darshan or Thiruvadhirai Festival

It is a festival observed by Saivaites or the devotees of Siva. The cosmic dancer Lord Siva gives darshan on this day. It is observed in all Siva temples. Very early in the morning special ablutions are done to the dancing idol of Siva and He is taken in a procession. On this day in the houses, people prepare a sweet called *'Kali'* a mixed vegetable dish called 'Koottu' and offer it to the deity and eat and distribute. Arudra Darshan is very famous in the Nataraja temple at Chidambaram.

Natyanjali Festival

It is a dance festival at the Nataraja temple at Chidambaram. It is a homage paid by all the dancers to the cosmic dancer, Lord Nataraja. It is celebrated near the thousand-pillared hall of the temple where 108 dancing poses of Lord Siva are depicted. The poses are from Tamil Nadu's classical dance Bharatha Natyam. Dancers all over India come to pay their tribute by performing dances. A colourful and enchanting programme of dances like Bharatha Natyam, Kuchipudi, Kathakali, Odissi and Kathak are performed.

Karthigai Deepam

It is one of the most ancient festivals of Tamil Nadu. We have references to this festival in Sangam literature. It is the festival of lights of Tamil Nadu. Deepam means light. Rows of earthen lamps are lighted in front of houses in the evening. Traditional snacks called *Appam, Pori* and *Adai* are prepared and offered to deities. The festival is celebrated in all Siva temples. The one at Thiruvannamalai temple is most famous. It is called *Annamalayar Deepam*. A big lamp on the rocky top of the mountain is lit. A big wick is prepared and 100 litres of ghee is poured and the lamp is lighted. It glows throughout the night. Despite heavy downpours, the light will be burning. Lakhs of devotees gather for this festival from all over India. Thiruvannamalai is one of the Pancha Bootha Sthala or five element places and the element represented here is the fire. A big bonfire is made in front of temples. In houses, crackers are fired. This festival marks the end of the rainy season in Tamil Nadu.

Saaral Vizha

This is a unique festival of recent origin. It is celebrated in Kuttalam where there is a number of waterfalls. During the season, water will be abundant in them and thousands of people gather there to bathe in them. The water has healing powers as it passes through various medicinal herbs before the fall. Kuttalam is near Tenkasi in Tirunelveli district. The Saaral Vizha is a unique festival which invigorates our body. The water pours on us like thousand slaps and relieves our pains and aches and makes us fresh. Proper safety arrangements are made and there are separate places for men and women.

Kavadi Festival

This is a religious festival. Kavadi is a flower-decked decoration carried on the shoulders. There are different types of Kavadies called Pal (milk) kavadi, Panneer (rose water) kavadi, Pushpa (flower) kavadi, Mayil (peacock feather) kavadi etc. Devotees of Lord Muruga dancing in a divine trance to the rhythm of beating drums carry this on their shoulders and climb the mountain. The kavadi festival is very famous in Palani, Tiruthani and Tiruchendur and the other shrines of the Arupadai Veedu or the six abodes of Lord Muruga which are mentioned earlier under the sub-heading Temples and Deities.

Music Festival

The music festival is celebrated every year in the capital city, Chennai. During December, all the 'Sabhas' or Music clubs arrange for this. The Music Academy, Annamalai Mandram, Narada Gana Sabha, Indian Fine Arts Society and other sabhas arrange for this festival in various places. At Kalakshetra, a dance festival is also conducted during this time. It is a festival for lovers of music. Research scholars and renowned musicians render vocal and instrumental recitals in various sabhas from the afternoon till late in the night. It is a festival that reflects the culture of Tamil Nadu. Music lovers from all over the world participate in it.

Besides, all the Muslim festivals like Ramzan, Bakrid, Milad-un-Nabi etc. and all the Christian festivals like the New Year Day, Ash Wednesday, Good Friday, Christmas etc. are also celebrated in Tamil Nadu. Thus, Tamil Nadu abounds with national, secular and religious festivals of all sorts - and it is apt to call it 'a land of colourful festivals and unbiased gaiety'.

LIP-SMACKING CULINARY OF TAMIL NADU

From time immemorial Tamil Nadu is noted for entertaining the guests with sumptuous feasts. It can provide a wide variety of lip-smacking, tasty, delicious food both vegetarian and non-vegetarian to visitors. With plenty of vegetables in its blend. Tamil Nadu provides a healthy fibrous food. Grams, lentils, rice, greens and vegetables with spices add aroma and taste to the food.

Breakfast

It is known as 'Kaalai Chitrundi' in Tamil. The main items of the breakfast are:

1. Rice idlies (steamed rice and orid dhal battered into fluffy cakes), 2. Dosai (A pancake of the same batter fried crisp in a pan), 3. Vadai (deep fried doughnuts of a batter of lentils), 4. Pongal (cooked rice with lentils and flavoured with ghee, pepper, cumin seeds, cashewnuts, ginger bits and curry leaves), 5.Uppuma or Kitchedi (cooked sooji or semolina with oil, mustard, cumin seeds and lentils), 6. Idiappam (steamed rice noodles), 7. Appam (a similar preparation like Dosai but baked). Side dishes - all these items are eaten with Coconut Chutney, Sambar (seasoned lentil broth), and chilli powder (a powder mix of various dried lentils, chilly and salt with oil poured on it). Finally, coffee is served.

Lunch or Meals

This consists of cooked rice, dhall, ghee, vegetable side dishes, Sambar and Rasam (pepper water), curd, pickles and pappads or appalam. A sweet dish, payasam or kheer, is also served. In the case of non-vegetarian, various non-vegetarian side dishes of mutton, chicken, egg, prawn, crab, fish etc. are available.

Tamil Nadu dishes are mildly hot and aromatic and tasty.

Chettinadu cuisine

It is a speciality of Tamil Nadu both vegetarian and non-vegetarian and suitable to those who like hot and spicy stuff.

Besides, all varieties of other food items are available in hotels. In Star hotels, Continental, Chinese and Indian dishes are available.

Tamil Nadu is famous for its *filter coffee*. The coffee seeds are roasted and ground. The powder is put in a filter and boiling water poured over it. In about 15 minutes, the coffee decoction is collected in the lower container of the filter. It is taken and added to milk with sugar and served hot. The coffee aroma and its taste gives a new pep to those who drink it.

Now we shall pass on to the places of tourist importance in Tamil Nadu. This tourist guide is intended to give comprehensive details of places, their location, how to reach them, what to see there, what to buy and other useful tips to tourists with contact telephone numbers of public utility and emergency services. We shall begin with the state capital - Chennai.

Chennai
(Madras City)

Chennai hitherto known as the city of Madras is the capital of Tamil Nadu and the fourth largest city of India. It is the capital of Tamil Nadu and the gateway to the south. Francis Day and Cogan, the then East India Company officials who obtained a grant from the local chief Iyappa Nayak on August 1639 to build a factory were the founding fathers of the city. Various records showed the origin of the name and definitely the name Madras existed even before the

Englishmen landed there. It was then called 'Madras Patnam'. A fort was built by the Englishmen and called Fort St. George as portions of it were completed on St. George's Day, the patron saint of England. After the fort was built, Iyappa Nayak insisted that the new settlement be named Chennappatnam after his father Chennappa Nayak. Thus the name 'Chennappatnam' came into being. In due course, Madras became the English name and Chennai the native name. Chennai lies on the 13° N. Latitude and 80° E. Longitude on a 17 km. stretch of the Coromandel coast and is virtually trisected by Adyar and Cooum rivers and the Buckingham canal. The present population is over 42 lakhs. Though its beginnings were a humble hamlet, it has now grown into a cosmopolitan metropolis by taking up the adjoining villages like Thiruvallikeni, Mylapore, Thiru-vanmiyur etc. which are thousands of years older than the recent city of just 360 years. Thus a tiny hamlet hardly a sq.km. area has now become a city of 174 sq.km. It is still an expanding city and one cannot rule out its scope of further extension in north, south and west as the Bay of Bengal grudges its expansion to the east.

Chennai presents a distinctive variation to North India in music, dance, art forms, food, language, people, habits, customs and costumes. Besides modern development in industries and commerce, its traditions and conventions still continue side by side making life wonderfully charming. One can see a harmonious blend of the old and the modern in all things - conventional vegetarian fare to fast foods, traditional nine yard sarees to the latest fashion designs, ancient temples to modern multi-storeyed buildings, Indo-Saracenic and Victorian architecture to modern, classical music and dance to ultra modern pop music and disco dances. It is, in short, a kaleidoscope of harmony in contrast.

Unlike most other modern cities with a smoky sky, Chennai is a modern city with a clear sky, long sandy beaches, parks, landmarks of history, rivers, temples, churches, mosques, dance and drama theatres, cinema houses, star hotels, lodges and other tourist infrastructural facilities that make a more convenient entry point and to initiate your tour of the land of the Tamils and South India.

How to get there?

Chennai has road, rail and air links to all parts of India and the world and easily accessible from anywhere under the sun. The international airport here, is connected by several

LEGEND	
⤫	Airlines
✈	Airport
🏛	Bank
☰	Beach
ʔ	Bird Sanctuary
🚌	Bus Stand
✛	Church
🏫	Educational Institution
🍽	Hotel / Restaurant
🏢	Government Office
✚	Hospital
🕌	Mosque
◉	Miscellaneous
☆	Places of Interest
▤	Police Station
✉	Post Office
🛍	Shopping
⛟	Taxi Centre
🛕	Temple

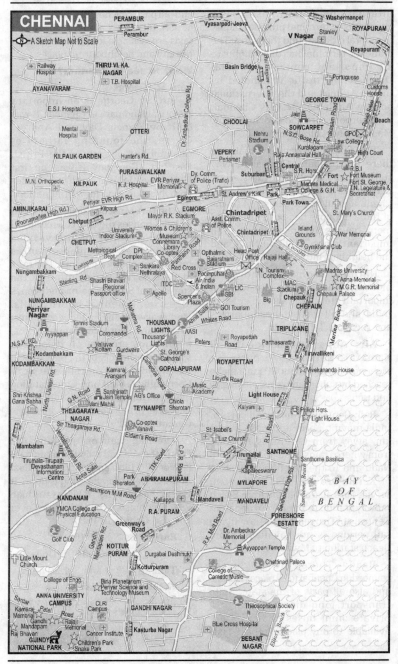

international airlines. The international terminal provides flights to several cities around the world. The domestic terminal has daily flights to all important centres in India. Domestic air traffic is handled by Indian Airlines and the international one by Air India. Besides Chennai, local airports are located in Trichy, Madurai and Coimbatore.

Two major railway terminals are there in Chennai - Central railway station and Egmore railway station. Central has broad gauge and connects Chennai to all major cities and towns of India. Egmore has both broad and metre gauges and links Chennai to all important places of Tamil Nadu and the neighbouring state of Kerala.

National highways and state highways connect the city with all important state capitals and cities of India and all district headquarters and towns of Tamil Nadu.

Air: Anna International and Kamaraj National Airports at Meenambakkam about 20 km. can be reached by suburban trains, city buses and taxis.

Rail: Central – trains to all parts of India moving north and west. Just a km. away from Central is Egmore, from where trains to all parts of Tamil Nadu and to the neighbouring state of Kerala are available. Suburban services are also available from Beach railway station to Tambaram and from Central to Tiruvellore. A new flying rail service is now available from Beach station to Mylapore.

Road: There are highways connecting Chennai to all places in India and also all parts of the state. State transport long distance coaches, private omni buses and taxis are available to any place. Prepaid taxis and airport coaches are available at airport. City buses, auto-rickshaws and taxis are available for travelling within the city and neighbouring places.

What to see in Chennai?

Fort St. George

Fort St. George is an important historical landmark in Chennai. It was built by Francis Day and Andrew Cogan, the founding fathers of Chennai and officials of the British East India Company. It was the first British settlement and was under French occupation for a brief period.

The Fort Museum formally opened in 1948 houses the fine collections of original writings of the various personalities who made Madras history for about a century. Portraits of past governors, painting of the storming of Srirangapatna and scenes of earlier Chennai adorn walls. Medieval weapons, collection of coins, silver wares, porcelain, manuscripts, engravings etc. are on display. A spectacular history of the past rolls in our minds. The marble statue of Cornwallis (1880) and Tipu handing over his children depicted on its pedestal bring before our eyes the Carnatic wars.

The flag staff on the ramparts facing the sea and atop the main gate is over 150' high and is still the tallest in India. Daily flag hoisting is done. It is said the Governor Yale was the man who first hoisted the Union Jack over Fort. St. George in 1687.

Entry Fees	: Rs. 5.00
	: $5.00 (US Dollar)
Timings	: 9 a.m. - 4.30 p.m.
Holiday	: Friday
Phone	: 91-44-25670276

St. Mary's Church, the oldest Anglican church in the city is built inside the fort. The foundation was laid on Lady's Day in 1678 and completed in 1680. It stands much the same as it was when built barring the spire and the tower which are later additions. It is full of mementoes of men who made the history of early Madras, and the narrow yard has tombs of various ages with inscription in several languages. These stones were presumably removed from an earlier grave. Its outer walls are four feet thick and bomb-proof. It is said to be the oldest Protestant church east of the Suez. A huge painting of the Last Supper in the Raphael style brought from Pondicherry when it was plundered in 1761 is a prized possession of the church. The marriage register of this church records the illustrious marriages of Elisa Yale with Catherine Hynmers and Robert Clive with Margaret Markeylyne. The Register of Baptisms, marriages and burials of the church are presented in the Fort Museum.

Other things to see in the fort are Administrative House where Robert Clive lived (at present occupied by the Pay and Accounts office), Wellesley House, King's Barracks and Cornwallis Cupola.

Now, the state legislature and secretariats are housed here besides the defence department offices.

High Court

The imposing Indo-Saracenic building of the High Court is an important landmark. Its stained glass arches and minarets are wonderful. The foundation was laid in 1889 and completed in 1892. Besides taking four years, it has consumed 13 lakhs. In its tallest minaret rising 160 feet above sea level, the Madras light-house was erected in 1894. It was a big gas-mantled lighthouse with huge reflecting discs. Formerly people were allowed to climb its spiralling staircase to have a bird's eye view of the city. The present new lighthouse is on the Marina. The former one called Esplanade lighthouse after being dismantled remains as an ornamental Doric column in the High Court compound itself. During the First World War in 1914, the German cruiser Emden bombarded near this place causing damages to the walls. Even today, a plaque in the eastern compound immortalises the event bearing the date 22 September 1914.

There was an imposing temple, where the High Court stands today, called Patnam Perumal Temple or Chennakesava Perumal Temple erected by Beri Thimmana in 1648. It was demolished by the Company and historical records reveal that the Company paid a compensation of 565¼ pagodas to the Hindus of Chenna-patnam providing alternative site near flower bazaar where Chennakesava and Chennamalles-wara temples were built side by side in 1780 and survives to this day. Another Indo-Saracenic building adjacent to the High Court on the western side is the Law College established in 1892. It was originally the first burial ground of the White Town and even today we can see the arched and spired memorial of David, son of Elihu Yale, the illustrious former governor. Just opposite the high court stands another building of sandstone built in the Jaipur-Jaina style - the Y.M.C.A. building. Another tall building which was once the tallest in the city - the 'Dare House' could also be seen in the Parry's Corner.

The Harbour

Chennai is today one of the major ports of India. In the beginning, ships used to be anchored off the Fort and landed passengers and goods in a narrow sand bank. The second Lord Clive shifted it to the present place and built a pier in 1789. Subsequently works began in 1897 to ensure safe anchorage and was completed in 1910. Thus was formed the man-made harbour of Chennai (Madras) which today stands first in India in handling container carriages–on an average about 2 lakhs container traffic a year. Opposite the harbour on the North Beach Road, stately buildings like the Collector's Office, the General Post Office, the State Bank of India building etc. entice the visitors.

Museum

The Government Museum is on the Pantheon Road in Egmore. National Art Gallery, Gallery of Contemporary Arts, Children's Museum, the Museum Theatre and the Connemara Public Library also lie in the Museum Complex. The museum was a gift to the government in 1851 by the Madras Literary Society which gave its valuable collections of geological specimens. It is the first government-sponsored museum in the country. It has the most beautiful bronze collection of international repute, numismatic and arms collection with various departments like Natural History, Comparative Anatomy, Systematic & Economic Botany, Mineralogy, Geology, Industrial Arts, Ethnology, Antiquities and Archaeology. The old building of the Connemara Public Library is a wonderful piece of architecture of Indo-Saracenic interior and stained glass roof. The museum theatre is a typical old English theatre with a pit and is a semi-circular amphitheatre.

Entry Fees

Foreigners	Rs.250/-
Adults	Rs.15/-
Children	Rs.10/-
School Concession	Rs. 5/-

Timings : 9.00 a.m.-5.00 p.m.

Holiday : Friday

Phone : 91-44-28193238/ 3778

Victoria Memorial

It houses the National Art Gallery. It is a fine building of the Mughal style of North India adapted to Madras requirements. It is faced with a pink-coloured sandstone characteristic of Mughal buildings. Its fine gateways resemble that of Akbar's dream palace at Fatehpur Sikri; and its large hall has a marble floor and a fine ceiling with relief ornaments in chunnam. The foundation stone was laid by George V who visited Madras as Prince of Wales. The exhibits include a fine collection of bronze images belonging to 10-13th centuries, 16-18th century Deccan paintings, 11-12th century splendour of handicrafts and superb Ravi Varma paintings. The whole compound of the Museum is adorned with cannons captured in various battles by the British army. These is also a sculpture park in the rear and a rare 18th century horse-coach which were common in the early colonial period.

The Marina Beach

Any tourist to Chennai should not miss this beautiful spot – a long stretch of sandy beach, the second longest in the world. A drive along the Marina is a fantastic ride. On one side you can see stately historic buildings and on the other the vast stretches of sand lashed by the Bay of Bengal. It is the real lungs of the city and people come in large number to enjoy the calm cool breeze - especially in summer there will be a sea of people. One can see long row of ships waiting to enter the harbour and catamarans returning to the shore with the bounty of their toil. Edibles and snacks are available and people enjoy them while they enjoy the cool breeze. The main attraction of the Marina are the Samadhis of two charismatic former chief ministers of Tamil Nadu, Thiru. C.N.Annadurai fondly called *"Arignar Anna"* (Intellectual elder brother) and Thiru. M.G. Ramachandran fondly called *"Puratchi Thalaivar M.G.R."* (Revolutionary Leader MGR). Even today, you can see large number of people paying homage to their beloved leaders. Opposite the Anna Samadhi, the Senate House, the Convocation Hall, the Library and the new centenary building of the first university of south India - the Madras University, are situated. The Senate House is a good specimen of Indo-Saracenic architecture with minarets, domes and stained glass windows. On the north, we have a modern swimming pool, the river Cooum and the Victory Memorial between Fort St. George and the iron bridge at a point called Cupid's Bow built by a committee of citizens of the city of Madras to commemorate the victory of allied armies in the First World War (1914-18). It is a beautiful monument with a planned garden and later victories of the Indian army are also recorded here.

On the southern side, a row of beautiful buildings which house government offices could be seen, *Ezhilagam* - 'the abode of beauty' is the first and foremost of them. But, the most beautiful ones are the Khalsa Mahal built between 1864 and 1868 and the tall tower adds grace to the Marina. These buildings were once the harem of Arcot Nawabs. Adjoining it, is the Presidency college where one can see the statue of Dr.U.V. Swaminatha Iyer, the Tamil scholar who brought to light Tamil classics of the Sangam age. Lines of glorious tributes paid to this Tamil savant by the national poet Bharathiar are inscribed on the pedestal. There is an old aquarium opposite this college. Upto this junction, the area is called Chepauk; beyond that is Thiruvallikeni with Marina Cricket Grounds, Warlock Park, University Examination Hall and Vivekananda House or Ice House where once the icebergs cut and brought from the lakes of Canada used to be stored. The beautiful statue of Dr. Annie Besant and the statue of Swami Vivekananda as an itinerant monk adorn this place. After Queen Mary's College, we have the state police headquarters and the Chennai station of the All India Radio. Opposite the radio station is the new lighthouse.

Along Marina's park-fringed promenade one could see stately statues of doyens of Tamil language and literature. They include Caldwell, Kambar, Ilango Adigal, Bharathiar, Bharathidasan, Thiruvalluvar, Avvaiyar, G.U.Pope and Fr. Beschi (Veeramamunivar). The Triumph of Labour, Mahatma Gandhi, Kamaraj and Chevalier Sivaji Ganesan are the other statues adorning the Marina. The Marina is maintained as litter-free zone by Chennai Corporation.

Valluvar Kottam

What was once a lake in the heart of the city and later a garbage-dump was reclaimed and refurbished by Chennai Corporation and on it was built the **Valluvar Kottam** – a fitting memorial to the greatest poet-saint of Tamil Nadu. It is shaped like the old and one of the biggest temple chariots, in fact a replica of the one at Thiruvarur. It is 33m tall with a life-size statue of Thiruvalluvar on its seat. In the front hall corridors of the chariot, all the 1330 Thirukkurals with their 133 chapters have been depicted in bass-relief. Its auditorium is the largest in Asia and about 4000 people could be accommodated. It is a befitting modern memorial erected in the Dravidian and Pallavan style of architecture. *Thirukkural* is a unique work translated in almost all the major languages of the world.

> **Entry Fees** : Rs. 3.00 (adult)
>
>   Rs. 2.00 (child)
>
> **Timings**   : 8 a.m. - 6 p.m.
>
> **Phone**   : 91-44-28172177

The Birla Planetarium

A Planetarium - one of the most modern - is located in Kotturpuram between Adyar and Guindy. With a seating capacity of 236, it is a boon to research scholars of Astronomy, Astrophysics, Space Science etc. Every day barring Mondays, two programmes depicting the position of constellations, moon panorama, galaxies, comets, occurrence of solar and lunar eclipses, space travel etc. are on show to the public. It is a modern tourist attraction and gives a new experience that dispels all superstitions about the heavenly bodies. Adjacent to it is the **Periyar Science and Technology Museum,** useful and interesting to students and lovers of science especially to those who wish to know scientific principles and techniques that govern our life.

> **Entry Fees** : Rs. 45.00 (Adult)
>
>   : Rs. 25.00 (upto 12 Yrs.)
>
> **Timings**   : 10.45 a.m, 1.15 p.m.,
>
>   3.45 p.m.

Tamil	:	12.00 noon
Programme		02.30 p.m.
English	:	10.45 a.m.
Programme		01.15 p.m.
Phone	:	91-44-24410025

Kalakshetra

Meaning 'Temple of Art', it is a cultural institution of international repute. It is renowned for Bharata-natyam, the classical dance of Tamil Nadu and 'Kuravanji', a dance drama of Tamil Nadu. It was founded by Rukmini Devi Arundale in 1936 to train, encourage and revive interest in the dances and traditions of Tamil Nadu. It is run on the ancient Gurukulam system where students stay with the gurus or teachers and learn the art treating them as their foster parents. Throughout the year, Kalakshetra performs dance and music recitals in different parts of the city. The venues and timings are published in all major newspapers and also available from the India Tourism Office at Anna Salai and from the Tamil Nadu Tourism Office, Saidapet. It is an interesting sight to see the students learning and performing arts under a sylvan setting, most of the time under the shades of trees in the open air. Dr. U.V. Swaminatha Iyer manuscript library could also be seen in the complex. It is a rare library of its kind preserving traditional literature on palm leaves. They are microfilmed and kept in the library for the use of research scholars of posterity. A number of ancient and rare books have also been published by the library and are available in the sales depot.

Theosophical Society

The Theosophical Society to help and encourage the study of comparative religion, philosophy and science was founded by Madame Blavatsky of Russia and Col. Olcott in the U.S.A. in 1875 and later moved its headquarters to Adyar in 1882. It is on the southern bank of the river Adyar at its estuary. The serene place of this retreat is amidst 270 acres of gardens and estates. The shrine of all faiths, the Garden of Remembrance and a century-old library having invaluable collection of oriental palm-leaf manuscripts and parchments and the Big Banyan Tree, one of the largest in the world are the main tourist attractions here. Every year towards the end of December, the annual convention of the Society is held.

Entry Fees	:	NIL
Timings	:	8.30 a.m. - 10.00 a.m.
		2 p.m. - 5 p.m.
Holiday	:	Sunday
Phone	:	91-44-24912474

Elliot's Beach

The Elliot's Beach is the place where former governors used to go for sea bathing and relaxation. The Schidt's Memorial on the shore washed by the waves is a favourite shooting location for Tamil movies. It was once a calm place of relaxation and a bathing spot but the old charm of it is gone due to crowded residential colonies that have come up. The major attractions nearby are a modern temple and a church – the Ashta Lakshmi Temple dedicated to the goddess of wealth is a multi- storeyed building different from the traditional temples and the church is the Shrine Velankanni. Both attract large number of crowds during festive occasions. The Elliot's Beach is in Besant Nagar.

Ripon Buildings

Fondly called the White House of Madras opened in 1913 by Lord Hardinge, the then viceroy of India, it has been built of brick and chunnam with little stone and has been surmounted by a graceful tower with a big clock resembling the Big Ben of London. The stately building has been built in the British style. The Chennai Corporation, the City Council and the Mayor's Office function here. The white building is a graceful landmark and during full moon days its charm increases and it looks like a dream palace.

Covelong (Kovalam Beach)

A small fishing village with a beautiful beach and backwaters on the way to Mamallapuram. A quiet spot for rest, relaxation and sea bathing. An excellent beach resort of the Taj Group, Fisherman Cove, is there. The ruins of a fort and a Muslim Durgah nearby are also worth visiting.

Muttukadu

It is about 36 km from Chennai on the Mamallapuram Road. It has been developed as a scenic picnic spot and a centre for water sports by the Tamil Nadu Tourism Development Corporation. The backwaters of Muttukadu provides ample scope for them. In February each year wind surfing regalia with competitions are held. Training and demonstration programmes are also held.

Timings	:	8.30 a.m. - 5.30 p.m.
Holiday	:	Tuesday
Phone	:	91-44-27472369

Gardens and Parks

Chennai was once a garden city – even though the gardens have vanished, the names of them, Kilpauk Garden, Sylvan Garden, Poes Garden etc. still cherish the memory. Though most of them have gone there are still some with the name. The Chennai Corporation maintains about 80 small and big gardens. **"My Lady's Garden"** is the chief garden. It is a well laid-out flower garden where the Corporation holds its annual flower show – a feast to the eyes indeed, usually inaugurated by the Governor of Chennai. Prizes will be given to the best maintained traffic islands and gardens. There will also be a show of flower arrangements, Bonsai trees, musical fountain, vegetables carving etc. during the flower show.

Napier Park in the heart of the city near Anna Salai beside the river Cooum, is another big Corporation Park with May Day Memorial. The **Panagal Park** in T.Nagar and **Nageswara Rao Panthulu Park** at Mylapore are other important major parks of the Corporation, that attract crowds. The Corporation band will play Carnatic music during evenings by rotation on a weekly basis.

The Guindy National Park is a deer sanctuary and an abode of a variety of birds, the black buck, spotted deer, civet cats, jackals, mongoose and monkeys. Adjacent to it is the **Snake Park** and reptilium where about 200 species of snakes including King Cobras and black serpents are reared besides lizards, chameleons, crocodiles and spiders. Snakes in cluster on tree branches and pits thrill the visitors. Venom extraction from snakes is done on Saturdays between 4.00 and 5.00 p.m. – a really heart-chilling experience to witness.

Entry Fees	: Rs. 5.00 (Adult)
	: Re. 1.00 (Child)
Timings	: 9.00 a.m. 5.30 p.m.
Holiday	: Tuesday
Phone	: 91-44-22353623
	91-44-22301328

Children's Park

An amusement park for children is adjacent to the snake park with various types of play materials really enjoyable to children. And one can see large number of tiny tots brought to the place on excursion.

Gandhi Mandapam

A stately memorial of the citizens of Chennai to the Father of the Nation has a gallery and five-pillared Mandapam with exquisite carvings. Gandhi Jayanthi and other important functions are held here and on every Sunday between 9.00 a.m. to 10.00 a.m. a large number of devotees of Sri Aurobindo and the Mother of Pondicherry gather to pray and meditate. Rajaji, Kamaraj and Bakthavachalam memorials are adjacent to it.

Arigner Anna Zoological Park

The zoological garden maintained by the Corporation of Chennai in the People's Park was handed over to the government and shifted to Vandalur. It is named as Anna Zoological Park and spread over an area of 1,265 acres. It is the largest in South Asia and has a rich variety of different species of mammals, reptiles and birds. The animals roam in natural surroundings. A battery-operated car is available to go round. There is a special enclosure for nocturnal creatures. Safari parks, an aquarium and a natural museum are the other attractions in the zoo. Buses ply from all places in the city to the zoo.

Entry Fees	: Rs 15 (Adult)
	Rs 10 (Child)
Timings	: 8.30a.m.-5.00 p.m.
Holiday	: Tuesday
Phone	: 91-44-22751089

Theme Parks around the City
Kishkinta

It is situated about 4 km away down Rajaji Salai at Tambaram. Suburban trains and buses take you to Tambaram. From there buses are available to Kishkinta. It is spread over 110 acres of land providing exciting high-tech amusement park set in beautiful surrounding. One can experience the never-before fun sensation here. The latest attraction is a man-made waterfalls called *Chennai Courtallam.*

V.G.P. Universal Kingdom

It is about 21 km on the road to Mahabalipuram south of Chennai. Buses are available from Adyar. It is another amusement and theme park with artificial beautiful settings and sceneries and structures. Many films are shot here. A number of exciting games and high-tech entertainment equipments and super-fast giant wheel are a speciality. Sea swimming is another attraction here. Pongal festival and flower and vegetable shows are also conducted here.

Entry Fee	:	Rs. 125.00 (Adult)
		Rs. 75.00 (Child)
Timings	:	9.00 a.m. - 7.30 p.m.
Phone	:	91-44-24491443/ 24491445

MGM Dizzee World
MGM Mary World
MGM Water World

Further south to V.G.P. Golden Beach is the Dizzy World. A high-tech amusement park with thrilling and heart throbbing entertainments which makes one really dizzy.

Entry Fees	:	Rs. 390.00 (Adult)
		Rs. 350.00 (Child)
Phone	:	91-44-27472129

Queens Land

Established in 2003, this amusement park is spread over a large area of 70 acres located on the Chennai-Bangalore Trunk Road, near Poonamallee. The largest cable car is a main attraction here. It covers a distance of 1.5 km in 30 minutes. There are many thrilling rides available to experience with.

Travelling in high or low speed mechanised boats around a beautiful island will be a memorable experience.

Entry Fee	:	Rs. 350.00 (Adult)
		Rs. 250.00 (Child)
Timings	:	10.00 a.m. - 6.30 p.m.
Holiday	:	Monday
Phone	:	91-44-26811136/ 26811124

The Crocodile Bank

It is another place of excursion about 34 km from Chennai and located between V.G.P. Golden Beach and Dizzy World. Here several species of crocodiles are reared in natural surroundings - the crocodiles basking in the sun and their sudden movement is an exciting sight. One can see crocodile eggs and feel the rough back of the crocodile here.

Temples in and around Chennai

There are over 700 temples in and around Chennai. Some of them are old, some built during the colonial periods and some modern. We shall here take up some selective temples known for their antiquity, sculptural beauty and popularity.

Kapaleeswarar Temple

Mylapore is one of the oldest towns of Tamil Nadu. Ptolemy, the Greek and the Arabs of the 11th century have mentioned it in their writing. It was an ancient seaport and appears to have existed for over 2000 years. Earlier, it was a Jain settlement and even before that the Buddhists were here. They called it 'Mayura Sabdha Pattinam' (The town of peacock sound). In Tamil, it has been called "Mayil Arpu" (Mayil means peacock and Arpu means sound). And Mayil-Arpu-oor became Mylapore in due course. There was a shrine on the shore dedicated to Thirthankarar

Neminathar. The famous Jain scholar Mayilai Nathan had lived here. He has written a commentary to "Nannool", a popular grammar of the Tamil language. Until recently a few mutilated Jain and Buddhist statues could be seen in a compound opposite to the Santhome Basilica.

The original Kapaleeswarar temple was built by Pallava but it might have been eroded by the sea or demolished by the Portuguese who settled here in 1522. Saint Thirugnana Sambandar and Appar are believed to have visited that temple. The present temple is supposed to be an exact replica of the old Pallavan temple built about 300 years ago. The temple's 120 feet gopuram (Portal tower) was built in 1906 and the stucco figures adorning it speak of puranic legends. The temple has a big tank. One of the 63 Nayanmars, "Vayilar Nayanar" was born here and a separate shrine exists for Him. Bronze images of the 63 Saivaite saints adorn the outeryard of the temple and "Arubathu Moovar" festival is the most famous attracting lakhs of people. The legend of this place is that the consort of Siva, Parvathi, worshipped Siva in the form of a Peacock (Mayil); hence the place is called Mylapore. Another legend is that one of the Saivaite saints, Thirugnana Sambandar performed a miracle by giving life to a girl named Poombavai whose ashes were kept in a pot.

There are also other temples dedicated to Lord Siva. In one of those temples, the Lord manifests as Lord Veerabadra, wielding a sword, a shield, bow and arrow in His hands. He wears a Chain of skulls around His legs. One of the earrings is of the type worn by women, and the other by men. Ganga and Moon can be seen on the Lord's head.

Mylapore is associated with Vaishnaviate traditions too and there are two Vaishnavaite temples, Madhava Perumal and Kesava Perumal in Mylapore. One of the first three Alwars – Peyalwar was also born here in a well. Even today, the birth of this Alwar is celebrated near a well in Arundale Street which is the birthplace of the Alwar. Saint Thiruvalluvar, the author of the illustrious Thirukkural was also born here and a temple dedicated to Him also exists.

Parthasarathi Temple

This temple also was built by the Pallavas in the mid-eighth century. Its tank is beautiful with lilies, hence this place is called *Thiru* - beautiful, *Alli*-Lily, *Keni*-Tank. *Parthasarathy* means the chariot driver of Partha or Arjuna and it denotes Lord Krishna. The image in the sanctum sanctorum is scarred with arrow wounds - testimony of the sculptor to the veracity of the chariot driver of the Mahabharatha war. One of the 12 Alwars (Vaishnavaite saints) Thirumangai Alwar of the 8th century had sung hymns on this shrine. The Chola, Pandya and Vijayanagar kings have made endowments and grants to this temple. Behind the temple is Bharathiar Memorial building – the place where he lived during his last days.

Temples of George Town

Unlike these two old temples, the temples of George Town were built after the new European settlement came into being. Chenna Kesava Perumal and Chenna Malleeswarar temples in Flower Bazaar, Kalahasteeswarar temple in Coral Merchant Street, Mallikeswarar temple in Lingi Chetty Street, Chintadri Pillaiyar Koil in Muthialpet, Kachchalleeswarar temple in Armenian Street, Krishnaswami temple in Muthialpet, the Kandasami Koil in Rattan Bazaar and the Kalikamba Kameswarar Temple in Thambu Chetty Street are some of them. The last one dates back to 1678 and Emperor Shivaji once worshipped Goddess Kalikamba here. One of the temples was built by prosperous merchants of the 18th century. The Adikesava Temple in Acharappan Street too belongs to this period.

Vadapalani Andavar Temple

It is located in Kodambakkam - the Hollywood of Chennai where many of the cinema studios like Vijaya, Vahini, A.V.M., etc. are located. The temple is dedicated to Lord Muruga. It is considered a very important shrine and on par with the shrine at Palani - the original Padaiveedu of Lord Muruga in the district of Dindigul. On Krithigai and Sashti days, one can see devotees carrying various types of Kavadis to pay their offerings.

Siva-vishnu Temple

It is in the busy area of Thyagaraya Nagar. Both Siva and Vishnu have separate shrines here. The temple is crowded during evenings. The Kasi Viswanatha temple in Kuppiar Street, W.Mambalam belongs to the 17th century. When it was built it was called "Mahabilva Kshetra". "Mahabilva" was in later days corruptly pronounced as Mambalam thus giving this name to this area. The Karaneeswarar temple at Saidapet is dedicated to Lord Siva.

The Mundaka (Lotus) Kanni (Eyed) Amman temple at Mylapore is the most famous Mariamman temple where animal sacrifice was performed before it was banned. The Mariamman is supposed to be a very powerful deity capable of fulfilling the just desires of the devotees. There is another old temple of the colonial period located in Pudupet near Harris Road called Kamaleswar Temple. Pachaiappa Mudaliar, the famous "Dubash" of the Company used to take his holy dip in the Cooum river daily – the river was so clean in those days – and worship the deity in this temple.

Villivakkam

This place, about 10 km by rail from Chennai Central, has to its divine pride two ancient temples, one dedicated to Lord Siva and the other to Lord Vishnu. The presiding deity of the former is Lord Agastheeswara and that of the latter is Lord Dhamodhara. Villivakkam is also connected by buses to other important parts of Chennai.

Jain Temples in the City

In George Town area near Adhiyappa Naicken Street, a Jain Mandir was built in 1899 in typical north Indian style. There are two more Jain temples in Mint Street. Another new Jain temple built in 1979 at G.N.Chetty Road in T.Nagar is of dazzling whiteness. A magnificent flight of steps lead to the sanctum sanctorum where the 16th Tirthankar Shanthinatha is seated. This temple belongs to the Svetambara sect of the Jains. It is two tiered and 70 feet high – the first of its kind in the south. Two more Jain temples are there in Chintadripet and another at Veppery.

A Sikh Gurudhwara is also located nearby behind the Teynampet Congress Ground. A modern Gurudhwara where the Sikhs of the city throng on festive days. The only Buddhist temple is at Egmore in the lane opposite the Egmore Railway Station.

Some Important Temples around the City

These temples are easily accessible either by buses or by taxis.

Ashtalakshmi Temple

This temple is located in Elliots beach. The name Ashtalakshmi is obtained because it is dedicated to Eight Manifestations of Goddess Mahalakshmi. The Navarathiri Festival is celebrated in a grand manner. Devotees from all over the city flock to this temple to attend this festival and also to take a cool breeze in the beach with family members.

Mathyakailash

Located in Adyar, this temple sits right in the centre of Parameshwar, Ambikai, Adityan and Thirumal. Here there are 'Sannidhis' for Anjaneyar and Bairavar besides the 'Nava-Grahas'. Situated at Adyar on the way to Taramani this beautiful temple in white marble is the delight of connoisseur.

Tiruvottiyur

This ancient temple is about 10 km on the Northern Trunk Road. It was once a part of Chennai city but then excluded. It is a Saivite shrine predating the Pallava period. Adi Sankara, the founder of Advaitham has visited this temple and has sung in praise of the deity. Saivaite saints Sundarar and Gnanasambandar too have visited this temple. It was rebuilt by Rajendra Chola I. It is also associated with Pattinathar of the 18 Siddhars. He attained salvation here and his Samadhi too could be seen. The presiding deity is Thyagarajaswami. It was a vedic centre during Chola period and the temple architecture is superb and belongs to the Chola period.

Tiruvanmiyur Temple

Another old temple exists in Thiruvanmiyur on the road to Mamallapuram. It is a 11th century Chola temple and the presiding deity is Lord Marundeeswarar. The author of Ramayana, Valmiki is said to have worshipped here. The name is due to his association. "Valmikiyur" in due course became "Vanmikiyur" and finally "Vanmiyur". There is also a shrine dedicated to Valmiki. Pamban Swamigal samadhi is also found near this shrine.

Tirupporur Temple

About 40 km south of Chennai is an old temple dedicated to Lord Muruga. "Soora Samharam", the defeat and salvation to the demon Soorapadman is an important festival. The temple contains several inscriptions.

Pallavaram Cave Temple

Pallavaram is a place of historical importance. Prehistoric tools were found here. During the Pallava period, it was a flourishing town called Pallavapuram. Mahendra Varma Pallavan has built a rock-cut cave temple on the slopes of the Pallavaram hill which is now a muslim durgah. It is about 15 km from Egmore and can be reached by suburban electric trains from Beach railway station or by buses.

Tirisulam Temple

It is a Chola Temple with 11-12th century inscriptions. It is dedicated to Lord Siva and the "Sivaratri" festival is very famous. The railway station is opposite the airport and called "Thirisoolam". The name is said to have been derived from Tirichuram, one of the family names who held sway on Chennai.

Tiruneermalai Temple

It is a nearby place of Pallavaram. A shrine is dedicated to Vishnu whose deity is called "Nirvannapperumal" from which the name "Thiruneermalai" is derived. It was once a forest shrine about which Alwars have sung hymns. The bronze images in this temple are very beautiful. This is an old temple of the Pallava period. The main temple is at the foot of the hill. There is also a shrine up the hill which can be reached by a flight of steps.

Kunrathur Temple

This place is adjacent to Thiruneermalai. It is the birthplace of saint Sekkizhar, the author of "Peria Puranam", a sacred book revealing the history of the 63 Nayanmars (Saivaite Saints). It was He who built the Nageswara temple here. It belongs to the 12th century. About a km away is the ancient hill shrine of 'Kunrathur Kumaran' sung by Arunagirinathar. There is a round rock here which produces musical notes when one strikes it with a stone.

Mangadu Bangaru Kamakshi Amman Koil: It is an ancient temple of Pallava times near Porur. Mangadu has golden idol of Kamakshi doing penance. People throng this temple on Fridays and holidays.

Thiruverkadu Temple

It is a Mariamman temple just 5 km away from city limits, a famous temple that attracts thousands of devotees on holidays especially on the 1st of January.

Koyambedu Perumal Koil

There is an old temple at Koyambedu where the city's main vegetable market is located. It is dedicated to Vishnu. There is an underground mandapam with a secret underground passage. It is said that during the muslim invasion, the idols were kept in this mandapam and later, after the danger was over they were taken out and installed.

Singaperumal Koil

About 48 km on the Grand Southern Trunk Road is this Vishnu shrine on a hillock covered by dense shrubs. This shrine houses a huge image of Yoga Narasimhar (the Lord with a lion's head and a human body) one of the 10 avatars of Lord Vishnu carved out on the face of the rock, the sanctum sanctorum shelters the god in the act of doing penance. The stucco image was fashioned by Pallava kings who built many cave temples in this area. The Chola kings were also patrons of this temple as inscription of the Chola King Rajaraja I (1000 AD) is also found here.

Tirukkalukkundram Temple

It is an important shrine on a 500 ft. hill midway between Mamallapuram and Chengalput. Two eagles come every day to have a morsel of food at noon time. After pecking a morsel they disappear as they arrived. This is a daily ritual. Hence, this hill is called the Sacred Hill of the eagles (Thirukkalukkundram).

Pallavas have built a shrine at the top of the hill and reliefs of Ardhanariswarar, Dakshinamurthi and Somaskandar could be seen on the rear and northern walls of the sanctum and Vedagireeswara lingam occupies the centre. Abutting the flight of steps on the way leading down, is another Pallava rock-cut cave etched with Dutch inscriptions exposing the later link with Dutch occupation. The Dutch establishment was in the nearby Sadras where even today one can see the remains of an old Dutch fort – it is about 10 kms from here.

At the foot of the hill stands big Siva temple with a majestic gopuram piercing the sky. Paintings and sculptures of Vijayanagar adorn the temple. On the east of the temple is the sacred tank *"Sangu Theertham"* or tank of conch.

Uttiramerur Temple

Uttiramerur could be reached by bus. It is on the road to Vandavasi from Chengalputtu. There are several ancient temples here. The Sundaravaradaperumal temple of the period of Dantivarma Pallava is of complex design. Three sanctums one above the other in storeys house Vishnu seated, standing and recumbent. The idols all are brick in stucco. In another shrine of the Chola period are the famous inscriptions that speak of the elected panchayat raj of the Cholas. The method of election, the qualification of the contestants etc. are clearly indicated. It exposes that local administration was purely a democratic set-up.

Thennangore Radhakrishna Temple

Further on the road to (Wandiwash) Vandavasi about 22 km from Uttiramerur, one can find the recently built beautiful temple of Radhakrishna in Thennangore. The temple is built like the Puri Jagannath temple and the idols are exact replicas of Panduranga of Pandaripur in North India. The temple was built by Haridoss Giri Swamiji, the disciple of Gnanananda Giri Swamiji. There are beautiful sculptures depicting scenes from the life of Lord Krishna. The sanctum has graceful idols of Panduranga and there is a Bhajan Hall, the pillars of which are nothing but statues of saints of the Bakthi cult. There is also a shrine for Gnanananda Giri and a Siva temple. Foreigners throng during Krishna Jayanthi festival and beautiful lodges are provided to them. Daily Bhajans are a speciality and so is every day free feeding of devotees. It is a most modern temple and a visit is rewarding.

Mamallapuram

It is popularly called Mahabalipuram and is 58 km south of Chennai. It can be reached by bus or taxi. A beautiful spot of wonder and amazing sculptures which no tourist to Chennai should miss.

Mamallapuram was once the flourishing port of the Pallavas – an old lighthouse built of stone exists intact till date, proclaiming the glory of Pallava trade and maritime supremacy. It is also the birthplace of one of the first three Alwars – Boothathalwar. Since Pallava kings were both Saivaites and Vaishnavaites, Mamallapuram has shrines of both beliefs. Though no formal worship is done today, large number of visitors come every day to enjoy the sculpture and splendour of Pallava art and architecture. The monolithic and scooped out cave temples are of different dates, 10 centuries old.

The Shore Temple: Lapped by the surging sea it stands gloriously on the verge of the Bay of Bengal. It has a Dravidian style vimana towering over 60 feet built in basaltic rock. A prismatic lingam is on the sanctum facing the sea and Vishnu is seen reclining on the ground (Stala sayana) in his chamber in the rear.

Pandava Raths or Monolithic Shrines are five in number out of which four are carved, out of a single rock, while the fifth is scooped from a small rock.The hut-like Draupadi Rath sports door-keepers, Durga with a worshipper cutting and offering his neck, and the outer walls of Arjuna's rath have most lovely and graceful figures of gods and mortals carved by a skilful sculptor. Nakula-Sahadeva rath stands with a huge monolithic elephant in front. Bhima's rath has two storeys and lion-based pillars. Dharmaraja's rath is the biggest and has 8 panels of exquisite sculptures.

Arjuna's Penance is the splendour of Mamallapuram. It is a huge rock in the canvas unfolding a scene of gods and demigods, birds, beasts and natural scenery. Some are of the opinion that it is in fact Bagirath's penance to bring the celestial Ganges to the earth. A natural cleft in the rock has been cleverly carved into the turbulent river Ganges with serpent gods worshipping like devotees along the banks frozen in their prayer – a superb poetry in sculpture which no visitor should miss.

The Mahishasuramardhini cave is carved into three shrines a bass relief of Somaskanda in the rear, Anantasayana - Vishnu canopied by Shesha, reclining on the serpent bed. Mahishasuramardhini is struck in bold relief in such an awe-inspiring way with the thrill of the beholder in the battlefield.

Krishna Mandapam is a rock-cut temple with pastoral scenes depicting the life of Lord Krishna.

Varaha Cave illustrates the legend of rescuing the earth Bhoodevi by Vishnu incarnated as a boar.

Besides one would be wonder-struck to see Krishna's butter ball a huge boulder with just a tip of it touching the rock giving the on- looker an impression that it may roll on him any moment. There is a huge rock tub said to be the bathing tub of Draupathi. Above, on the rocky hill is a shrine of Vishnu without the deity. One can also see the old rockbuilt lighthouse and the modern lighthouse side by side. Mahabalipuram is a real feast to the eyes that could read an epic in lively sculpture.

Tiruvidanthai is a few kilometres north of Mamallapuram where stands a famous Vaishnavaite shrine built by early Cholas. A huge stucco image of Varaha holding Bhoodevi (Earth) can be seen.

The **Tiger Cave** is located a couple of miles in the south on the seashore – facing the sea. There is a beautiful monolithic stage where cultural programmes were held in olden days.

Kanchipuram Temples

75 km from Chennai, Kanchipuram is one of the great mythological cities and *"Nakareshu Kanchi"* is a popular saying in Sanskrit that means "Kanchipuram is the best city". It was the capital city of the Pallavas and the northern capital of the Cholas. Even during the Vijayanagar period, it was an important centre. It was also a centre of learning and a centre for Buddhists and Jains in early time. The Chinese traveller Hieun-Tsang who has visited Kanchipuram praises its glory and painfully notes the declining trend of Buddhism in his accounts. It is also a world famous centre for silk weaving. Kanchi Pattu - 'the silk of Kanchi' – is cherished by one and all and one can really see silk looms in action and find out how beautiful sarees are made. It is a temple city and innumerable ancient temples could be seen at every turning. A selective list of most important temples are given here. The whole city is divided into Siva Kanchi, Vishnu Kanchi and Jain Kanchi.

Kailasanathar Temple

This Siva temple is one of the earliest temples built by Rajasimha Pallava in the late 7th century A.D. The front was added by Mahendra Varma III later on. It is the only temple of the original Pallava architecture without additions by Cholas and Vijayanagar kings and remains a fine specimen of freshness and simplicity of early Dravidian architecture. True to its name, Kailas or Paradise, it shelters all the gods in various aspects in several niches along the circumambulatory path around the sanctum sanctorum. One has to crawl through a small opening to enter it and has to come out of a pit at the end. It is believed that by doing this exercise one will reach Kailas after one's sojourn on the earth. Puranas unroll themselves through sculptures to our view. Pallava paintings are also visible in fragments in some niches. These murals remind us the magnificence of the temple as it would have looked when it was first built. The office of the Archaeological Survey of India is nearby and one could get more details about the history and importance of Kanchipuram.

Vaikunthaperumal Temple

This Vishnu shrine was built between 674-850 AD by the Pallava king Parameswara Varman and Nandivarman II. Here the Pallava history is revealed in reliefs all along the corridors. Their dresses, costumes, jewellery and habits are captured in exquisite splendour. The shrine has two storeys and enshrines Vishnu in them. Such storeyed temple is called "Maadak Kovil" in Tamil. The walls have rich puranic sculpture. Lion pillars adorn the cloisters inside the outer wall.

Ekambaranathar Temple

This Siva temple is the largest and is spread over nine hectares. Its huge gopuram or portal tower is 192 feet high and its massive outer walls were constructed by Krishna Devaraya, the great Vijayanagar king in 1509. The original shrine dates back to the Pallava period, additions have also been made by Cholas. Five separate enclosures and a thousand-pillared hall and a beautiful big tank are inside the temple. 'Eka Amra' means a single mango tree and the lord is known as Ekambaranathar. It is one of the five element (Prithvi or earth) shrines of Siva and the Lingam is made of earth. A single mango tree is seen behind the sanctum – a very old tree indeed the age of which is fabulously said to be 35,000 years, with four branches representing the four Vedas. It is also said that the fruit of each branch has a different taste. Near the tank is a small cell for Valiswara, erected by Mahendra Varma Pallavan. At the back of the Lingam, Siva and Parvathi image is sculptured. The hall of Nataraja, the cosmic dancer has some interesting frescoes in the ceiling. The 'Mavadi Sevai' festival attracts huge crowds.

Kamakshi Amman Temple

This is the most important temple and the chief deity of Kanchipuram. 'Kanchi Kamakshi' is a popular saying and it has been sanctified by Adi Sankara and He has stationed before the goddess a Sri Chakra said to be containing the efficiency of power of the Devi. There is no separate sanctum for Siva here. There is a separate sanctum for Adi Sankara.

Varadaraja Perumal Temple

This Vishnu temple was built during the Vijayanagar period. This is another big temple having 5 enclosures with massive outer wall and a hundred-pillared hall. One exquisite, sculptural marvel is a huge chain carved out of single piece of stone. The sanctum on a small hillock faces west and displays murals in its ceiling. One should not miss to see the golden lizard here. The 100-pillared hall is a perfect specimen of Vijayanagar art and architecture.

Muktiswarar and Matangeswarar temples are also Pallava relics with fine specimens of art and architecture. Ashtapujam temple is in the heart of Vishnu Kanchi where the multihanded Vishnu armed to the teeth with various weapons is seen in the act of rescuing Gajendra, the elephant devotee from the clutches of the crocodile. There is another temple dedicated to Lord Vishnu called "Ulagalantha Perumal" which depicts the Viswaroopa taken by Vishnu to defeat Mahabali, the demon king. The deity raising one of its legs measuring the space (sky) is featured here – an awe-inspiring and thrilling sight. The famous commentator of Thirukkural, Parimel Azhagar was once the Poojari of this temple.

Jain Kanchi

In the south-west beyond the river Vegavadhi – one of the tributaries of Palar – stands a group of Jain temples. This place is known as 'Tiruparuthi Kundram'. This belongs to the early Chola period. There is a sangeetha mandapam (music hall) in this temple dedicated to Vardhamana Mahavira – the roof of which is adorned with paintings, illustrating the lives of Tirthankaras. Rare Jain manuscripts are also preserved in this temple.

There are a few of the most important temples in Kanchipuram and there are many of them old and new. The most important of the recent ones is the Kumarakkottam - a temple dedicated to Lord Muruga. The divine abode of the holy Sankaracharyas called Jagadgurus who reside in Kanchi at Their headquarters and give darshan to devotees is popular as 'Kanchi Kamakoti Peetam'. Tourists can reach Kanchipuram by rail or by bus and hiring a taxi or autorickshaw will do to cover the temples mentioned, in a single day.

Maduranthakam - Erikatha Perumal Koil

Maduranthakam is about 80 km south of Chennai on the trunk road to Tiruchy. The biggest lake of the district is here, with a bund of about 13,000 ft in length and a depth of about 100 ft when full. It irrigates about 3000 acres of surrounding villages. This lake was cut by the Cholas. In the close of the 18th century when Colonel Lionel Place was the collector, furious monsoon brought unprecedented rains and the lake was full and there was danger of the bund giving way at any moment. When the collector encamped here and was examining the bunds he saw the huge figure of Rama with his bow in his hand on the bund. The rain stopped and the breach was averted by divine grace. The collector, in token of his respect and gratitude built a sanctum for Sita – the consort of Rama – in the temple that stands near the bunds of the lake. Lord Rama here, is hence known as 'Eri Katha Rama' or Rama, the one who guarded the lake.

There is also a Siva temple and the Bairava statue here which are of exquisite splendour. There once flourished a vedic centre in this place.

Vedantangal Bird Sanctuary

Vedanthangal, the paradise of ornithologists, is five km away from Maduranthagam. It is one of the largest bird sanctuaries in India. It is spread over 30 hectares and a lake full of trees half submerged is a convenient breeding site for birds of all feathers. Over 1,00,000 migratory birds visit every year. The season for bird-watching is mid-October to mid-February. The varieties include herons, spoonbills, pelicans, sandpipers, white gulls, cormorants, blue-winged teals and swans. Though this sanctuary has been existing for a very long time, only in 1798 was this fact publicised. There is a watch-tower to see the birds. The ideal time is the afternoon when diurnal birds begin to return and the nocturnal birds leave.

At **Malaivaiyavur,** about 6 km from the sanctuary, there is a famous hilltop temple dedicated to Lord Srinivasa Perumal.

Sriperumpudur Temple

It is midway between Chennai and Kanchipuram and the birthplace of saint Ramanuja, the propounder of Vishistadvaita philosophy. The shrine has been improved by Vijayanagar kings. The pillars are exquisite and bear testimony to Vijayanagar architecture. The image of Ramanuja is also installed in this Vishnu shrine.

Rajiv Gandhi Memorial

It is located here in the spot where he was killed by the human bomb — one can always see a stream of visitors to this memorial paying homage to their departed charismatic leader.

Tiruttani Murugan Temple

This famous Murugan shrine is about 80 km from Chennai and can be reached either by train or by bus. It is the place where Lord Muruga, after killing Demon Surapadman, softened His fury. The shrine stands on a basaltic hill reached by a flight of steps or by vehicle through a road. On New Year Day, lakhs of pilgrims climb the steps chanting Bhajans. The temple is of Pallava origin. Saints like Arunagirinathar, Kachiyappa Munivar, Muthusami Dikshitar and Ramalinga Adigal have sung songs in praise of Tirutthani Lord Muruga. During Krithigai days, kavadis are taken up the hill by a large number of devotees. On the slope of the hills is a herbal farm.

In the eastern end of the town downhill on the river bank is a temple dedicated to Siva. Veerattaneswara is the presiding deity. This was built by the Pallava king Aparajitha. It is a black granite temple of the closing years of Pallavas with an apsidal vimana with parivara devathas in niches all round the outer wall. The sanctum here is a forerunner of present-day shrines.

Thiru Alangadu Temple

This is a unique Siva temple 37 miles west of Chennai. The Nataraja bronze idol is with the rare dancing pose called *Oorthuva Thandava* lifting his leg upwards. This was done to subdue Kali in a dance bout as being a female She could not do so out of modesty. An image of dancing Kali is also kept here. It is the place where Karaikkal Ammaiyar one of the 63 Saivaite saints attained Mukthi. Her image is a unique piece of art exposing the features of an old lady, bones protruding, shrivelled bosom and sunken eyes.

Tirupati Temple

This temple town is in the state of Andhra Pradesh 137 km from Chennai. Daily 2 train services and every half an hour bus services are operated from Chennai. Besides, private vehicles and tourist coaches are also available. Down the hill there is a shrine for Alarmelmanga Thayar, the consort of Lord Vishnu and Govindaraja temple. 13 kms up the hill Tirumala, is the famous shrine of Sri Venkateswara popularly known as Balaji. In Tamil, this is called *'Vengadam'*. One has to cross seven hills to reach the temple. Pucca road is available, besides many pilgrims prefer to climb the seven hills on the steps.

Lakhs of people throng from all parts of India every day and one has to wait in the queue for 3 or 4 hours and on festive occasions more than 8 to 9 hours to have darshan of the deity. Thousands of devotees tonsure their heads here and they make a vow to do so if their desires are fulfilled. Tirupati temple has the largest revenue everyday touching several lakhs of rupees. Each day is a wedding day to Lord Venkateswara and by contributing a fixed sum one can perform this ceremony to the Lord. *Tirupati laddu and vada* – the prasadams of this lord are sold to public. Laddu is a popular item and no pilgrim ever misses to buy it, standing for hours in long queues. Umpteen lodges and Devastanam (temple) guest houses and cottages are available.

The places mentioned above and located around Chennai could easily be reached by bus or taxis and after a day trip tourists could return to Chennai for their night stay.

Churches in and around Chennai

Santhome Basilica

Santhome Church is associated with the apostle doubting Thomas. He is believed to have landed here in 52 AD to spread Christianity. At that time, this part was known as Mylapore. It is said that he used to preach on the sands of old Mylapore which has been devoured by the sea. Later on, he had some enemies and had to live in a cave near Saidapet about 6 km away from Mylapore on the banks of river Adyar, called Little Mount. From there, he had to retreat further to a hill now called St.Thomas Mount where he was killed in 72 AD. His mortal remains were buried on the beach where he preached. Later on, a church was built over it. Afterwards it was transferred to another church built further inland. In 1606, it was rebuilt as a cathedral and in 1896, it was made into a basilica. The church is a magnificent building built in Gothic style with beautiful stained glass windows portraying the stay of St. Thomas. The central hall has 14 wooden plaques depicting scenes from the last days of Christ. A three feet statue of Virgin Mary believed to have been brought from Portugal in 1541 adorns the church. In this basilica, a small hand bone of St. Thomas and the head of a lance are kept as sacred relics.

St. Mary's Church

It is the first Anglican church built inside the Fort St.George, details of which can be had under the heading Fort St. George.

Portuguese Church

This is the church of Our Lady of Assumption and is the first church built in British India (1642 AD). It was in existence before Mary's of Fort. St. George. Even now it survives on Portuguese Church Street in northern George Town .

Church of St. Mary of the Angels

This is the Catholic church built with the permission of the Company. It was built on the site of a Portuguese cemetery in 1755. The inscription on the gates of it dates back to 1642, and it is still preserved at the cathedral's entrance. In this cathedral are some beautiful oil paintings of the crucifixion and Mary Magdalane. The movement chapel attached to it is the last resting place of the Embience, Armenian family of that name. It is popularly known as St. Antony's Church.

The Armenian Church

This was built in 1772 on the site of the old Armenian cemetery. A courtyard garden and gleaming pews of this church are wonderfully preserved. This church has the biggest bells in Chennai. This church of the Armenian orthodoxy is next door to the Church of St. Mary of the Angels.

St. George's Cathedral

This Anglican church was built in 1814-15 and consecrated in 1816. It was considered at that time the finest, outside London. Its spire is 140 feet high and used to be an imposing majestic monument in those days with its broad green lushy open space on Anna Salai near the Gemini Circle. Now the church has lost its panoramic appearance as a major portion of the open space is occupied by the American Consulate and the Anna flyover raising high nearby. The spire which was visible on all sides could now be seen only at a narrow point in the Cathedral Road.

Luz Church

This church in Mylapore on the Luz Church Road is the oldest church construction still in existence. This is popularly known even today as '*Kaattu Koil*' (Forest Temple) in Tamil as there was a thick jungle around it in those days. There is a legend behind the construction of this church. Some Portuguese sailors in danger on the sea were guided by a divine light to safety. After they landed on the beach, they saw the light still glowing and followed it till it disappeared. On that spot they built the Luz Church and dedicated to 'Our Lady of Light'. There is an inscription bearing the date 1516. Luz Corner the busiest part of Mylapore got its name from the church.

St. Andrew's Kirk

The Scots built this Kirk on the Poonamallee High Road (now Periyar E.V.R. Salai) and consecrated in 1821. It stands with an imposing look near the Egmore Railway Station. Its dome is unique and the marble paved aisles are magnificent.

Little Mount Church

This is half way between Santhome and St. Thomas Mount. It is the place where St. Thomas took asylum when he was pursued by enemies. It is called *Chinna Malai* in Tamil. There are two churches here, the new one built half

way up the hill in 1971 has been dedicated to Our Lady of Health. Another church built by the Portuguese earlier in 1551 is the blessed Sacrament Chapel still in existence, connected to the new church. The old one is a cave in which St. Thomas was hiding and doing prayers and penance. To the east of the cave is an opening with a palm print nearby. Legend says that this narrow opening was the portals of a tunnel through which St. Thomas escaped to St.Thomas Mount and the palm print is the hand print of St.Thomas. A cross cut into the rock is believed to be the cross before which St. Thomas prayed. There is also a spring nearby which St. Thomas is supposed to have struck to quench the thirst of his followers. It is said that the water has curative powers even today. Every year on the fourth Saturday and Sunday after Easter, the Little Mount festival is celebrated and thousands of devotees throng on these days.

St. Thomas Mount Church

St. Thomas Mount is a 300 feet hill called "*Parangi Malai*" in Tamil, on the verges of the present city limits. The Portuguese had rebuilt a church here at the behest of King Emanuel. It was originally a chapel of the Nestorian Missionary. It was on this mount that St. Thomas is said to have been speared to death. 'The Bleeding Cross' here is a miracle. Hearsay tradition says that it was chiselled by St. Thomas. During May in 1558, it first publicly bled and is said to have bled periodically ever since. There is a painting of Virgin Mary and child Christ, supposed to have been painted by St. Luke and brought to India by St. Thomas. A flight of steps lead to the top of the mountain.

Shrine Velankanni

This modern church is in Besant Nagar (vide Elliot's Beach).

Important Mosques
Wallajah Mosque (Big Mosque)
It is popularly known as the Big Mosque on the Triplicane High Road in Chepauk. It was built in 1789. It is the biggest in the city with a spacious open space. All the muslims in the city gather here on important days. It is an impressive and historic mosque associated with Nawab Wallajah's family. There is another mosque in the muslim area nearby, called Zam Bazaar historically associated with the Prince of Arcot family in a crowded part of the city.

Thousand Lights Mosque
This historic mosque stands on Thousand Lights area at the junction of Peters Road and Anna Salai. This area with numerous lanes and narrow streets is associated with members of the Nawab family as the street names reveal. The name is derived from the lighting of a triangular wedge of a building constructed by Nabab Umdat-ul-umrah around 1800 for Shias assembling during Moharram. It is one of the major mosques of the city.

Kasi Viranna Mosque
It is in Moore's Street in George Town. Kasi Viranna, a chief merchant was very close to the Golconda Sultan and he even had a muslim name Hassan Khan. He built the mosque in 1680 before he died.

Besides these temples, churches and mosques, numerous in each category have come up in various parts of the city. Only a few of them very important and having historical background have been listed here.

Chennai is still an expanding city and new residential colonies are springing up every now and then and with them the places of worship also multiply.

Shopping
Several state-run and private emporia in Chennai sell handicrafts of different kinds – rose-wood, sandal-wood, ivory, bronze, silver, leather, silk and handwoven fabrics, sarees and jewellery are also available.

Where to stay in Chennai
HOTELS

Five Star Deluxe
• **ITC Hotel Park Sheraton and Towers**, 132, T.T.K. Road, Chennai-600 018 ℗ 24994101 Fax: 044-24995101 Email:reservations.sheratonpark @itcwelcomgroup.in
• **Le Royal Meridien** 1, G.S.T. Road, St. Thomas Mount, Chennai - 600 016. ℗ 22314343, Fax: 044-22314344 Email:reservation@leroyalmeridien-chennai.com
• **Taj Coromandel**, 17, Mahatma Gandhi Road, (Nungambakkam High Road), Chennai - 600 034. ℗ 28272827 Fax: 044-66000089, 28257104 Email: coromandel.chennai@tajhotels.com

Five Star
• **Connemara**, 2, Binny Road, Chennai - 600002. ℗ 28520123 Fax:044-28523361 Email:tajcon@ giasmd01.vsnl.net.in
• **The Rain Tree**, 120, St. Mary's Road, Alwarpet, Chennai - 600 018. ℗ 42252525 Fax : 044-42252627
• **The Fisherman's Cove**, Covelong Beach, Kanchipuram Dist. Tamilnadu - 603 112. ℗ 04114-272304 to 272310
• **Trident Hilton**, 1/24, GST Road, Chennai-600 027. ℗ 22344747. Fax: 044-22344555 Email: reservations.chennai@tridenthotels.com
• **Welcomgroup Chola Sheraton**, 13, Cathedral Road, Chennai-600 086. ℗ 28110101. Fax: 044-28278779. Email: chola@welcomgroup.com

Four Star
• **Ambassador Pallava**, 30, Montieth Road, Egmore, Chennai - 600 008. ℗ 28554476, 28554068 Email: pallava@ambassadorindia.com
• **Benz Park Tulip**, 41, Tirumalai Pillai Road, T.Nagar, Chennai - 600017. ℗ 28159999 Fax : 044 - 28158995
• **GRT Grand Days**, 120, Sir Thyagaraya Road, Pondy Bazaar, T.Nagar, Chennai - 600 017. ℗ 28150500. Email: grtgranddays@vsnl.com
• **Hotel President**, 16, Dr. Radhakrishnan Salai, Mylapore, Chennai - 600 004. ℗ 28472211. Fax: 044-28532299, 28533336. Email: reserve@president.com
• **Hotel The Aruna Chennai**, 144, Sterling Road, Nungambakkam, Chennai - 600 034. ℗ 28259090, 28233561-565 Fax:044-28258282. Email: arunasales@ gmail.com

• **Savera Hotel,** 146, Dr. Radhakrishnan Road, Mylapore, Chennai - 600 004. ✆ 28114700 Fax: 28113475. Email: hotsave@md2.vsnl.net.in

Three Star

• **Breeze Hotel,** 850, Poonamallee High Road, Kilpauk, Chennai - 600 010. ✆ 26427772, 26428202, 26430593, 98400 60616. Fax: 044-26413301 Email: breeze@vsnl.com

• **Days Inn Deccan Plaza,** 36, Royapettah High Road, Chennai - 600 014. ✆ 66713333 Fax: 044-66713344. Email: info@deccanhotels.com

• **Hotel Abu Palace,** 926, EVR Periyar Road, Chennai - 600 084. ✆ 26412222, 26431010 Fax: 91-44-26428091. Email: abuin@vsnl.com

• **Hotel Aadithya,** 155/1, Arcot Road, Chennai - 26. ✆ 23650055, 23651808 Fax: 044-23650808 Email: aadithyamdsind@eth.net

• **Hotel Dee Cee Manor,** 90, G.N. Chetty Road, Chennai - 17. ✆ 28284411, 28282696 Fax: 044-28282775 Email: dcmanor@vsnl.com

• **Hotel Ganga International P Ltd.,** 47, Bazullah Road, T. Nagar, Chennai - 17. ✆ 28141321-1322. Fax: 044-28145193

• **Hotel Kanchi,** 28, Ethiraj Salai, Egmore, Chennai - 600 105. ✆ 2827 1100 (10 lines). Fax: 044-28272928 Email: reservation@hotelkanchi.com

• **Hotel Mars** 768, Pammal Main Road, Pallavaram, Chennai - 600 043. ✆ 22402586, 22641523 Fax: 044-22404064 Email: hotelmars@yahoo.com

• **Hotel Maurya International,** 168-169, Arcot Road, Chennai - 26. ✆ 23650049 (8 lines). Fax: 044-23650052

• **Hotel Palmgrove,** 5, Kodambakkam High Road, Nungambakkam, Chennai - 600 034. ✆ 28271881 Fax: 044-28231977

• **Hotel Radha Park Inn International,** 171, J. Nehru Salai, Inner Ring Road, Arumbakkam, Chennai - 600 106. ✆ 66778899 Fax: 044-24756644 Email: parkinn@vsnl.com

• **Hotel Royal Southern,** S.R.M. Nagar, Chennai - 603 203. Email: srmhotels@net4india.com

• **Hotel Shelter,** 19-21, Venkatesa Agraharam St., Mylapore, Chennai - 600 004. ✆ 24951919 Fax: 044-24935646. Email: shelter@vsnl.com

• **Madras Hotel Ashoka Private Limited,** 33, Pantheon Road, Chennai - 600 008. ✆ 28553377 Fax: 044-28553668

• **Mowbrays Inn** 303, TTK Road, Alwarpet, Chennai - 600 018 ✆ 24970555, 24984326, 24993915. Fax: 044-24984319, 24971764 Email: mowbrays@md3.vsnl.net.in

• **New Victoria Hotel,** 3, Kennett Lane, Egmore, Chennai - 600 008. ✆ 28193638 (10 lines). Fax: 044-28190070 Email:hotelnewvictoria@vsnl.com

• **New Woodlands Hotel (P) Limited,** 71-72, Dr. Radhakrishnan Road, Mylapore, Chennai - 600 004. ✆ 28113111 (26 lines). Fax: 044-28110460 Email: newwoodlands@vsnl.com

• **The Dakshin** 35, Venkatanarayana Road, Nandanam, Chennai - 600 035. ✆ 24330866/0871/0948/6574/6575 Fax: 044-24322639 Email: deokarg@hotmail.com

• **The Grand Orient,** 693, Anna Salai, Chennai - 600 006. ✆ 28524111 Fax: 044-28523412. Email: empeegrandorient@vsnl.com

• **The Residency,** 46, GN Chetty Road, T.Nagar, Chennai - 600 017. ✆ 28253434 Fax: 044-28250085. Email: resmds@vsnl.com

Two Star

• **Hotel Dasaprakash,** 100, Poonamallee High Road, Chennai - 600 084. ✆ 28255115 (8 lines).

• **Hotel Maris,** 11, Cathedral Rd., Chennai - 600 086. ✆ 28110541 (10 lines). Fax: 044-28114847

• **Hotel Pandian** 15, Kennet Lane, Egmore, Chennai - 600 008. ✆ 28191010/20 Fax: 044-28193030 Email: hotelpandian@vsnl.com

• **Hotel Peninsula,** 51, GN Chetty Road, T.Nagar, Chennai - 600 017. ✆ 28150001-2815007 Fax: 044-28150008 Email: peninsul@ md3.vsnl.net.in

• **Hotel Premier,** 22, Poonamallee High Road, Chennai - 600 003. ✆ 25383311.

• **Hotel Ranjith,** 15, Nungambakkam High Road, Chennai - 600 034. ✆ 28270521, 28277688. Fax: 044-28277688 Email: hotelranjith@yahoo.com

• **Hotel Sindoori Central,** 26/27, Poonamallee High Road, Chennai - 600 003. ✆ 25386647. Fax: 044-25387022 Email: sindhotels@vsnl.com

One Star

• **Hotel Swagath,** 243-244, Royapettah High Road, Chennai - 600 014. ✆ 28132971 (21 lines).

• **Tourist Homes Private Limited,** 45, Gandhi Irwin Road, Egmore, Chennai - 600 008. ✆ 28250079.

• **VGP Universal Kingdom,** East Coast Road, Injambakkam, Chennai - 600 041. ✆ 24491101, 24491442, 24491446 Fax: 044-24490514

Others

• **Admiralty Hotel,** 5, Norton Road, Mandaveli, Chennai - 600 028. ✆ 24641121

• **Beverly Hotel** 17, Rajarathinam Road, Kilpauk, Chennai - 600 010. ✆ 26481299 Fax: 044-26613172. Email: beverly@vsnl.com

• **Buena Vista,** Beach Road, Neelangarai, Chennai - 600 041. ✆ 24492222 Fax: 044-24495008. Email: info@bv-india.com

• **Buharis Blue Lagoon Hotel,** 79-A, East Coast Rd., Neelankarai, Chennai - 600 041. ✆ 24491425.

• **Guru Regency** No. 8 to 12, Balfour Road, Kilpauk, Chennai - 600 010. ✆ 26449090, 26449191 Fax: 044-26453298. Email: pmg22@hotmail.com

• **Hotel Blue Diamond,** 934, Poonamallee High Road, Chennai - 600 084. ℭ 26412244. Fax : 044 - 26428903

• **Hotel Shan Royal,** 85, Poonamallee High Road, Chennai - 107. ℭ 26221212, 26194648 Fax : 044-26286998

• **Hotel Garden,** 68-A, Purasawalkam High Road, Chennai - 600 007. ℭ 26422677, 26422188, 26424484, 26424540, 26424492-93, 26424547

• **Hotel Impala Continental,** 12, Gandhi Irwin Road, Egmore, Chennai - 600 008. ℭ 28250564, 28193097

• **Hotel L.R. Swami Narayanan,** 83, Usman Road, T.Nagar, Chennai - 600 017. ℭ 24339796

• **Hotel MGM Grand,** New No. 31, Santhome High Road, Mylapore, Chennai - 600 004. ℭ 24980320/99/11 Fax: 044-24980360

• **Hotel Nayagara** 15, II Cross, United India Colony, Kodambakkam, Chennai - 600 024. ℭ 24818283 Fax : 24819112

• **Hotel Peacock,** 1089, Poonamalle High Road, Chennai - 600 084. ℭ 25322981 (8 lines), 25321080 (10 lines).

• **Hotel Picnic Plaza,** 2, RK Mutt Road, Mylapore, Chennai - 600 004. ℭ 24941730.

• **Courtyard by Marriot,** 564, Anna Salai, Teynampet, Chennai - 600 018. ℭ 66764000, Fax : 044-66764001

• **Nilgiri's Nest,** 105, Dr. Radhakrishnan Road, Mylapore, Chennai - 600 004. ℭ 28115111, 28115222/28110716, 28111772-73 Fax: 044-28111719 Email: nilgirisnest@sify.com

• **Picnic Hotel,** 1132/1, Poonamallee High Road, Chennai - 600 003. ℭ 2538 8809/28 Fax: 044-25366850 Email: picnic@dataone.in

• **MGM Diamond Beach Resort** 1/74, New Mahabalipuram Road, Muttukadu, Chennai - 603 112. ℭ 27472487

• **Y.W.C.A. Guest House** 1086, Poonamallee High Road, Chennai. ℭ 26613178

• **Youth Hostels** Indira Nagar, Chennai - 600 020. ℭ 24420233.

Important Information

• Govt. of Tamil Nadu Tourist Office, Panagal Building, Saidapet, Chennai-15. ℭ 24321694.

• Tourist Information Centre, Central Railway Station ℭ 25353351.

• Tourist Information Centre, Egmore Railway Station ℭ 28252165.

• Tourist Information Centre, Domestic Terminal, Chennai Airport ℭ 22340569.

• Tourist Information Centre, International Airport ℭ 22349347.

• Tamil Nadu Tourism Development Corporation, Head Office, ℭ 28545684.

• Tamil Nadu Tourism Development Corporation, Dr. Radhakrishnan Salai, Chennai - 4. ℭ 28547344 Fax : 28546620.

• Govt. of India Tourist Office, 154, Anna Salai, Chennai-2 ℭ 22852429, 28254785 Fax : 28252193.

• Tourist Information Centre (Govt. of India), Domestic Terminal, Chennai Airport. ℭ 22560569, 22560338.

• Tourist Information Centre (Govt. of India), International Terminal, Chennai Airport ℭ 22560682.

• Maharashtra Mandal, 61, E.V.K. Sampath Road, Chennai ℭ 22560328.

• Publications Division, Sales Emporium, 731, Anna Salai, Chennai ℭ 28267643.

State Information Centre (Govt. of Tamil Nadu)

• Mahakavi Bharathiyar Memorial House, T.P.Koil St, Triplicane, Chennai-5. ℭ 28591393.

• Hindu Religious & Charitable Endowments, Nungambakkam High Rd., Chennai-34 ℭ 28279402.

• Music College, Chennai-28. ℭ 24937217.

• Tamil Nadu Iyal Isai Nataka Mandram, Chennai-28 ℭ 24936848, 24937471

• Kalakshetra, Tiruvanmiyur, Chennai. ℭ 24520836, 24524057

• Automobile Association of South India ℭ 28521162, 28524061

• Youth Hostel Association of India ℭ 24820976

• State Guest House, Chennai. ℭ 25366921-24

Kanchipuram
(Temple Town)
How to get there?

It is 71 km. away from Chennai and well connected by a network of good roads. Frequent bus services are available from Kanchipuram to Chennai, Bengalooru and other places. There is a Railway Station. Nearby Airport: Chennai Tirusulam Airport. Rail link from Chennai via Chengalpattu upto Arakkonam. Road link to all major cities.

Places to see:
TEMPLES

1. Ekambaranathar temple
2. Vaikunta Perumal temple
3. Kailasanathar temple
4. Varadarajaswami temple
5. Kamakshi Amman temple
6. Muktheeswarar temple
7. Mathangeswarar temple

8. Ashtabujam temple
9. Ulagalanda Perumal temple
10. Kumarakottam
11. Jain temple, Thiruparankundram
12. Kanchi Kamakoti Peetam Math.

Full details about these temples can be had under the heading 'Temples in and around Chennai' in the chapter 'Chennai'.

CHURCHES

Protestant Church - near Railway station; Roman Catholic Church - Konerikuppam.

MOSQUES

Jama Masjid, Hajaratha Burhana, Avulia Durgah and Hamid Avulia Durgah.

ANNA MEMORIAL

It is in Little Kanchipuram or Vishnu Kanchi. Dr. C.N. Annadurai, the former Chief Minister of Tamil Nadu and the founder of D.M.K. was born here. His ancestral house here has been converted into a memorial. Various exhibits like photographs, the articles used by him and important events of his life are portrayed here. As he is associated with the Dravidian movement and the nationalist movement one can see the evolution of these important movements which made a breakthrough in the lives of the Tamils who hailed him as their elder brother – 'Anna'.

HISTORICAL IMPORTANCE

From time immemorial it has been hailed as one of the holy cities of India. Buddhism, Jainism, Saivism and Vaishnavism thrived here. It was the northern capital of the Cholas, the main capital of the Pallavas and even during the Vijayanagar period, it was an important centre. The Pallava, Chola and Vijayanagar art and architecture flourished here and the temples of this city are living monuments of them. It is at present the head-quarters of Kanchipuram district and the Collector's office is located here.

HANDLOOM INDUSTRIES

Kanchipuram silk sarees are known all over the world. Beautiful high grade pure mulberry silk of various hues are woven into sarees by traditionally trained weavers reputed for texture, lustre, durability and fine finish. These sarees are exported to foreign countries. About 5000 families are engaged in this industry. Sarees are available at loom prices here and through cooperative societies.

NEARBY PLACES OF EXCURSION

• Sriperumpudur - 29 km. •Tiruttani - 42 km. • Vedantangal bird sanctuary - 60 km.

Full details of the above places are given under the heading 'Temples in and around Chennai'.

Where to stay?

• **Hotel Tamil Nadu (T.T.D.C.)**, 78, Kamakshi Amman Street, Kanchipuram. ✆ : 222533. Grams: Tamil Tour
• **Municipal Rest House.**
• Umpteen hotels and private lodges are also available.

Mamallapuram

(The splendour of Pallava art)

How to get there?

It is 60 km away from Chennai and linked by a good road running along the coast of the Bay of Bengal connected to Chengalpattu and Kanchipuram via Thirukkaluk-kundram. Nearest railway station: Chengalpattu. Nearest Airport: Chennai. Daily tourist coaches of T.T.D.C. and umpteen bus services are available.

Places to see

1. Shore temples, 2. Pandava raths, 3. Krishna Mandapam, 4. Rock-cut caves – nine in number, 5. Old

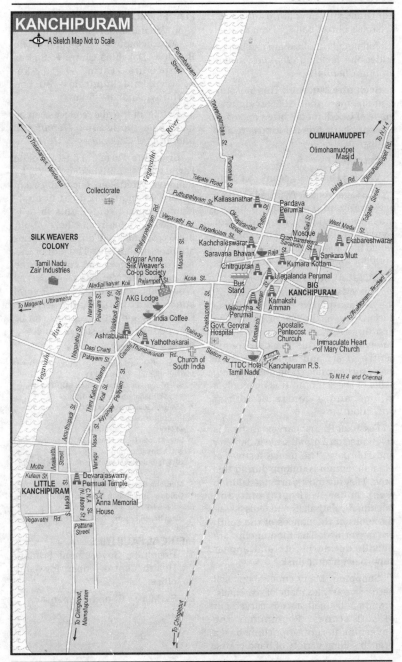

KANCHIPURAM

Ⓝ A Sketch Map Not to Scale

Perumbakkam Street

River
Vegavathi

Thiravengamani St.

To Thiruttani, Vandavasi

OLIMUHAMUDPET

Olimohamudpet Masjid

To NH.4

Pattai Rd.

Olimuhamudpet Rd.

Tolgate Road

Collectorate

Puttupalayam St.

Kailasanathar

Pillayarpalayam Rd.

Vegavathi Rd.   Rayarkolam St.

SILK WEAVERS COLONY

Tamil Nadu Zair Industries

Arignar Anna Silk Weaver's Co-op Society

Aladipillaiyar Koil

Rajampet St.

Madam St.

Kosa St.

Chakkupetai St.

Pandava Perumal

Okkapiranthar Street

Puttari St.

Sali St.

Mosque

West Mada St.

Ekabareshwarar

Ekambareswara Sanandhi St.

Sankara Mutt

Kumara Kottam

Ulagalanda Perumal

BIG KANCHIPURAM

Kachchaleswarar

Saravana Bhavan

Raja St.

Chitruptan

Bus Stand

Vaikuntha Perumal

Kamakshi Amman

Kamakshi St.

Apostalic Pentecost Churcuh

To Palakkonam, Arcotram

To Magaral, Uttiramerur

Narayan St.

Palayam St.

Vinkadi Koil St.

AKG Lodge

India Coffee

Govt. General Hospital

Ashtabujam

Desi Chetti

Palayam St.

Megaladhu St.

Vegavathi River

Gandhi Rd.

Thumbavanan Rd.

Railway

Station Rd.

Yathothakarai

Church of South India

TTDC Hotel Tamil Nadu

Kanchipuram R.S.

Immaculate Heart of Mary Church

To N.H.4 and Chennai

Thiru Kalch Nambi

Koil St.

Vasai St.

Aiyangar Palayam

Amuthvaadi St.

Analkathu Street

Motta Kulam St.

LITTLE KANCHIPURAM

N.Mada St.

Vegavathi Rd.

Pattana Street

Devarajaswamy Perumal Temple

C.N.A. St. (N.Mada St.)

Anna Memorial House

To Chingleput, Mamallapuram

To Chingleput

lighthouse & new lighthouse, 6. Krishna's butter ball, 7. Tiger's cave.

Full details about them can be had under the heading *'Temples in and around Chennai'.*

Sculpture Museum: This museum contains more than 3000 sculptures made of wood, metal, brass and even cement. Some fine paintings are also on display.

Entry fee :   Rs. 2/-

Visiting Hours : 9.00 am - 5.00 pm

Massage, Yoga & Ayurveda : There are many places here offering massage, reiki, yoga and other Ayurvedic practices. The charges would be somewhere between Rs. 400 - 500 for a session of 30 - 45 minutes.

HISTORICAL IMPORTANCE

This was a flourishing port during the Pallava period and later Chola period. The birthplace of one of the first three Alwars – Boothathalwar. The Pallavas made this place a unique centre of art and architecture. At every turning, one could find amazing skills of the sculptor. It is now only a village and a centre of tourist attraction.

Festival: Pongal harvest festival is celebrated on a grand scale in January and February. The dance festival of Mamallapuram is unique during this time. They are mostly arranged during week-ends. Bharatanatyam, Kuchipudi, Kathakali and Odissi – all the types of the dances of the south are performed. The monuments are floodlit during nights and appear superb even after dusk.

Shopping: Many small shops sell decorative articles made of sea-shells, granite and small statues carved out of soft stones. Poompuhar the government-run emporium has a branch selling variety of handicrafts.

PLACES AROUND MAMALLAPURAM

- Vedanthangal Birds Sanctuary
- Muttukkadu • Covelong - The Beach • Dakshina Chitra • Sadras
- Crocodile Farm - 14 km
- Thirukkalukkundram - 30 km.
- Thiruvidandhai - 5 km.

Details of the above places can be had under the heading *'Temples in and around Chennai'.*

Crocodile Farm : The Crocodile Farm was established in 1976 by Romulve Whittaker. Located 14 km before Mamallapuram (Chennai-Mamallapuram route), this farm is spread 3.2 hectares, where about 5000 crocodiles of 6 different species are bred in captivity. The aim of this farm is to protect and conserve the endangered reptiles such as crocodiles, Alligators, etc. Several species of Indian and African Crocodiles and other reptiles can be viewed here from a safe distance.

Where to stay?

- **Ramakrishna Lodge,** 8, Othavadai Street, Mamallapuram. ✆ 27442331
- **Sri Murugan Guest House,** 42, Othavadai Street, Mamallapuram. ✆ 2742552
- **Mamalla Bhavan Annexe,** 104, East Raja Street, Mamallapuram. ✆ 27442260 Fax : 91-44-27442160
- **Silver Moon Guest House,** 2A, Othavadai Cross Street, Mamallapuram. ✆ 27443644
- **GRT Temple Bay,** Mamallapuram. ✆ 27442251 Fax : 91-44-27442257
- **Mamalla Beach Resort,** ✆ 27442375
- **Golden Sun Beach Resort,** ✆ 27442245 Fax : 91-44-27442900
- **Ideal Beach Resort,** ✆ 27442240 Fax : 91-44-27442243

MEDICAL FACILITIES

1. Hospitals, Government Primary Health Centre - near Township office.

2. St. Mary's Church Dispensary

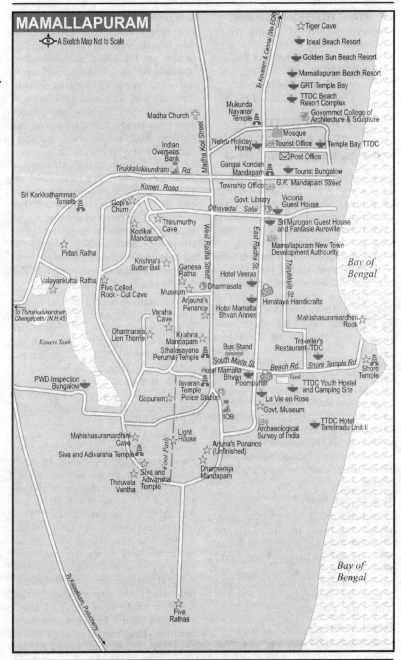

MAMALLAPURAM

N — A Sketch Map Not to Scale

To Kovalam & Cennai (Via ECR)

☆ Tiger Cave

🛏 Ideal Beach Resort

🛏 Golden Sun Beach Resort

🛏 Mamallapuram Beach Resort

🛏 GRT Temple Bay

🛏 TTDC Beach Resort Complex

Mukunda Nayanar Temple

🏛 Governmet College of Architecture & Sculpture

Madha Church ✝

Madha Koil Street

Nehru Holiday Home

🕌 Mosque

🏛 Tourist Office Temple Bay TTDC

✉ Post Office

Indian Overseas Bank

Gangai Kondan Mandapam

🏛 Tourist Bungalow

Tirukkalukkundram Rd.

Township Office G.K. Mandapam Street

Koneri Road

Govt. Library

Victoria Guest House

Sri Karkkathamman Temple

Gopi's Churn

Othavadai Salai

🏛 Sri Murugan Guest House and Fantasie Auroville

Thirumurthy Cave

Kodikal Mandapam

West Radha Street

East Radha St.

Mamallapuram New Town Development Authourity

Pidari Ratha

Krishna's Butter Ball

Ganesa Ratha

Bay of Bengal

Valayankuttai Ratha

Five Celled Rock - Cut Cave

Museum

🏛 Dharmasala

Hotel Veeras

👜 Himalaya Handicrafts

To Thirukkalukundram, Chengalpattu (N.H.45)

Varaha Cave

Arjauna's Penance

Hotel Mamalla Bhvan Annex

Mahishasuramardhini Rock

Koneri Tank

Dharmaraja Lion Thorne

Krishna Mandapam

Sthalasayana Perumal Temple

Bus Stand

Traveller's Restaurant TDC

Thirukkula St.

PWD Inspection Bungalow

South Mada St.

Hotel Mamalla Bhvan

Beach Rd. Shore Temple Rd. ☆ Shore Temple

Isvaran Temple Police Station

Poompuhar

Tank

TTDC Youth Hostel and Camping Site

Gopuram

IOB

La Vie en Rose

☆ Govt. Museum

TTDC Hotel Tamilnadu Unit II

Mahishasuramardhini Cave

Light House

Archaeological Survey of India

Siva and Adivaraha Temple

Foot Path

Aruna's Penance (Unfinished)

Thiruvala Ventha

Siva and Adivaraha Temple

Dharmaraja Mandapam

To Kalpakkam, Puducherry

Bay of Bengal

Five Rathas

43 >

IMPORTANT TELEPHONE NUMBERS

* Government of Tamil Nadu Tourist Office: 27442232
* Archaelogical Survey of India : 27442226
* Police Station: 27442221
* Town Panchayat Office: 27442223

Puducherry
(Pondicherry)
(The lingering French Culture)

Puducherry is 162 km south of Chennai. It was the former French settlement. Even before that, it was known as Vedapuri and once maritime trade flourished here. Roman coins, wine jars and other articles reveal Roman connections and its antiquity is considered to be before the Christian era. It was under the rule of the Cholas, Pallavas and the Vijayanagar kings. Later it came under the Golconda Sultan and the French bought it from him in 1763 and founded their settlement. Besides Puducherry, another place Karaikal about 150 km south of Chennai on the seashore and Yenam in Andhra Pradesh and Mahe in Kerala also form part of the Union Territory of Puducherry. Even after Indian Independence, Puducherry remained under French rule and only in 1954 was the *de jure* transfer to India made by France.

How to get there?

Puducherry is linked by a good network of roads to almost all the important places in South India. Buses ply every half an hour to Puducherry from Chennai. It is also linked by rail with Chennai, Trichirappalli and Villupuram. A small airport has also come up in Puducherry.

Places to see

Sri Aurobindo Ashram: The main attraction of Puducherry is Sri Aurobindo Ashram. Sri Aurobindo who was the stalwart freedom fighter of the pre-Gandhian era, following spiritual Adesh (voice or order) came to Puducherry in 1910, then a French territory, and remained here for ever practising Yoga. He was later joined by a French lady, Mirra known as the Mother. After the mother's coming, the followers increased in number and the Ashram came into being. After Sri Aurobindo's retirement to recluse in 1926, Mother shouldered the entire responsibility of the Ashram. Ever since, the Ashram has grown in leaps and bounds and today there are about 2000 inmates - Sadhakas practising in action the integral or supramental yoga of Sri Aurobindo.

The main Ashram building where Sri Aurobindo and the Mother's samadhis are enshrined is open to public from 8.00 a.m to 5.00 p.m. with a recess from 12.00 noon to 3 p.m. Anyone who happens to be there by 9.00 a.m. can take special permit and visit the room where Sri Aurobindo resided and did his splendid spiritual work. The things used by Sri Aurobindo and a rare collection of beautiful artifacts are kept there. In the reception counter the books of Sri Aurobindo are on sale. One could also buy pictures, calendars and diaries there – all connected with Sri Aurobindo and the Mother. The information centre will give you all details. The educational institutions run by the Ashram, the gymnasia and the playground activities and the cultural programmes and exhibitions organised every now and then by the Ashram could also be seen after obtaining permit from the reception counter. One can also take one's breakfast, lunch and dinner in the

Ashram dining hall by paying a small amount. Ashram guest-houses scattered nearby provide accommodation too at reasonable rates and most of them would be full – only early birds will find a niche in them.

There are some important days observed in the Ashram and public are allowed to have darshan of Sri Aurobindo's and the Mother's rooms. Thousands of devotees will gather on those days. The most important days are:

(i) January 1st - Prosperity Day

(ii) February 21st - Mother's Birthday

(iii) August 15th - Sri Aurobindo's Birthday

(iv) November 17th - The Mother's Samadhi Day

(v) November 24th - Supramental Day

(vi) December 5th - Sri Aurobindo's Samadhi Day

Beach: Puducherry is on the coast of the Bay of Bengal and the 1500 metre stretch beach is an ideal place for swimming and sunbathing. 4 metre tall statue of Mahatma Gandhi, a beautiful artificial mountain park near the Ashram playground, the statue of Puducherry's illustrious governor Dupleix and the War Memorial built by the French to commemorate the soldiers who sacrificed their lives for the victory of the First World War, the 150-year-old lighthouse are other attractions of the beach. The beach is maintained clean and of late boulders have been erected to prevent sea-erosion. Sri Aurobindo Society's beach office and the Puducherry Government Tourist Office are on the beach road.

French Institute: The only present link with France in Puducherry is this institute. It is an internationally acclaimed institute on Dumas Street founded in 1955 by Dr. J. Fillozet, the renowned French Indologist. It has a brilliant collection of rare books on Science, Technology, Ecology, Cartography, Pedagogy, Indian languages and culture. The Romain Rolland Library run by the government has a collection of 60,000 books some of them being rare French volumes.

The collection of the French Institute includes approx. 8600 palm-leaf codics (including 360 bundles of texts written on paper) and 1144 transcripts of manuscripts on paper in Devanagari script including five illustrated manuscripts. The Institute has published four volumes of descriptive catalogues. It is unique in that it is the largest collection of Saiddhantika manuscripts in the world.

The French Institute Manuscript Resource Centre has been in operation since August 2003. The MRC has so far documented 2500 manuscripts. The collection was registered in the World Memories of the UNESCO in July 2005 and was declared a "Manuscripts Resource Centre" in 2004 in recognition of the valuable collection.

For details contact : ℂ 0413-2334168 Ext - 123 Fax : 0413-2339534

JIPMER : Jawaharlal Nehru Institute of Post-graduate Medical Education and Research, started in 1979, it is one of the most prestigious institutions of its kind in India. This is one of the foremost medical institutions in the country and is located at the western entry point to Puducherry. This place is called *Gorimedu.*

Botanical Garden : The botanical garden planned by C.S.Perrotet in 1826 is near the old bus stand off the West Boulevard. It has a good collection of exotic flower plants, both alien and indigenous. There is a toy rail to amuse children and the Jawahar Bal Bhavan - a unique all-India organization to train children in various arts is also located here.

Aquarium : Another attraction in the Botanical Garden is the aquarium which has some rare species of ornamental fish.

Museum : The 1984 museum near the park facing the beach houses the antiques apart from the Roman coins and other articles of Roman origin unearthed from Puducherry. This reveals the connections of ancient times. There are also sections of archaeology, geology, and sculpture, handicrafts, artifacts, ornaments and things obtained in Arikamedu, a place in the nearby village Ariyankuppam. The bed used by Dupleix, a palanquin and a pousse-pousse that resembles a hand-pulled rickshaw are also on display.

Park : There is a well laid out park facing the beach and opposite the governor's residence. Most people take rest during the afternoon under the shady trees. The statues of Bharathiar and Bharathidasan have been erected here. One main attraction is the sculpture park interspersed in the garden with beautiful images and ornamental pillars looted by Dupleix from Gingee. In the centre is a cenotaph, raised by Napoleon, called Ayi Memorial - a woman who donated her tank to quench the thirst of people which is now the symbol of Puducherry.

Bharathiar & Bharathidasan Memorials : The national poet Bharathi took asylum in Puducherry when the British atrocities against freedom fighters were rampant. The house where he lived in Puducherry on the Dharma Raja Koil Street has been converted into a fine memorial by the Puducherry government. Rare photographs, manuscripts written in Bharathiar's own hand, volumes of his works and the papers he published are on display. Some of the things he used and some rare photographs of his associates are also on display.

Bharathidasan, the true revolutionary poet and disciple of Bharathiar is a native of Puducherry. The house where he resided has also been converted into a fitting memorial in Bharathidasan Road.

Anandharangam Pillai's House: The famous dubash who was right hand to Dupleix and who recorded the events of his days in his diary. Anandharangam Pillai's house could be seen in Ranga Pillai Street. The beautiful ornamental carvings on tables and stately doors with carvings and the articles used by him are on display here.

Mudaliarkuppam : Boating facilities are available at this village. T.T.D.C. operates Row boats, Pedal boats and Motor boats. A Snack bar will also be provided shortly. It is felt that this boat house will attract the tourists traveling on 'the East Coast Road' in large numbers and provide good quality entertainment. This village is located in Kancheepuram Dist. 92 Km. from Chennai and 36 Km. down Mamallapuram on the East Coast Road. Timing 10.00 a.m. to 6.00 p.m. Contact : T.T.D.C., Tourism Complex, Chennai-5. ✆ 25368358.

TEMPLES

Villiannur : Sri Gokilambal Thirukameswara Temple is located

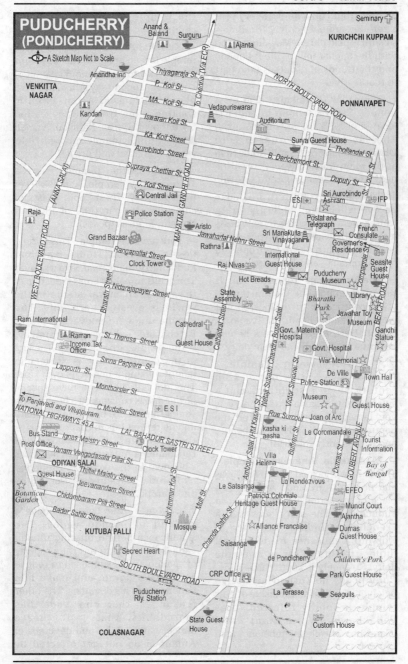

PUDUCHERRY
(PONDICHERRY)

Ⓝ—A Sketch Map Not to Scale

Seminary

KURICHCHI KUPPAM

Anand & Baland
Surguru
Ajanta

VENKITTA NAGAR

Anandha Inn

Thiyagaraja St.
P. Koil St.
MA. Koil St.
Iswaran Koil St.
KA. Koil Street
Aurobindo Street
Supraya Chettiar St.
C. Koil Street
Central Jail
Police Station

Kandan

Vedapuriswarar

Auditorium

To Chennai (Via ECR)

NORTH BOULEVARD ROAD

PONNAIYAPET

Surya Guest House
L. Thollandal St.
B. Derichemont St.
Duputy St.
ESI
Sri Aurobindo Ashram
IFP

Louis St.

Raja

Aristo
Jawaharlal Nehru Street
Rathna
Raj Nivas
Hot Breads

Grand Bazaar
Rangapallai Street
Clock Tower

Nidarajapayer Street

Sri Manakulla Vinayagam

Postal and Telegraph
French Consulate
Governer's Residence

International Guest House
Puducherry Museum

Seaside Guest House

Library

WEST BOULEVARD ROAD

TANSA SALAI

MAHATMA GANDHI ROAD

Bharati Street

State Assembly

Bharathi Park
Jawahar Toy Museum

Gandhi Statue

Ram International
Raman
Income Tax Office

Cathedral
Guest House

Cathedral Street

St. Theresa Street
Sinna Pappare St.
Lapporth St.
Monthorsier St.
C. Mudaliar Street

Govt. Maternity Hospital
Govt. Hospital
War Memorial
De Ville
Police Station
Town Hall

To Panjavadi and Viluppuram
NATIONAL HIGHWAYS 45 A

ESI

Museum
Guest House

LAL BAHADUR SASTRI STREET

Netaji Subash Chandra Bose Salai

Rue Surcouf
Joan of Arc

Bus Stand
Post Office
Ignas Maistry Street
Yanam Vengadasala Pillai St.
Clock Tower

ODIYAN SALAI

Guest House
Thillai Maistry Street
Jeevanandam Street
Chidambaram Pilli Street
Bader Sahib Street

Botanical Garden

KUTUBA PALLI

Ambour Salai (Hd Kasim St.)

Vada Simone St.

Buffron St.

kasha ki aasha
Le Coromandale

Villa Helena

Le Satsanga
Patricia Coloniale
Heritage Guest House

Saisanga

Alliance Francaise

de Pondicherry

La Rondezvous

Dumas St.

GOUBERT AVENUE

Tourist Information

Bay of Bengal

EFEO
Muncif Court
Ajantha
Dumas Guest House

Children's Park

Chanda Sahib St.

Eliai Amman Koil St.

Mull St.

Mosque

Sacred Heart

SOUTH BOULEVARD ROAD

CRP Office

La Terasse

Park Guest House

Seagulls

Puducherry Rly. Station

State Guest House

Custom House

COLASNAGAR

10 kms from Puducherry. Every year a ten-day annual festival (Brahmotsavam) is held during May-June along with the appearance of the full moon and thousands of devotees take part in that festival.

Tirunallar (Karaikal) : The most famous Saturn temple in India is located here, 5 km west of Karaikal. The sanctum sanctorum of Lord Dharbaraneswara Temple holds Siva as the main deity. However, its shrine dedicated to Saneeswaran (Saturn).

The blessings of Saturn are said to be overwhelming, while its wrath causes great misery. The temple hosts a mammoth festival (Shani peyarchi), each time Saturn moves from one sign of the zodiac to another.

The Varadaraja Temple : This is the most important Vishnu temple (12th century) in town, located just west of Gandhi Road, off Tyagaraja Street. Here Narasimha sits behind Venkatachalapathy, the main deity.

Vedapureeswarar Temple : Another Siva Shrine but of 18th century stone inscriptions and a swayambhulinga in Puducherry is very famous. Recently renovated, the gopuram (tower) adds to its beauty and is brilliantly colourful.

Manakkula Vinayakar Temple : This temple is located behind Raj Nivas and near to Aurobindo Ashram is a place of attraction for the tourist in Puducherry. The story goes that a Frenchman finding the place of worship a nuisance made several futile attempts to throw away the deity. Strangely it kept reappearing. Convinced, he turned an active beleiver. By locals, Ganesha of this temple is fondly referred to as Vellakkaran (White Man) Pillai (Ganesha). The elephant belonging to the temple is an attraction for children.

Karaikal Ammayar Temple : This temple has an image of the lady saint who is said to be among 63 saints of Lord Siva. Legend says that Lord Siva disguised himself as an ascentic seeking alms from a lady called "Punithavathi" from Karaikal. A small and beautiful temple erected right where she lived and prayed.

Sri Moolanthar Temple : This is a 10th century Temple, about 25 km from the city. The temple boasts of some granite carvings of Bharata Natyam Mudras (poses).

Panchavatee Temple : This temple lies in between Tindivanam and Puducherry main road, exactly near Thiruchitrambalam cross road, one of the tallest anjaneyar statue in the world is erected here only. The Panchamuga Anjaneya temple at Panchavatee is known for bestowing better health to the devotees. The idol of the central image is 36 feet in height making it one of its own kind. The idol is believed to have special power and is considered a healer. The Temple has indeed become a landmark and no tourist bus in that route skips the Temple. This vision of Panchamuga Anjaneya with five faces - his own in the centre, surrounded by Garuda, Hayagreeva, Narasimha and Varaha.

Devotees offer Lord Anjaneya a garland of ulundu vadas. The significance behind offering ulundu vada is that ulundu has the property of cooling and is supposed to reduce Anjaneya's ugram and make him beneficent to his devotees. The other reason is that the vada has ingredients that will please Saneeswaran, Rahu and devotees of Anjaneya do not get affected by planetary positions. If you move from Tindivanam to Puducherry you may find the temple Panchavatee at 29th Kilometre. From Puducherry towards Tindivanam road its one km ahead. Swami Abhishekam Daily 5.30 am to 6.30 am.

Pooja Timings : 08.30 am - 11.00 am and 04.00 pm - 08.00 pm.

For further details contact : 0413-2678823, 0413-2671232

Vattaparai Amman : In Thiruvamathur village is the famous Vattaparai Amman. It is a round-shaped rock and in olden times if any dispute arose instead of going to court they came here and standing before the deity will tell only the truth and nothing but the truth. The deity is supposed to be so powerful that any false witness would be severely dealt with by Amman, so none dared to utter falsehood. Many disputes were thus solved here.

Masthan Saheb Durga : This Durga is dedicated to Masthan Saheb Syed Dawood Buhari, a Sufi saint who came to Karaikal from Buhara two centuries ago. He died aged 120, in 1829. Various miracles are attributed to him. The above 170 year-old Kandhuri Festival (November) is celebrated. It starts with the hoisting of a huge flag on a pole-reminiscent of a ship mast and a sea-fairing tradition. And winds up, 10 days later with a spectacle of floats lit with electric colours.

Villiannur Church : The Church of the Capuchins was the first built in Puducherry and the only building that survived the destruction of the town in 1761. Today it is but a shell, however it has an interesting gabel.

The Church of the Immaculate Conception, the Cathedral, was built in 1791 on the place of a former church. It was built based on a design of an existing church in France and has varied ornamental decorations.

The Holy Heart of Jesus is an example of Gothic masonry work. It contains rare and beautiful stained glass panels depicting events of the life of Christ.

The Notre Dame des Anges (1852) is a beautiful built Church facing the ocean. Its clear lines, Greek-Roman architecture and mellow colours add to its harmony and the interior finish of shell-lime (Chettinad) plaster is superb.

IN AND AROUND PUDUCHERRY

Auroville: Auroville is composed of a cluster of properties some 12 km north of Puducherry. It can be easily reached via the East Coast Road (ECR) which connects Chennai and Puducherry. The visitor centre and Matrimandir can be reached by travelling eight kilometres westwards from the signposted turnoff at the ECR. Turning east leads directly to Auroville Beach, several hundred metres away.

Auroville (City of Dawn) is an experimental township in Viluppuram district in the state of Tamil Nadu, India near Puducherry in South India, whose stated purpose is to realize human unity in diversity. It is a popular tourist destination, and has been described as a "New Age metropolis conceived as an alternative exercise in ecological and spiritual living." The township starkly stands out from the surrounding traditional Indian villages and farms.

Auroville was founded in 1968 by Mirra Alfassa, known as The Mother. She was a collaborator of Sri Aurobindo, who believed that human evolution had not finished. The

Mother believed that this experimental community would evolve humans by bringing a more advanced consciousness called the supramental. The Indian government endorsed the township, and in 1966, UNESCO, the United Nations cultural organization, passed a resolution endorsing the project.

The Matrimandir : It is an unfinished golf-ball-like giant globe covered with golden discs located in the middle of the town. It was conceived by The Mother as "a symbol of the Devine's answer to man's inspiration for perfection." Silence is maintained inside the Matrimandir is called Peace area. The Peace area in which the structure is situated is characterised by three main features : the Matrimandir itself with its twelve gardens, twelve petals and future lakes, the Amphitheatre and the Banyan Tree.

A spiraling ramp leads upwards to an air-conditioned meditation room of polished white marble inside the Matrimandir. At its centre, a 70 cm crystal ball in a gold mount glows in column of sunlight.

Matrimandir has a solar power plant and is surrounded by perfectly manicured gardens.

Promenade : A lovely beach within bike range from the city centre in the north is a pleasant surprise. With a 1.5 km long promenade, this is the most delightful part of the city. A stroll, sunbath, or a swim enhances the quality of experience. On the beachfront are located many sites such as a statue of Mahatma Gandhi surrounded by eight exquistely carved monolithic pillars and a war memorial.

Yanam : This is one of the regions in the Union Territory of Puducherry, which is 870 kms away from it. It is situated on the East Coast of the Indian Peninsula at 16 degrees 42' northern latitude, and between 82 degree 11' Eastern longtitude bounded on all sides by the East Godavari District of Andhra Pradesh State. Temperatures in Yanam range from 27^0C to 45^0C in summer and 17^0C to 28^0C in winter.

The town of Yanam lies on the spot where the River Coringa (Atreya) branches off from Gauthami into two parts. The entire region, consisting of Yanam town and six villages is treated as Municipality for purposes of local administration. The region, which covers an area of 30.0 Sq.km. has a population of 31,362 according to the 2001 census. The region is bounded on the east and south by river Gauthami Godavari river which discharges itself into Bay of bengal after flowing almost 14 kms towards east from Yanam.

For further details contact : 0884 - 2321694, Email : dio.yanam@nic.in

Mahe : Mahe is a tiny point in the Geographical map of Kerala, the million earner for the distant Puducherry Government, 647 kms away from Puducherry. In this former small French Town which covers an area of 9 Sq.km, over 36,000 inhabitants live in peace. This petit French Town is situated on the West Coast of the Indian Peninsula between 11 Degrees 42' and 11 Degrees 43' Northern Latitude, and between 75 Degrees 31' and 75 Degrees 33' Eastern longtitude, just between Badagara and Thalassery, 58 kilometres from Kozhikode, 24 kilometres from Kannur in Kerala State and is a busy trade centre.

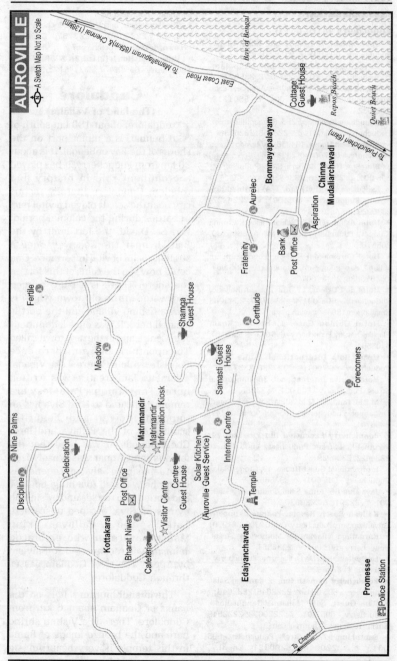

AUROVILLE

A Sketch Map Not to Scale

To Mamallapuram (55km) & Chennai (138km)

East Coast Road

Bay of Bengal

Cottage Guest House

Repos Beach

Quiet Beach

To Puduchcheri (6km)

Bommayapalayam

Chinna Mudaliarchavadi

Aspiration

Aurelec

Fraternity

Bank

Post Office

Shamga Guest House

Certitude

Fertile

Meadow

Samasti Guest House

Forecomers

Nine Palms

Discipline

Celebration

Matrimandir

Matrimandir Information Kiosk

Internet Centre

Kottakarai

Bharat Niwas

Post Office

Visitor Centre

Solar Kitchen (Auroville Guest Service)

Centre Guest House

Cafeteria

Temple

Edaiyanchavadi

Promesse

Police Station

To Chennai

Accommodation

Puducherry (STD: 0413)

• **Government Tourist Home,** Kolas Nagar, Puducherry - 605 001. ✆: 2358276-8

• **Government Tourist Home,** Uppalam, Puducherry - 605 001. ✆: 2358276, 2358278

• **Ajanta Sea View,** 50, Goubert Avenue, Beach Road, Puducherry - 605 001. ✆: 5501819, 2349032

• **Anandham Residency,** 255, Rangapillai Street, Puducherry - 605 001. ✆: 2226368, 2226358

• **Aristo Guest House,** 124,(50-A) Mission Street, Puducherry - 605 001 ✆: 2336728

• **Blue Star Hotel,** Kamaraj Salai, Puducherry - 605 001. ✆: 2338536, 2336836

• **Executive Inn (Pvt) Ltd,** 1-A, Perumal Koil Street, Puducherry - 605 001. ✆: 2224422, 2330929

• **Hotel Ashok (ITDC) (Beach Resort),** Chinna Kalapet, Puducherry - 605014. ✆: 2655160, 2655166.

• **Hotel Coromandel Kailash,** Poornakuppam Village, Ariyankuppam, Puducherry - 605 007. ✆: 2618836, 2618400

• **Hotel de I'Orient,** 17, Rue Romain Rolland, Puducherry - 605 001. ✆: 2343067, 2343068 Email:orient1804@satyam.net.in

• **Hotel Golden Gate,** 1, 1000 ft Road, Elapillaichavady, Puducherry - 605 013. ✆: 5503187, 5208564

• **Hotel Ram International,** Anna Salai, Puducherry - 605 001. ✆: 2337230, 2337239

• **Hotel Suriya International,** 36, Rangapillai Street, Puducherry - 605 001. ✆: 2338686

• **M.P.M. Inn,** 126, M.M.Adigal Salai, Bus Stand, Orleanpet, Puducherry - 605 005. ✆: 5207247, 2206701.

• **Pondicherry Executive Inn Pvt Ltd.** 14, Perumal Koil Street, Puducherry - 605 001. ✆: 2224422, 2330929

• **International Guest House,** 47, Gingee Salai, Puducherry - 605 001. ✆: 2336699

• **Jaya Inn,** 66, Anna Salai, Puducherry - 605 001. ✆: 2229137, 2226830

• **Kailash Beach Resort,** Pooranankuppam, Ariyankuppam, Puducherry. ✆: 2619700, 2619701

• **Karnataga Nilayam,** 1, Montorsier Street, Puducherry - 605 001. ✆: 2332351

• **Le Dupleix,** Rue De La Casarne, Puducherry - 605 001. ✆: 2226999

• **Pondicherry Ramesh Inn,** 5, Kamaraj Salai, Puducherry - 605 001. ✆: 2222645, 2222646

• **Ram Guest,** 546, Mahatma Gandhi Road, Puducherry - 605 001. ✆: 2220072, 2222549 Email : ramguest@hotmail.com

• **Santhi Inn,** 57, J.N. Street, Puducherry - 605 001. ✆: 2220946, 5200321 Email : santhinn@hotmail.com

• **The Promenade,** Beach Road, Puducherry - 605 001. ✆ 2227750, 2227757 Email : promenade@sarovarhotels.com

• **Vailankanni Hotels (P) Ltd.** 2A, S.V. Patel Salai, Puducherry - 605 001. ✆: 2337451, 2334407

Cuddalore

(The land of Vallalar)

Cuddalore, about 180 km south of Chennai, is a minor port on the shores of the Bay of Bengal. It is about 20 km from Puducherry. It has played a prominent role in history and religion. Cuddalore literally means city near the sea. It played a vital part in battles during the colonial period. Fort St. David, the fort built by the British near the sea was once a strategic point of vital importance. One could now see the ruins of this fort on the shore. There is a palm fringed backwater in the old town which is now a fishing village and the port is located here. It was once a dominant Jain Centre and in the new town called Thiruppathiri- puliyur, there once flourished a Jain Centre. Loka Vibaga, a famous Jain treatise was written here. The famous Pataleeswara temple dedicated to Lord Siva has an imposing tower and beautiful sculptures of the Pallava and later Chola periods. It was here that the famous saint Appar was proselytized from Jainisim to Saivism. Legend has it that he was tied to a huge boulder and hurled into the sea and by singing hymns on Siva, escaped unscathed. Later, the Pallava king Mahendravarman who embraced Jainism was reconverted to Saivism by Appar. The river Gedilam passes through Cuddalore.

Thiruvendhipuram : It is on the banks of Gedilam about 6 km from Cuddalore. There is a Vishnu shrine here and the bronze image of Rama in this temple is very beautiful – a rarity that cannot be seen anywhere else. Devanayaka Perumal is the presiding deity. There is a picturesque bathing ghat in the temple. Sri Vedanta Desikan, a famous Vaishnavaite saint is said to have lived here for 15 years.

Thiruvadigai Temple : It is a beautiful Siva temple on the banks of Gedilam about 3 km from Panrutti – a place renowned for cashewnuts and jackfruits. The Pallava Viruttaliswarar is the presiding deity. It was originally a Jain temple and Mahendravarman, the Pallava king demolished it and built this beautiful temple. It is renowned for its artistic images and stucco figures on the vimanam and gopuram. Even now a big Jain statue in sitting posture could be seen unsheltered in the temple. Some frescoes could also be seen on the ceiling of this temple, though damaged. A Vishnu temple and Gunapara Iswaran another Siva temple built with the demolished Jain temple could also be seen in the vicinity. Manavachagam Kadanthar's samadhi is also located in Panrutti town.

Vadalur is an important place associated with saint Ramalinga Adigal, southwest of Cuddalore. He is the author of *Thiruvarutpa* and a spiritual superman of yester years. He finally settled in this place and built an octagonal structure called 'Satya Gnana Sabha' here. This spot was chosen purposefully by him because one could see all the four towers of Chidambaram temple from here. The sanctum of this sabhai or temple is separated from the main hall by seven screens and only on 'Thai Poosam Day' in December-January all of them are lifted, otherwise only three will be removed. *Jothi* or eternal light is worshipped here. There is also a dharmasala which feeds all the people

who come here. It is said that the hearth lighted by Ramalinga Adigal is still kept burning. Nearby is Mettukuppam where one can see the room in which the saint locked himself and instructed not to open it till a stipulated time. People in anxiety opened it before the due date and to their surprise no trace of him could be seen there.

Neyveli - the Lignite Town : The lignite town Neyveli is near Vadalur and one can see the giant bucket wheel excavator digging the earth to reach the coals. Another attraction is the Artesian wells. It is a planned township. Thermal electric power is also produced here. With permit, one could visit the open mines and see the busy activities of the digging of the brown coal and the pumping of water on which the coal deposit is virtually floating under the earth. The high pressure water underneath has to be pumped before the coal is cut.

Devanampattinam Beach : It is a fine beach with sandy stretches and an ideal location for sea bathing. Since Cuddalore is a minor harbour one could see a row of ships anchored at a distance which are reached by catamarans and boats. New housing colonies are coming up here now.

How to Reach?

Cuddalore can be reached by rail and buses. Road link to all important places are available. Umpteen buses ply every day to Cuddalore or via Cuddalore.

Where to Stay?

Though it is the district headquarters, good lodges worth the name are not available. The best is to stay at Puducherry and visit Cuddalore and the nearby places. There are also some lodges and food is available in many hotels.

Tiruvannamalai
(The Place of Salvation)

Tiruvannamalai is a historic holy place, about 175 km from Chennai. It is the 'Mukthi Sthalam' (Place of Salvation) for several saints like Gugai Namachivayar, Seshadri Swamigal, Ramana Maharishi, Arunagirinathar etc. and the place is studded with caves and shelters of holy men. It is one of the 'Pancha Bootha Sthalams' (places of five elements) and the element here is Fire or Agni. It is called 'Sonachalam' in Sanskrit meaning red mountain – symbolic of fire.

How to get there?

It is about 175 km from Chennai and many buses ply daily. It is 66 km from Pondicherry and 68 km from Villupuram. As it is on the Katpadi-Villupuram meter gauge railway track, one can also reach it by train.

What to see?

Arunachaleswarar Temple : This is the most famous Siva temple and as mentioned earlier, one of the five element forms of Siva. It is at the foot of the hill - Tiruvannamalai. The temple is dedicated to Jothi Lingam or God incarnate as fire. It is an ancient temple. The Cholas, Vijayanagar kings, Hoysalas and the Nayakas of Thanjavur have all done various works and extended the temple to the present magnificence. It has imposing gopurams (portal towers) on all four sides and provides a majestic look. It is said that there are about 100 temples here but the chief one is this. The main gopuram is 66m high and has 13 storeys. The work was started by Krishna Devaraya and completed by Sevappa Nayaka of Thanjavur. There are many circumambulatory corridors and two large tanks inside the temple. There is a 1000-pillared mandap with floral paintings in its ceiling. Inscriptions of various rulers and chieftains abound the temple walls. Legend has it that Lord Siva stood in the form of a huge pillar of fire and the attempt of Vishnu to find his feet and the attempt of Brahma to find his head were futile. The lofty mountain is symbolic of this incident. Every year during Karthigai Deepam (November-December) a huge bonfire atop the hill is lighted in a cauldron serving as a lamp and thousands of tons of ghee poured in it with bales of cloth for wick. Lakhs of people from all over India throng to have a darshan of the sacred fire – Annamalai deepam which is visible around for many days despite heavy rains. The Kili Gopuram or parrot tower inside is very auspicious since Saint Arunagirinathar is said to have taken the form of a parrot while attaining salvation shedding his mortal coils. A sculptural representation of this could be seen on this gopuram. The Pathala Lingam or underground Lingam where the Saint Ramana Maharishi did penance is a main attraction in this temple. The samadhis of Seshadri Swamigal and Ramana Maharishi on the path round the mountain attracts streams of pilgrims - graceful places of peace and serenity. On full moon days, people throng here to walk round the mountain and reach the temple for worship. This is known as 'Girivalam' or going round the mountain. The Tamilnadu Tourism Development Corporation runs special buses from Chennai on these days.

A few kilometres east is a hamlet where the parapets of a tank is profusely covered with erotic sculptures rivalling Khajuraho. The legend has it that a Vijayanagar

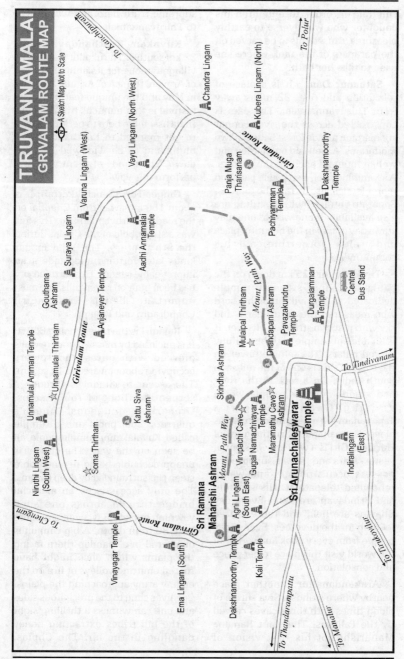

TIRUVANNAMALAI
GRIVALAM ROUTE MAP

A Sketch Map Not to Scale

To Kanchipuram

To Polur

Chandra Lingam

Kubera Lingam (North)

Vayu Lingam (North West)

Dakshnamoorthy Temple

Girivalam Route

Varuna Lingam (West)

Panja Muga Tharisanam

Pachiyamman Temple

Suraya Lingam

Aadhi Annamalai Temple

Gouthama Ashram

Anjaneyer Temple

Central Bus Stand

Durgaiamman Temple

Mulaipal Thirtham

Mount Path Way

Dhandapani Ashram

Pavazakundru Temple

Girivalam Route

Unnamulai Amman Temple

Unnamulai Thirtham

Skindha Ashram

To Tindivanam

Kattu Siva Ashram

Niruthi Lingam (South West)

Soma Thirtham

Virupachi Cave

Gugai Namachivayar Temple

Maramathu Cave Ashram

Sri Arunachaleswarar Temple

Indiralingam (East)

Mount Path Way

Sri Ramana Maharishi Ashram

To Chengam

Girivalam Route

Vinayagar Temple

Agni Lingam (South East)

Ema Lingam (South)

Dakshnamoorthy Temple

Kali Temple

To Tiruvoilur

To Thandarampattu

To Manalur

chieftain in order to enlighten his daughter who was averse to earthly pleasures, caused this to be carved on the parapets of the tank where she used to take her bath.

Sathanur Dam : It is a place of relaxation and rest, 22 miles away from Thiruvannamalai. The dam is constructed across the river Pennar submerging a huge forest between two mountains. A well laid out garden and well lit fountain enchant the visitors. A swimming pool, a crocodile park and motor launch also attract the tourists. Separate cottages with boarding are also available. If one wishes one may stay a day or two in the beautiful place and relax forgetting all his commitments.

Tirukkovilur : 25 km down on the banks of Pennar stands a temple dedicated to Thirivikrama the Lord who measured the entire earth and sky with just two strides of His feet. It is an ancient temple with beautifully carved pillars. The temple tower on the eastern side is one of the tallest in South India. On a rock in the river bed stands another temple worth visiting. **Gnananandagiri's Tapovanam** is a main attraction in this place. Gnanananda Giri, the guru of Haridoss Giri is a well known saint of yester-years and he was supposed to possess occult powers and was a renowned telepathist. His samadhi and Brindavan are here. Every day Bhajans are held and there is free feeding for the devotees. Even today people from every nook and corner of the world visit this place to get peace and consolation.

Arakandanallur: Another place nearby where stands a Siva shrine of olden times with three caves carved by the Pallavas. The saint Ramana Maharishi got his first vision of

supreme truth here and was drawn to Thiruvannamalai.

Kuvakam Koothandavar Koil: 22 km south of Thirukoilur stands this village famous for its annual festival of Aravan, the son of Arjuna. It occurs in May and the unique feature of this festival is that eunuchs from all over India assemble here to perform a vow to get married to Koothandavar at night and to be widowed by next dawn. Thousands of them visit and perform this vow.

Gingee Fort (Senchikkottai): It is about 150 km away from Chennai on the road to Thiruvannamalai. This fort was a stronghold of the Cholas during the 9th century. The Vijayanagar kings later fortified and made it an impregnable citadel. This fortified city has been built on seven hills, the most important being Krishnagiri, Chandragiri and Rajagiri.

Rajagiri is the tallest rising 600 ft. It is enclosed by massive granite walls pierced with gates and towers occupying about an area of 12 sq. km. The ascent to citadel is through a serpentine flight of rough steps. Granaries, dungeons, queen's quarters, cool pools and a temple called Kuvalakanni temple could all be seen on the way. The citadel is unapproachable being perched on a steep cliff surrounded by deep chasms. The only access is by an artificial bridge thrown across one such yawning gap of 25 ft. wide and more than 80 ft. in depth. A big cannon is quartered in a mandap there facing the plains which once might have roared emitting volleys of fire on the enemy army approaching the plains. Beehives cling to the precipitous sides and one can witness a thrilling sight of the hill tribes extracting honey dangling in the air. The Cholas,

Vijayanagar kings, Rajputs, Marathas, French, Nawabs, the Nayaks and the English evinced keen interest in keeping the strategic citadel.

The small hill is ascended by a flight of steep steps cut on the buttress of the fort. There is an audience hall atop and one could experience the cool fast winds embracing him/her. The fort is immortalised in the ballads of Raja Desingh – a hero of the Moghul period who with undaunted courage defied the Moghuls. When he was killed treacherously, the entire harem committed sathi – self immolation. Even today a pit near the tank called *Chakkara Kulam*' is shown as the place where it happened.

The tutelary deity of Raja Desingh was Lord Vishnu called Ranganatha and can be seen on the hill at **Singavaram**, 32 kms north. It is a cave temple furnished by Mahendra Varma Pallavan. The God is in the recumbent posture here. In the prakara of this temple, one could see the relief of a chilling spectacle of a devotee severing his head as an offering to Durga.

Panamalai : On the road to Villupuram from Gingee on the southern side lies this place. Here Pallava king Rajasimha has built a famous temple to Thalapuriswara–a Siva temple. There are some fine frescoes existing in good condition illustrating the Pallava style.

Mandagappattu : About 17 km on the way to Gingee from Villupuram stands this famous rock-cut cave temple of Pallava king Mahendra Varma who had the *nom-de-plume* of Vichitra Chittan and who boasts that he has built temples that will last for ever as they are made without mud and wood.

Mel-Sittamur : It is on the way to Tindivanam from Gingee. Temples dedicated to Jain Tirthankaras could be seen here. It is the headquarters of the chief Jain monk and possesses rare Jain manuscripts. In the beginning of Christian era when portions of Mylapore were submerged under the sea, the Jain temple that existed there was shifted to this far-off place inland. Whatever could be salvaged were removed and brought to this place. There are some fine carvings in the temple. Jain research scholars visit this temple. A good number of Jains scattered nearby come for worship.

Dhalavanur : Another rock-cut temple exists here, built by Mahendra Varman, the Pallava king. The temple is called *Satru Malleswaram*. The name derives from Satrumalla one of the titles of Mahendra Varman.

Thiruvakkarai : It is near Tindivanam on the banks of the river Varaha Nadhi. Here is a temple, part of which was erected by Sembian Mahadevi, the Chola queen. It is curious in many respects. The entrance way is not aligned in a line. The Nandi of this temple is planted away from its usual place in front of the sanctum. There is an unusual mudra of the Chathura Dance pose of Nataraja. It is a place famous for trees that have become rocks and fossilised due to passage of time. They are displayed in a special park. During full moon days, hundreds of people gather here to worship the multi-handed Kali known as Vakra Kali Amman enshrined near the front gopuram.

By a strange convention, in this temple, the regular Pooja is performed in the period known as 'Ragukalam' or the period under the influence of Ragu.

Sanyasikuppam : On the way to Pondicherry from Tindivanam one can reach this place where an elaborately carved stone bull stands. **Valudavur**, a nearby place has the ruins of a fort, once the residence of Mahabath Khan, the minister of Raja Desingh.

Where to Stay?

Tiruvannamalai (STD: 04175)

• **Hotel Ramakrishna**, 34-F, Polur Road, Tiruvannamalai. ✆ : 2225004 Fax : 2225008
• **Hotel Deepam**, 9, Car Street, Tiruvannamalai.
• **Swathi Lodge**, 27, Othavadai Street, Tiruvannamalai. ✆ : 2226426/27
• **Trishul Hotel**, Kanakaraya Mudali Street, Tiruvannamalai. ✆ : 2222219

☞ *We have covered here almost all the important places of tourist interest on the way to Tiruvannamalai and the nearby places that could be covered en route to Tiruvannamalai.*

Vellore

(The Fort Town)

Vellore is 145 km from Chennai. It was the last capital of Vijayanagar empire, now a busy town, a market for various agricultural commodities and the district headquarters. There are some rare places of tourist importance in and around Vellore. One could stay here comfortably and visit the places. The climate is generally hot with cool nights–a typical example of inland climate where there is considerable difference between high and low temperatures. 'A temple without idol, A river without water and A fort without forces' is a local saying about this town.

How to get there?

Vellore is very well connected with important places by good roads. There are buses every half an hour to Vellore from Chennai. There is also a rail link on Chennai-Bangalore route. Katpadi is the nearby junction and from Katpadi there is a metre gauge link to Vellore. The nearest airport is at Chennai.

Places to See

Vellore Fort : It is a moated fort of the Vijayanagar period built around the 16th century preserved in good condition even today. It was built of granite blocks with a moat watered from a subterranean drain fed by a tank. It was built by Chinna Bomminayaka, a chieftain of the Vijayanagar emperors, Sadasivaraya and Srirangaraya. It was later in the hands of Muthraza Ali, the brother-in-law of Chanda Sahib. It then passed into the hands of Marathas from whom it came under David Khan of Delhi in 1760. Then it was under Tipu Sultan. Finally, it came to the British after the fall of Srirangapatnam. At first, Tipu's children were kept in safe custody here. It is like the Windsor Castle of South India and the only one of its kind. Even before the first war of Indian Independence in 1857, a revolt against the British broke out here in 1806 which is in fact the harbinger of the 1857 Sepoy Mutiny. Various public buildings and private offices including the police training centre and a jail are inside the fort.

Jalakanteswara Temple : A Siva temple that was built at the same time the fort was built around 1566. It is a fine specimen of the later Vijayanagar architecture. The carvings are superb and even today looks fresh. One can't see Vijayanagar relics of this sort outside Hampi. The British were so enthralled by the wonderful sculpture that they contemplated to shift the temple completely to a museum in England, but fortunately a severe storm intervened and the project was dropped. Following the occupation of

Muslim rulers, it was used as a garrison and desecrated. The idol was removed and worship terminated. It went under the custody of the Archaeological Survey of India and is preserved as a museum. In 1981, the idol which was removed by the threat of Muslim invasion was moved back into the temple and worship carried on.

A Golden Temple near Vellore : Tamil Nadu can boast of its own Golden Temple now. The Golden Temple is about 140 km from Chennai at Sripuram (Spiritual Town) in Tirumalaikodi in Vellore district.

Sri Narayani Peedam, a private religious charitable organisation, built this Sri Lakshmi Narayani temple. And the glittering monument also boasts of some glittering figures.

This temple covering 55,000 Sq.ft. has intricate carvings and sculptures in gold. It is a unique temple whose Vimanam and Ardha Mandapam have been coated with gold both in the interior and exterior. Twelve layers of gold foils have been pasted on copper sheets embossed with the designs of Gods and fixed on the walls. About 400 goldsmiths and coppersmiths, including craftsmen from Tirumala-Tirupathi Devasthanam, have completed the architectural marvel in gold in six years. The approximate cost of the temple is Rs.600 crore.

A breathtaking wonder of intricate designs, the temple dedicated to Goddess Narayani is in the midst of lush greenery spread over 100 acres.

Except the pathways, even the roofs and the pillars of the temple are made of gold as about 1.5 tonnes of the metal went into its making.

The asram can be contacted at :
Om Sakthi Narayani Siddar Peedam Charitable Trust, Malaikodi, Ariyur, Vellore 632 055. ✆ 0416 - 2271202

C.M.C. Hospital : The Christian Medical College Hospital having over a thousand bed strength is renowned all over the world. Even patients from Malaysia, Sri Lanka and the Middle East come here for treatment. Founded by an American missionary in 1900, it has the support of 74 churches and organizations worldwide.

Places around Vellore

Dr. Vainu Bappu Observatory: This observatory at Kavalur has the biggest telescope in Asia. It is a powerful 2.34 metre telescope. One can observe heavenly bodies clearly from here. It is named after the great Indian astrophysicist Dr. Vainu Bappu who was responsible for the erection of various observatories in this country and the Indian Institute of Astrophysics was founded by him. He also discovered a new comet named after him as Bappu-Boll-New Kirk, the other two suffixes stand for the other two scientists who added more details to the newly found comet. There is a beautifully laid out garden in front of the observatory which was designed by Vainu Bappu himself. He also made important contributions in calculating the luminosity and distance of stars with his colleague Wilson and it is known all over the world as *'Bappu–Wilson Effect'*.

Thiruvalam : An ancient Siva temple where the Nandi, instead of facing the deity faces the opposite direction. It was once the capital of Banas, who were vassals to Pallavas and the temple was built by them. The puranam of this place narrates the story of contest between Lord Muruga and Lord Ganapathi for the fruit presented by Naradha to Lord Siva. Ganapathi got the fruit by just going round His parents Siva and Parvathi while Muruga who literally went round the world was outwitted. Till recently it was the abode of Mouna Swamigal.

Vallimalai : A few miles off Thiruvalam and 25 kms from Vellore lies this hilly range which was once an abode of Jain monk and even today one could see the relief images of Tirthankaras carved on the slopes. At the bottom of the hill and in a cave on the top are temples dedicated to Lord Muruga. Vallimalai is also called as Parvatharajan Kundram. In the interior of the wooded slopes lived Vallimalai Swamigal who introduced the novel system of visiting temples on the New Year's Day.

Ratnagiri : This is about 15 kms from Vellore and there is a Murugan Temple on the top of Ratnagiri and by a flight of steps from the roadside one could reach this temple. It is an old temple but recently renovated with additions.

Sholinghur : Here the low range of hills culminates in an arc and thus forms a sort of natural fortification. The Cholas and Banas keeping its strategic value formed a settlement here and four temples have come up here, two on the hills and two on the plains. This range is also called *Gadikachalam* in Tamil. The tall hill rising like a spire has the Lord Yoga Narasimha Swami, one of the incarnations of Lord Vishnu and the temple is reached by a stiff climb. The deity is a huge idol in Yogasana pose. The small hill adjacent has the Hanuman temple. In a cleft, there is a pool of curative water. Mentally afflicted people stay here for 40 days and get cured of their illness. On the plains stands a Vishnu shrine improved by Vijayanagar kings and a Siva shrine of the Chola period.

Arma Malai : This hill is between Kudiyattam and Vaniyambadi and a little north of the highway. There is a cave with Pallava paintings of Jain character.

Kadambur Hill : This is near Ambur where one can see the natural cave where Anvaruddin was hiding. There is a beautiful Siva temple with a tank on the top. There is also a cool spring in a cleft. The cave about 200 sq. ft. with a small cleft through which cool breeze enters is worth a visit.

Yelagiri Hills : It is on the west of Vellore, an isolated attractive picnic spot. It is in the Eastern ghats at an elevation of 1000 metres. It is popularly known as *Poor man's Ooty*. A salubrious climate, beautiful sceneries and a temple to Lord Muruga attract visitors. Especially in summer, people in large numbers visit this place. Since this place is an ideal location for organising one day or two day trekking, often trekking expeditions are arranged. The Chairman, Youth Hostels Association of India, Tamil Nadu Branch, 24, 2nd Street, Balaji Nagar, Chennai - 600 014 could be contacted for further details.

Pallikonda : On the way back to Vellore one can alight at Pallikonda where Lord Ranganatha lives in an island (Ranga), in Palar. A beautiful Krishna idol dancing with a ball of butter adorns a cell in the prakara.

Thirumalai : It is 10 km north of Polur near Vellore. Two Jain temples are located in the hill. A Jain temple could be seen here. The main attraction is the paintings of Jain figures, monks, serpents, gods etc.

Padavedu : It is 10 km west of Arani near Vellore. It was the original home of the Sambhuvarayas who ruled independently this area as feudatories of the Cholas. There are two temples here, one dedicated to Renukadevi and the other to Ramaswami. In the Ramaswami temple, Hanuman is holding a book in his hand – a very unusual idol. He is supposed to be reading the Ramayana.

Thiruparkadal : It is an island in the river Palar and near Arcot on the way to Vellore. There are two shrines here, one dedicated to Lord Siva called Karapuriswara, built by early Cholas, and the other dedicated to Lord Vishnu. There are two idols in the Vishnu temple – one a recumbent Ranganatha and the other, Lingodhbhava, where out of the Lingam emerges Lord Vishnu.

Arcot : It is on the Chennai-Vellore road. It is aptly called a City of Durgahs, for at every turning one will stumble on a durgah – a tomb of a Muslim saint. The tomb of Sadat-ullakhan, an edifice of green polished marble, the ruined palaces of the Arcot Nawabs, the English fort on the banks of Palar could all be seen here.

Where to Stay?

Vellore (STD: 0416)

• **Hotel Prince Manor,** 83, Katpadi Road, Vellore - 632 004. ✆ 2227106 Fax: 0416-2253016 Email: hotelprincemanor@vsnl.net

• **Hotel River View,** New Katpadi Road, Vellore. ✆ : 2225047, 2225251, 2222349 Fax: 0416-2225672

• **Palace Cafe,** 21, Katpadi Road, Vellore - 632 004. ✆ 2220125

• **Nagna International Lodge,** 13/A, KVS Chetti Street, Vellore. ✆ 2226731

• **Srinivasa Lodge,** 14/1, Beri Bakkali Street, Vellore. ✆ 2226389

• **VDM Lodge,** 13/1, Bakkali Street, Vellore . ✆ 2224008

Many hotels and lodges are available in Vellore. Hotel Sangeet, the India Lodge, Palace Lodge and Venus Hotel are some of them. Staying at Vellore one could easily visit all the places mentioned above. So far, we have covered almost all the important places of north Tamil Nadu. Now, we shall see the most important places in mid-Tamil Nadu (Nadunadu).

Chidambaram

(The abode of the Cosmic Dancer)

Chidambaram is a major tourist centre that opens the real gateway to the land of temples. It is the abode of the cosmic dancer Sri Nataraja. It is also a centre of learning, a centre of culture, a centre of pilgrimage, and a centre of Dravidian art and architecture. The original name of this place was Thillai Vanam (Forest). Thillai (Excecasia Agallcha) is a kind of thick shrub. The real meaning of Chidambaram is conciousness of the sky (space) [cit - consciousness, ambaram - sky (space)]. It is one of the five element places of Lord Siva and the element represented here is the sky (space) - ambaram. Hence, the name Chidambaram. The Pandyas, the Pallavas, the Cholas, the Vijayanagar kings have all worshipped the dancing Nataraja and enriched the temple with various works including the gold plating of the vimanam (dome)of the sanctum. Besides, the temple was also used as a garrison by the Marathas, the French, the British and by Hyder Ali for over 35 years during the Carnatic Wars. The famous Natyanjali festival is held here every year to pay homage to the Cosmic Dancer.

How to get there?

Chidambaram is 245 kms from Chennai and is well connected with several towns in the state. From here, there are bus services to Chennai, Pondicherry, Nagapattinam and Madurai. It is also connected with metre gauge rail link, main link going to Rameswaram via Kumbakonam, Thanjavur and Trichirappalli. The nearest airport is at Trichirappalli from where Indian Airlines connections are available to Chennai, Madurai and Sri Lanka. Umpteen buses ply daily to Chidambaram and via Chidambaram to various places.

Places to See

The Nataraja Temple : The temple called *Ponnambalam* or *Kanaga Sabai* is one of the oldest temples of the Chola period. It is a unique temple where Lord Siva is worshipped in an idol form instead of the usual 'Lingam'. It is spread over an area of 40 acres with 4 tall portal towers piercing the sky on each side having five sabhas or courts. The towers were built by Kulotunga Chola, Kopperumchinga, Vikrama Chola and Krishna Devaraya in the East, South, West and North respectively. The eastern gopuram (tower) is 40.8 metres high and carved on it are 108 dance poses of Bharathanatyam, the classical dance of Tamil Nadu. The western tower has also similar carvings. The other two depict the various Thiruvilaiyadalgal or puranic Holy Pranks of Lord Siva. The tallest is the northern tower soaring to a height of 42.4 m.

The presiding deity is Lord Nataraja installed in the Kanaga Sabha, the roof of which is gold-plated. The icon is the most bewitching dancing pose of Lord Siva. Adjacent is the shrine of Govindaraja (Vishnu) reclining on the serpent Adisesha and from His naval rises a lotus stem with a bloomed lotus on which is seated Brahma with His four heads. Therefore one can worship all the trinity of the Hindu faith – Brahma, Vishnu and Siva, at the same time, in this temple. In no other temple, it is possible. Two other shrines, one dedicated to Subrahmanya and the other to Ganesha could also be seen

in this temple. A huge Nandi looks devotedly on His Lord and master through an aperture on the wall. As already stated Lord Siva is represented in the form of 'Akasha' - Sky (space), and it is one of the Pancha Bootha Sthalas of Lord Siva. Behind the idol, a screen conceals a mystery popularly known as *Chidambara Rahasyam* (mystery). While burning camphor is shown to the idol, the screen is removed momentarily to reveal a sparkling light which is symbolic of the removal of the sheath of ignorance to understand the Supreme Truth. There are two mandapams inside the complex, one 100-pillared and the other 1000-pillared. There is a big tank mirroring the north gopuram. The Nrithya Sabha is an artistic work of elegance with its minutely chiselled pillars carved to resemble a chariot drawn by horses. Govindaraja Perumal Sannathi in the Temple attracts vaishnavite devotees.

The Srimulanatha complex and the shrine of goddess Sivakami contain beautiful paintings in the ceiling.

Festivals in the temple

1. Arudhra Darshan in December-January

2. Aani Thirumanjanam in June

3. 10-day Panguni Uthiram festival in March-April

Natyanjali Festival : It is jointly organised by the Department of Tourism, Govt. of Tamilnadu, The Ministry of Tourism, Government of India and Natyanjali Trust in Chidambaram. It is generally held in February and opens on the Maha Sivarathri Day. Prominent dancers of India perform their dance and offer it to the cosmic dancer Nataraja in the vicinity of his sanctum sanctorum. It is a unique tourist attraction and all the dances of India, both classical and modern, are performed.

Thillai Kali Temple : Kali was the original Goddess of Thillai Vanam i.e. Chidambaram. Lord Shiva had to perform Urdhuva Thandava by raising one of His legs up, to subdue Her in a dance competition. Hence, She has to leave the place offering it to Nataraja. So, Her temple is located in the northern outskirts about 1.6 km from the shrine of Sri Nataraja.

Annamalai University : This university is located on the eastern side of the railway station. It is a residential university founded by Raja Sir Annamalai Chettiar. It is renowned for Tamil research studies and Tamil music. It offers education in various faculties like Arts, Science, Medicine, Agriculture, Fine Arts and Engineering. There is also a marine biology department at Porto Nova.

Places around Chidambaram

Pichavaram : 16 kms east of Chidambaram lies a most beautiful scenic spot spread over 2800 acres of mangrove forest. It is formed in the backwaters which are interconnected by the Vellar and Kollidam systems offering abundant scope for water sports, para-sailing, rowing and canoeing. The Pichavaram mangroves are the healthiest mangrove occurrences in the world. A number of islands interspersing vast expanse of water covered with green trees make this place enchanting. The backwater is separated by a sand bar from the sea making it an extraordinary place of loveliness. Tamil Nadu Tourism Development Corporation offers boating, accommodation and restaurant facilities.

Sri Mushnam : It is located northwest of Chidambaram. There is a big Vishnu temple of Bhuvarahaswamy (incarnation of Vishnu as a boar) here. It is one of the eight Swayam Vyaktakashethra (Spontaneous manifestation without being installed by anyone) in the south.

Melakadambur : It is located west of Chidambaram. The temple here is of the Pala art. Pala dynasty ruled over Bengal and produced masterpieces of art of a unique style. The Nataraja found in this temple dances on a bull and the idol belongs to Pala art.

Sirkazhi : Another Siva shrine 20 km from Chidambaram. It is the birthplace of one of the top 4 Saivaite saints named Thirugnana Sambandar and the legend proclaims that Goddess Parvathi breastfed the child Gnanasambandar as he was crying in the tank bund. The tank is inside the temple and is known as 'Mulaippal Thirtham' (Breast Milk Holy Water). During the month of April, a festival in memory of this legend is celebrated here. The temple is a Madakkoil – a structure with a storey attached.

Thiruvenkadu (Swetharanyam): It is 28 km from Chidambaram. The temple is dedicated to Agora Virabadra - a fierce aspect of Siva. An image of Bhikshadanamurthi (Mendicant Siva) unearthed here is an early Chola bronze casting of Lord Siva as a nude mendicant with the writhing cobra clinging on his thighs. The image is now in safe custody in the Thanjavur Art Gallery. This is also the abode of *Budha (Mercury)* one of the Navagrahas (nine planets).

Ulagalanda Perumal Temple : It is one of the 108 Divya desam. It is located on the Mayiladuthurai-Chennai state highway in Sirkazhi town.

Vaitheeswaran Koil : Down south of Chidambaram is located this temple of Lord Siva. The presiding deity is called Vaitheeswara - Lord of Healing. There is a tank inside the temple free from frogs called Siddha Amritha Theertha – a sacred pool reputed to contain nectar which has curative powers. Another name for this place is *Pullirukku Velur*. The sculptures are very wonderful here. It is the place of one of the Navagrahas - **Angarahan (Mars)**.

Tirupunkur : It is the place where Lord Siva's mount Nandhi moved a little away from obstructing the Darshan of Lord Siva to Nandanar, the harijan devotee.

Mayiladuthurai (Mayavaram): This town can be reached by bus from Chidambaram. The river Cauvery bisects the town into Uttara Mayuram and the town proper. A fine bathing ghat is provided to bathe in the river. Dakshinamurthi shrine is famous here and the God of Wisdom sits in yoga pose on a Nandhi. At the bathing ghat, there is another Nandhi in the mid-stream where the waters swirl around him. It is said that it is a punishment to the arrogant Nandhi. Nandhi realised his fault and became repentant. He was allowed to stay in the middle to attain liberation on the full moon day of the month of Aippasi (November-December) when all the holy rivers converge here. A dip in this place on that holy day is believed to be as holy as a dip in the river Ganges.

The Mayuranathaswamy temple is in the heart of the town. It is a Siva temple with an imposing nine-storeyed tower. The goddess Durga in the northern niche is a fine piece of workmanship and differs from Durgas of other temples. A chilling sight is the offering of a devotee who is in the act of severing his head.

Vazhuvur : This place on the southern side of Mayavaram is about 12 km away. It is renowned for its bronze images of exquisite splendour. The Lord of this temple is called Krithivasa, one who wears the elephant skin. This is one of the eight places where Siva danced to destroy demons. The dance hall is called *Gnana Sabai* - Hall of Wisdom. Behind Gajasamharamurthi is kept a Yantra which is known as Vazhuvur Rahasyam (mystery). The Gajasamharamurthi idol is a bronze image of the 11th century and is also the only one of its kind – a fusion of grace and vigour. The Bikshadana or Siva as mendicant is another marvel in bronze. He holds the Damaru (Hand-drum) in one hand, the Kapala in the other and is seen feeding a deer with His fingers with flowing locks of hair on which are perched the Crescent and the Ganges and the coy Uma with Skanda cuddled in Her arms makes the onlooker spellbound.

Perambur : 14 km away from Mayiladuthurai is a Subramania temple. Though small, the image is of granite and beautifully carved with 6 faces in the pose of Samharamurthi. Snakes abound this place, but no one has so far been bitten. The snakes just hiss at those who enter the Iluppai garden stealthily to pilfer.

Therazhundhur: The birth place of Kambar who rendered the epic Ramayana in Tamil, is 10 km away from Mayiladuthurai on the way to Poompuhar. There is a temple of sculptural value here and people point out a place called Kamba Medu as the birthplace of Kambar.

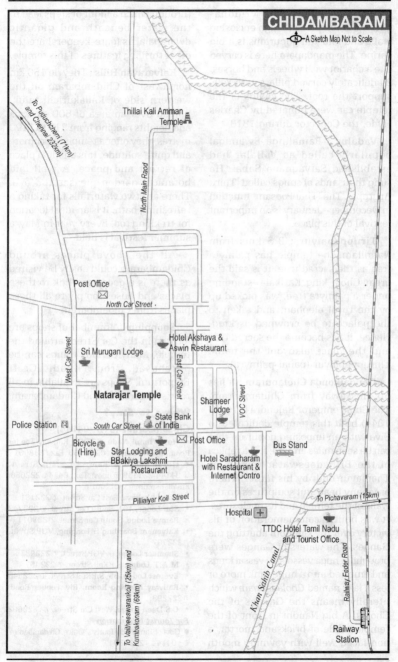

CHIDAMBARAM

N - A Sketch Map Not to Scale

Thillai Kali Amman Temple

To Puducherri (71km) and Chennai 232cm)

North Main Raod

Post Office

North Car Street

Sri Murugan Lodge

West Car Street

East Car Street

Hotel Akshaya & Aswin Restaurant

Natarajar Temple

Police Station

South Car Street

State Bank of India

Shameer Lodge

VOC Street

Bicycle (Hire)

Star Lodging and BBakiya Lakshmi Rostaurant

Post Office

Hotel Saradharam with Restaurant & Internet Contro

Bus Stand

Pilliaiyar Koil Street

To Pichavaram (15km)

Hospital

To Vaitheeswarankoil (25km) and Kumbakonam (69km)

TTDC Hotel Tamil Nadu and Tourist Office

Khan Sahib Canal

Railway Feder Road

Railway Station

Vriddhachalam: The Vriddha-giriswarar temple with high enclosing walls and four tall gopurams is a big shrine. The mandapam here is carved like a chariot with wheels and horses. 24 delicately carved pillars with Yalis support the roof. The chains of the temple car were donated by Charles Hyde, the Collector during 1813.

Vadalur : Ramalinga Swamigal popularly called as Vallalar had established Satyagnana Sabai. He sung thousands of songs called 'Thiru Arutppa'. The 'Thai Poosam' function in December - January is an important festival of this place.

Tiruppanaiyur : 3.5 kms from Nannilam, the temple has palmyra tree as the sacred tree. It is said the great Chola king Karikala, standing under a palmyra tree, was picked up by the royal elephant and taken to the palace to be crowned as king. Hence, it has become the sacred tree and the place also got the name Thiruppanaiyur (panai-palmyra).

Gangaikonda Cholapuram : It lies 50 kms away from Chidambaram. The Chola emperor Rajendra I (1012-1044) built this temple dedicated to Siva with an imposing gopuram that can be seen miles around. It is a replica of the Brihadeeswarar temple at Thanjavur built by his father. There are many beautiful sculptures on the walls of the temple and its enclosures. It was built in commemoration of his victory over the kingdom abutting the Ganges. The waters of Ganges were brought in huge vessels by vassal kings and emptied into a huge tank more or less a lake named *Cholagangam* which literally means the Ganges of the Cholas. A big Nandhi in front of the temple made of brick and mortar, a lion-faced well with yawning mouth through which a flight of steps lead to the water beneath and gigantic dwarapalakas (gate-keepers) are the other thrilling features of this temple.

Kalvarayan Hills : They lie 150 km northwest of Chidambaram on the western side of Kallakurichi taluk. Spread over an area of 600 sq. kms and heights ranging from 315 to 1190 metres, they offer a temperate climate and quite solitude. It is an ideal place of retreat and peace. A well laid botanical garden pleases the eye. There are two waterfalls for taking a refreshing bath. It is an ideal location for trekking too. Every year in May, a summer festival is held.

All the above places around Chidambaram could easily be visited as there is a good road link to these places and buses too ply to all these places from Chidambaram.

Shopping : A number of shops are located in the Car Street around the temple. Many curious things can be purchased from Khadi Craft Emporium. Shops are available in all tourist centres around Chidambaram.

Where to Stay?

Chidambaram (STD: 04144)

- **Hotel Tamil Nadu (TTDC),** Railway Feeder Road, Chidambaram. ℗ 238056 Fax : 238061
- **Hotel Saradha Ram,** 19, VGP Street. ℗ 04144-221338 (5 lines), Fax : 04144-222656, Email: hsrcdm@vsnl.com
- **Hotel Akshaya,** East Car Street. ℗ 222181
- **Star Lodge,** 101, South Car Street. ℗ 222743
- **Ramya Lodge,** South Car Street. ℗ 223011
- **Kalyanam Boarding & Lodging,** VGP Street. ℗ 222707
- **Shameer Lodge,** 6, VGP Street. ℗ 222983
- **M.A.T. Lodge,** S.P.Koil Street. ℗ 222457
- **Everest Lodge,** 55, S.P.Koil Street, ℗ 222545
- **Railway Retiring Room,** Rly. Feeder Road, ℗ 222298
- **O.S.Deen Lodge,** West Car Street, ℗ : 222602

For Tourist Information
- Govt of Tamilnadu Tourists' Office, Chidambaram. ℗ : 04144 - 222739

Poompuhar

(The Glorious Port of the Sangam Age)

Poompuhar or Kaviripoompattinam as it was known manifests the ancient glory of the Tamils. It was the chief port of the Chola kingdom during the Sangam Age. Sangam literature and the two great epics Silappadhikaram and Manimekalai give us glimpses of its glory. It was an international seaport and one could hear there many languages spoken by the merchants of various countries. The city contained separate quarters for foreigners and both day and night bazaars called *Nalangadi* and *Allangadi* were busy selling a plethora of articles like spices, gold, fancy wear, garments, liquor, pearls and precious stones and various edibles. Vast emporia were dealing on these goods. There were organised syndicates of merchants who also participated in the polity of the Cholas. Though it is reduced to a small village today, one could see evidences of its past glory in and around Poompuhar.

How to get there?

Poompuhar is in the Sirkazhi taluk of Nagappattinam district. Tourists have to alight at Mayiladuthurai Junction and proceed to Poompuhar by road. Those who come from Chennai have to alight at Sirkazhi and proceed by road. Poompuhar is linked to Mayiladuthurai as well as Sirkazhi by road, the distance being 24 kms and 21 kms respectively.

Tourists from Chennai to Poompuhar by private carriers can take the route via Tindivanam, Pondicherry, Cuddalore and Sirkazhi. Those coming from Madurai, Ramanathapuram and Tirunelveli may proceed via Melur, Tiruppattur, Karaikudi, Tharangampadi and Akkur. They can also come by Pudukkottai,

Thanjavur and Mayiladuthurai .

Distance by rail route is as follows:

Chennai-Sirkazhi 260 kms;
Chennai-Mayiladuthurai 281 kms;
Thanjavur-Mayiladuthurai 70 kms;
Trichy-Mayiladuthurai 120 kms.

One can also travel by bus to Mayiladuthurai or Sirkazhi from anywhere in Tamil Nadu and reach Poompuhar from there.

Antiquity of Poompuhar : Foreign notices of this ancient port could be seen in the travelogues of *Periplus* and *Merris Erithroly*, Ptolemy and Pliny. Pali literature like Milindapanha, Buddha Jataka tales, Abithama Avathar and Buddha Vamsakatha too mention this place. Buddhism flourished here 2000 years ago and evidences have been found out of the donation of a pillar by a Buddhist Somaya Bikkuni of Poompuhar during the second century B.C. Brahmi inscriptions dating back to 2nd century B.C. too speak of the city. The inscription at Sayavanam temple in Poompuhar also records its history. The Chola kings of the Sangam Age ruled the city with pride and embellished it in various ways. Most of them speak of a great festival called 'Indra Vizha' devoted to Lord Indra. Evidences have been found of its continuance till the later Chola period.

The plan of the city : From literary evidences, the plan of the city has been elicited as follows: (1) The city was divided into two well marked divisions as Pattinappakkam and Maruvurpakkam. (2) The market-place of Poompuhar was sandwiched in between Nalangadi, the day market and Allangadi, the night bazaar. (3) The seashore was occupied by ferocious undaunting fisher folks. (4) The warehouses were also located there. Artisans, merchants, sweet-vendors, butchers, potters and diamond-cutters lived in Maruvurpakkam. (5) Kings, nobles, elite citizens, rich traders and farmers, physicians, astrologers, the king's barracks and court dancers lived in Pattinappakkam. (6) Vellidai Murugan, Elanchi Mandram, Nedunkal Mandram, Bootha Chatukkam and Pavai Mandram were located in Pattinappakkam. (7) The city also had well laid-out gardens like Elavanthigai Cholai, Uyya Vanam, Champapathi Vanam and Kaveri Vanam. (8) Temples for Lord Siva, Chathukka Bootham, Indra, Balarama, Soory (Sun), Machathan, Chandra (Moon), Arugan (Jain), Thirumal (Vishnu) were there besides Buddha stupas and seven Buddha vihars, Champapathi Amman temple, brick idols and Ulagu Arivai Mandram. (9) There were avenues and separate sacred passages for temple idols to take bath in the river. (10) There were ring wells on the fringes of the city. (11) There was a separate quarter for foreigners besides separate market-places. (12) All along the river banks, cool and shady trees were planted. This in short is the plan of Kaviripoompattinam or Poompuhar. 'Puhar' means estuary and the city was at the estuary of the only perennial river of Tamil Nadu - Cauvery.

Excavation at Poompuhar : Archaeologists have unearthed interesting evidences supporting the literary evidences. The excavations were initiated in 1910. The Archaeological Survey of India found out several ring wells near the seashore. The excavations near Champapathi Amman and Pallavaneswaram temples brought to light the existence of various buildings. Remains of a brick building and a boat jetty were discovered in Keezhaiyur. A water reservoir and the remains of several buildings were also found. Relics of a sixty feet Buddha vihar was found in Pallavaneswaram. A Buddha marble paadha (feet of Buddha) of the size 3½' × 2½' with holy symbols akin to those at Amaravati and Nagarjunakonda. The coins that were in use during the early Chola Karikalan period were also found out. An ancient Roman copper coin too was unearthed at Vellaiyan Iruppu. Copper coins of Rajaraja Chola were also unearthed. An eighth century gold-plated copper statue of Buddha in meditation was also unearthed in Melaiyur in 1927. The Tamil Nadu Archaeological Department has discovered the remains of several buildings recently. This department in collaboration with The National Institute of Oceanography, Goa, has launched an offshore exploration of Poompuhar. This venture, it is hoped will bring out the magnificence of this erstwhile international seaport of South India.

Revival of Poompuhar's Ancient Glory : Dr. Kalaignar Karunanidhi, the illustrious statesman cum literateur and Chief Minister of Tamil Nadu who evinced keen interest in reviving the past glory of Poompuhar gave a crystal form to the lost city on the basis of literary evidences and through his initiation and efforts rose Silappathikaram Art Gallery, Ilanji Mandram, Pavai Mandram, Nedungal Mandram and Kotrappandal, in this place, with artistic splendour. Streams of visitors pour in every day.

What to see in Poompuhar

Silappathikaram Art Gallery: It has a beautiful seven-tier building of exquisite sculptural value. The first storey is 12' high and the following storey each has a height of 5' atop of which is erected a kalasam with a height of 8' - the total height being 50 feet. The art gallery depicting scenes from one of the five major epics of Tamil 'Silappathikaram' was opened in 1973. These lovely scenes are lovingly immortalised in stone on the walls of the gallery. It is in short a treasure-house of Tamil Nadu.

The Makara Thorana Vayil at the entrance of the Art Gallery gives an imposing look to the whole structure. It has been designed on the model of Magara Thorana Vayil found in Surulimalai Mangala Devi temple and rises to a height of 22½'. There is an anklet-shaped tank in the art gallery with statues of Kannagi (9½') and Madhavi (8') on both sides of it.

Ilanji Mandram, Pavai Mandram, Nedungal Mandram and Kotrappandal have been reerected here and they remain here attracting the public with their artistic splendour. All these public places have been mentioned in Silappathikaram, the epic poetry of the Tamils. They served various purposes besides being ornamental. For instance, *Ilanji Mandram* is a place of beauty with a miracle tank which cured all illnesses. *Nedungal Mandram* is a pillar of splendour and those afflicted with mental disorder or those who have been poisoned or bitten by snake, if they go round and worship they will be cured. *Pavai Mandram* is a place of justice and if injustice is done the Pavai (idol) there would shed tears. *Kotrappandal* was the ornamental shamiana presented by the king of the Vajjra country.

One can also stroll along the Bay of Bengal which appears to be washing the shores in repentance of its cruelty devouring this glorious land. The estuary where the river Cauvery enters the sea could also be seen.

Other Places of Interest around Poompuhar

Thirusaikkadu (Sayavanam): Situated 2 kms away from Poompuhar estuary is this Siva temple of Thiru Sayavaneswarar and Kuyilinum Inia Nanmozhi Ammai. The Saivaite Saints or Nayanmars have sung hymns in praise of this temple. Chola inscriptions are also found here.

Thiruppallavaneswaram : This is an ancient and beautiful temple in Poompuhar. Iyarpagai Nayanar and Pattinathar and the hero and heroine of Silappathikaram, Kovalan and Kannagi were also born here. This temple was built by the Pallavas. The inscription of Vikrama Chola calls this place *'Puharnagaram'* - Puhar city.

Melapperumpallam and Keezhapperumpallam : These two places are situated very near to Poompuhar and Thiruvengadu. The Valampurinathar temple at Melapperumpallam has Chola inscriptions. Nayanmars have sanctified this temple in their hymns. Keezhapperumpallam is at a distance of 2 km from Poompuhar and one of the *Navagrahas, Kethu* (serpent's tail), has a separate sanctum here.

Thiruvakkur : A famous Siva temple is here. It is constructed on Madakkoil (Storeyed Temple) pattern. Nayanmars have sung hymns on this temple. Sirappuli Nayanar, one of the 63 Saivaite saints, was born here.

Sembanarkoil : A temple of historic significance, it is called Thirusemponpathi in Thevaram. It is near Poompuhar on the bus route to Tarangambadi.

Punjai : It is near Semponnarkoil. A beautiful Siva temple sung by Nayanmars. It is hailed for the architectural wonders of the Cholas.

Thirukkadaiyur : It is on the road to Tarangambadi from Mayiladuthurai. It is one of the eight temples (Atta Veerattanam) glorifying the heroic victories of Lord Siva. Siva released Markandeya from the clutches of Yama, the God of Death and made him a perpetual youth. A beautiful bronze representation of this event could be seen here. The lingam here bears the rope marks of Yama. This place is also known for its fame in patronizing Bharathanatyam as evidenced by the inscription of Kulottunga Chola III. It is also a famous Sakthi Sthalam. The holy hymns of Abirami Anthathi was sung here by Abirami Bhattar, whose devotion made the Goddess bring the full moon on a new moon day. The Lord of this place is known as 'Amirthagateswara' (Lord of the nectar pot and people select this place to celebrate their 60th birthday so that they be rewarded with longevity by the grace of this God.

Anantha Mangalam : This place near Thirukkadaiyur is famous for its 'Dasa Bhuja Veera Anjaneya' (Ten-headed Hanuman).

Nangur (Thirunangur) : Eleven of the 108 holy places of Vaishnavaites are near Nangur. The Nangur Vishnu temples were sanctified by Thirumangai Alwar, one of the 12 Vaishnavaite Saints. The stucco figure of Nara Narayana in one of these temples is an architectural marvel. Some of them are Madakkoils (storeyed temples) and date back to the early Chola Paranthaga, 907 A.D. Evidences are available in Siam for its flourishing as a centre of trade in those days.

Thalaignayiru : This temple nearby contains an interesting inscription prescribing rules for the election of the village assembly. Those who were not members for the previous ten years and above 40 years alone are eligible to contest an election.

Tarangambadi (Tranquebar): It is on the coast of the Bay of Bengal, south of Poompuhar. It is the place where the first Tamil printing press was erected and casting of Tamil alphabets were done. The Christian missionary brought out The Bible here as the first printed book in Tamil.

It was a site of Danish settlement and has the remains of the Dansborg Fort built by Ore Godde, the Commander of the Royal Dutch Navy in the 17th century. This fort was constructed in 1620 with two storeys and the top echelons of the Dutch officials resided here. Though the ramparts are ruined, the rest of the buildings are in good condition.

The Church of Zion : It was built in 1701 in the corner of King Street and Queen Street. After several modifications in 1782, 1784, 1800 and 1839, the church as it stands today has an impressive vaulted roof.

The Town Gateway : It is 200 years old and has historical and architectural values.

Danish Fort : Even today it exhibits Danish architecture and is under the control of Tamil Nadu Archaeological Department and has an archaeological museum open to public on all days except Fridays.

Masilamaninathar Temple : It was built in 1305 AD by the Pandya king Maravarman Kulasekara. Its outstanding architectural beauty spellbind the onlookers, despite the front portion damaged due to sea erosion.

Rehling's Gaid : It is named after Johannes Rehling who was the Danish governor and owned this house between 1830 and 1841. It is the biggest building in Tarangambadi. Presently St. Theresa's Teachers Training College is functioning here and it is well preserved.

British Collector's House : It is on the eastern end of King's Street opposite the Dansborg Fort. It is another important landmark 150 years old with beautiful round columns, a central courtyard and a garden.

Transport: Buses ply frequently from Poompuhar, Sirkazhi, Mayiladuturai and Nagappattinam to Tarangambadi.

Where to stay?

Nagapattinam (STD : 04365)

● **Hotel Tamilnadu**, Nagappattinam.✆ 224389, 225114
● **ATM Lodge**, ✆ 250758
● **Deen Lodge**, ✆ 250032
● **Subham Lodge**, 47, West Car Street, Vaitheeswarankoil.✆ 279102, 279302

Visiting Time:
Silappathikaram Art Gallery
8.30 a.m. to 1.00 p.m. - 2.30 p.m. to 8.30 p.m.
Entrance Fee : Adult Rs. 2/-
Child (5 to 10 years) Re. 1/-

Nagappattinam
(Maritime Supremacy)

Historical Antiquity: This town was known from very early times as a trading centre and even today it is a minor port. It was the headquarters of a region during the Chola period and was a pride of the Cholamandalam coast. The other name of this place is Cholakula Vallippattinam. The Burmese historical text of 3rd century B.C. mentions this place and gives evidence of a Buddha vihar built here by the emperor Ashoka the Great. The Chinese traveller *Hiuen Tsang* also mentions it in his travel accounts.The ancient Buddhist literature names it as 'padarithitha'. Avurithidal, the name of a part of Nagappattinam might

have been derived from padarithitha, the name of a fruit tree common in this region.

Buddhist monks of Sri Lanka had close connection with this place. Anaimangalam copper plates of Kulothunga Chola mentions that 'Kasiba-thera', a Buddhist monk renovated this Buddhist temple in 6th century A.D. Pallava king Rajasimha (695-722 A.D.) permitted a Chinese king to be buried in a Buddha vihar in Nagappattinam. The Anaimangalam copper plate also reveals that Vijayathunga Varman of Sri Vijaya kingdom built two Buddha vihars in the names of Rajaraja and Rajendra named respectively Rajarajapperumpalli and Rajendrapperumpalli. The latter was also called *Soodamani Vihar.* Excavations by the Archaeological Department at Velippalayam in Nagappattinam unearthed more than 300 Buddha statues. They are kept in the Govt. Museum at Chennai. Kayaroganam Shiva temple here existed in the 6th century and was sanctified by the hymns of three Nayanmars.The Vishnu temple here has been sung by Thirumangai Alwar of 9th century. This town was a famous trading centre during the Vijayanagar period. The Portuguese settled here in 1554 during the Thanjavur Nayaka rule. Then Christianity began to take root and the famous Velankanni church came into existence.

In 1658, the Dutch supremacy prevailed and ten Christian churches and a hospital were built by them. They also released coins with the name 'Nagappattinam' engraved on them. The British were the last owners of this place after a prolonged struggle in 1781. Gold coins bearing the name of East India Company were issued from here. They were called

'Nagappattinam Varagan'and 'Nagappattinam Sornam' and were in circulation during the Thanjavur Maratha rule. Nagappattinam has thus a vast history of over 2000 years. Today, it is the headquarters of Nagappattinam district.

How to get there?

Nagappattinam is very well connected to all important places in Tamil Nadu by rail and road. Buses ply every hour from Chennai to Nagappattinam. Train facilities are also available from Nagappattinam to Thanjavur, Trichy, Nagore and Chennai. Bus services are also available for these places. Tamilnadu State Transport Corporation operates tourist buses to nearby places. Hired vehicles are also available. Cars and autorickshaws could be hired to visit places around Nagappattinam.

The nearest airport is at Trichy, a distance of 141 kms. Air Lanka and Indian Airlines operate services to Sri Lanka. The Indian Airlines operates services to Chennai and Madurai from Trichy.

Places to see in Nagappattinam

Harbour, Lighthouse and Beach : Nagappattinam is a minor port of India today. Hence, the harbour which was once a maritime pride is busy even today. The lighthouse is nearby and could be climbed. The beach, a fine stretch of sand is worth visiting. Sea bathing could also be done.

Temples

Kaayaroganam Siva Temple: The three Nayanmars, Appar, Sambandar and Sundarar have sung the hymns in praise of this temple. It is an old temple existing from 6th century A.D. This is a Karonam and one of the Vidanga Sthalams. A cult called Lakulisa - the mendicant aspect of Siva

- spread from Karonam in Gujarat to all parts of India. In South India, two temples of this cult came into being, one at Kanchipuram and the other here. The Thyagaraja here is known as Sundaravidangar. It is made up of a precious stone Komedhagam (lapis lazuli). The Nagabarana Vinayagar and the bronze Panchamuga (five-headed) Vinayagar on a lion mount are of exquisite workmanship in this temple.

The image of Thyagaraja in a niche of Thyagaraja Sabha is of excellent craftsmanship.

Neelayadakshi Amman temple is more familiar to devotees than Kaayaroganam.

Soundararaja Perumal temple is the Vishnu temple glorified by Thirumangai Alwar of the 9th century. This temple has a unique bronze of Narasimha slaying Hiranya, the demon and blessing his son Prahalada the devotee, of Narayana.

Mosques
1) Durgah at Nagai Pudhur Road
2) Durgah near new bus stand
3) Durgah at Moolakkadai Street

Churches
1) Lourdhu Madha Church
2) Maharasi Madha Church
3) T.E.L.C. Church
4) Protestant Church

Library
The District Library

OTHER FACILITIES
Telephone, telex and courier services are available. Hospitals and private clinics and pharmacies too are available.

Places around Nagappattinam
Nagore : It is 5 km north of Nagappattinam. The Durgah (faith of

all religions) of Saint Hazareth Syed Shahul Hamid Quadir Wali is here. He is believed to shower His grace without distinction of caste, creed, colour or class. People of all faiths flock here to get solace. Hindus call him Nagoor Andavar. The Kanduri festival during October and November is very famous. Four minarets serve landmark to this durgah and the biggest one of them was built by Pratap Singh, the Thanjavur ruler and his son Tulajaji endowed it richly. The tomb of the saint in the centre is approached by seven silver-plated doors.

Thirunallar : The famous Siva temple lies 5 kms from Karaikkal, a Puducherry Union Territory off Tharangambadi. The Siva temple is a Dharbaranyam and the presiding deity is Dharbaranyeswara. His consort is Bhogamanantha Poornambikai Amman. In the prakaram niche at the entrance is **Lord Saneeswarar (Saturn)** and lakhs of people worship here to propitiate Him when He enters a particular constellation of the zodiac once in 2½ years. Nala Theertham is a famous tank where the devotees take a dip smearing oil on their body. The original Nataraja idol of this temple is at Thiruchendur with the engravement Thirunallar on it. It is said that the Dutch removed this idol from here and reaching Thiruchendur, they also removed the idol of Muruga of that temple and when they set sail, a fierce storm appeared and they dropped them into the sea and escaped. Later, the idols were rescued from the sea by a miracle and both of them have been installed at Thiruchendur.

Velankanni : It is on the coast of the Bay of Bengal 14 kms south of Nagappattinam. The shrine basilica of Our Lady of Velankanni here on the shore is popularly called 'Sacred Arokkia Madha Church'. The church is dedicated to Virgin Mary and has an imposing façade with tall spires and the wings present the shape of a cross. In a niche in the altar is enshrined the statue of Our Lady of Health. Numerous legends prevail of the miraculous power of this lady, and lakhs of people converge here during the 'Feast' festival occurring in August. The greatest of miracles is the offerings thrown into the sea by devotees in Myanmar, Malaya and South Africa reaching this churches safely being picked and conveyed by fishermen. Such articles are exhibited in a hall here.

Sikkal : This place is on the bus route from Nagappattinam to Thiruvarur. Here is an age-old Siva temple in which the Sikkal Singaravelar bronze idol is so beautiful that it spellbinds the onlooker with rare craftsmanship and grace. This deity, Lord Muruga attracts crowds from far and near. The presiding deity of this temple is Navaneethes-warar. The festival in Chitthirai (April-May) is most famous. In the car festival, the bejewelled idol of Singaravelar receives the Vel (spear) from Parvathi - Vel Nedum Kanni (Long spear-like eyed) Amman to destroy the demon Surapadman. It is said that the idol profusely perspires at that time.

Tiruchenkattankudi : It is about 13 km from Nannilam famous for Asthamurthi Mandapam. The image of Seeralan, the son of Siruthonda Nayanar, who was cooked for meals to Siva and resuscitated by Siva, is in the prakara. Its idol of Ganapathi is said to have been brought from Vatapi of the Chalukyan kingdom after an expedition by Chola and installed here. Siruthonda Nayanar was the General Paranjothi who led Chola's forces. Thiruchenkattankudi is the place where Siruthondar lived and the episode of Seeralan's resurrection happened. Tiripurantaka and Nataraja in this temple are fine specimens of Chola art.

Ettukkudi : 28 kms away from Nagappattinam this temple is famous for Lord Muruga. Saint Arunagirinathar has sung hymns on the Lord here.

Vedaranyam (Thirumaraikkadu – Forest of Vedas): This place is 58 kms from Nagappattinam. The author of Thiruvilaiyadal Puranam Paranjothi Munivar (13th century A.D.) was born here. It is an ancient temple and the earliest inscription dates back to Parantaka Chola (905-945 A.D.). The presiding deity is Vedaranyeswara and it is one of the 'Saptha Vidanga Sthalams'. The miracle of this place is that the Vedas after worshipping the Lord had locked the main gates of this temple and worship had to be conducted through another passage. When Appar and Sambandar came here, the former sang hymns at the request of the latter to open the gates and thus the gates were automatically opened.

During the independence struggle this place attained fame because of Gandhiji's Salt Satyagraha. Sardar Vedaratnam Pillai and Rajaji took part in the Satyagraha (1930-32) and courted arrest. A memorial has been erected to commemorate the event.

Kodikkarai (Point Calimere): Just 10 kms from Vedaranyam and 68 kms from Nagappattinam is this sanctuary famous for birds. Black bucks, spotted deer, wild pigs and vast flocks of migratory birds like flamingoes could

all be seen here. In winter, the tidal mud-flats and marshes of the backwaters are covered with fowls like teals, curlews, gulls, terns, plovers, sandpipers, shanks and herons. Most of them are sea birds. At a time, upto 30,000 flamingoes could also be seen here. In the spring, quite different set of birds like koels, mynas and barbets are attracted by the profusion of wild berries. The best time to visit is November to January. April to June is the lean season with very little activity. The main rainy season is from October to December.

A forest rest-house is available. You can get to Kodikkarai by bus from Nagappattinam, Thanjavur, Mayiladuthurai and by train through Mayiladuthurai-Thiruthuraipoondi section.

Where to Stay?
Nagappattinam (STD : 04365)

• **Quality Inn MGM Vailankanni**, No. 64, F/2, Nagapattinam Main Road, ✆ 263900, 263336, Fax: 04365-263336 Email: qimgmv@vsnl.net

Tiruvarur
(Birthplace of the Musical Trinities)

The District of Tiruvarur has been carved out as a separate district due to trifurcation of Thanjavur District. According to this division, 7 taluks namely Kodavasal, Tiruvarur, Needamangalam, Mannargudi, Nannilam, Tiruturaipoondi and Valangaiman were detached from Thanjavur district to form this new district.

Tiruvarur is one of the oldest towns which has been popular as cultural headquarters for many centuries. This ancient town in Chola heartland is famous Sri Thyagaraja temple.

Sri Thyagarajaswami Temple : The most ancient temple patronised by almost all the kings reigning the south is the Thyagarajaswami shrine of Tiruvarur. This temple is associated with the legend of Sundarar to whom the God served as a messenger of love and arranged his marriage with Paravai and Sangili Nachiars. Thyagaraja like Nataraja dances — He performs the Ajapa dance here. Hence, He is known as 'Ajaba Natesar'. However, the presiding deity is Lord Vanmikanatha.

The temple complex is spread over 20 acres with the eastern gopuram dominating. In front of the western gopuram is the Kamalalaya Tank covering an area of 25 acres with an island temple in the centre. Vanmikanatha shrine is the earliest edifice, Akileswari a coming next and Thyagaraja the last. Many mandapams crowd the temple. The biggest one is the Devasiriya Mandapam. The Akileswara shrine contains beautiful sculptures of Ardhanareeswara, Durga, Karkalamurthi and Agastya in its niches. Paintings of Vijayanagar period adorn the ceiling of Devasiriya mandapam.

Outside the temple is a beautiful sculptural representation of Manuneedhi Chola who ran his chariot on his own son to mete out justice to the cow whose calf was killed by his son, caught under the chariot.

The temple car here is a beautiful structure and the biggest on which model is the Valluvar Kottam in Chennai built. The car festival is famous and attracts large crowd. The original car was burnt in 1922 in an accident and is now replaced in all its original grandeur. As in Srirangam, here the goddess Piriyavidai Amman is called 'Padi Thandal' (one who never goes out of the portals) and is never taken out in procession.

The Nandhi in this temple, unlike the other Nandhis in sitting pose, is seen standing before Thyagaraja. The deity is on Ratna Simhasana (throne made of precious stones). In the southwest corner of the inner prakara Nilotpalambigai is seen blessing her child Muruga sitting on a maid's shoulder. Goddess Kamalambigai is in yogasana pose during penance in another sanctum. Navagrahas are not as usual in a circle around the sun but standing in a row.

Tiruvarur is the birthplace of musical trinity Thyagaiah, Shyama Sastri and Muthusamy Dikshithar. Rare musical instruments — Panchamuga vadyam with five heads representing the five heads of Siva and a nadaswaram called Barinayanam — could also be seen in this temple.

Places around Tiruvarur

Kizhvelur : A mile from Kizhvelur station on the Tiruvarur-Nagore line is a temple of Agastyalinga. The Nataraja image here is unique having ten heads, all armed with trident, round, shield, mazhu, noose, club etc. - a craftsmanship of inimitable intricacy. There is a separate sanctum here for Kubera the God of fortune, rare indeed in the south.

Nannilam: 20 km from Tiruvarur is the place called Nannilam. It is here in Narimanam we get petrol. The crude petroleum pumped from the oil wells here is taken to the refinery at Ennore, Chennai. The installations of ONGC for drilling oil wells could be seen here.

Tiruvanjiam : It is 10 kms west of Nannilam. The sandalwood tree is the Sthala Viruksha here. Images of Durga, Bhairavar, Rahu and Kethu are of fine workmanship in this temple. Vanjinatha the deity is mounted on the Yama Vahana during Masi

Dhasami festival (February-March).

Engan : The most beautiful and captivating idol of Lord Muruga is located in this temple, 6 miles from Koradacheri on the Nagore-Thanjavur railway line. The idol of Shanmuganathar has been carved with minute details – even holes are pierced in His ears to insert ear-rings. The same sculptor who made the idol at Sikkal cut off his right thumb to avoid carving another image superior to the Singaravelar. But Lord Muruga appeared in his dream and bade him to make another image at Ettukkudi. He then blinded his eyes as it excelled Singaravelar of Sikkil. Again he had a command to commission another image at Engan. He sought the help of a woman to assist him as he was blind. While working, his chisel cut the finger of the lady and the spurting blood fell on his eyes. His eyesight was immediately restored and he exclaimed 'Engan' (my eyes) and completed this superb idol. Hence, the place got its name 'Engan'.

Vidayapuram : 4½ kms from Koradacheri is this place where Rajaraja I has built a beautiful Siva temple. The presiding deity is called Meenakshisundareswarar. The idol of Meenakshi, the consort of Siva is noted for its artistic perfection and grace.

Koothanur: 25 kms from Tiruvarur is the renowned place associated with the Tamil poet Ottakkoothar. There is a unique temple here to Goddess of learning - Saraswathi. The idol in sitting posture is elegant and artistic.

Thillai Vilagam : This place is about 25 kms south of Tiruturaipoondi. It is a famous Vaishnavaite sthalam visited by all. The image of the presiding deity Kothandarama is of intricate workmanship even the veins are beautifully exposed. There is a sanctum for Nataraja too in this Vishnu temple. There is another shrine of Kothandaramar at Vaduvur on the Mannargudi route. This village is also known as Dakshina Ayodhya.

Mannargudi : The most important Vaishnavaite shrine is here. It has the name **Rajamannargudi** as the presiding deity here is Rajagopalaswamy. The shrine is spread over 15 acres. The image of the presiding deity Rajagopalaswamy is 12 feet tall. There are 16 gopurams, 7 prakarams with 24 shrines, 7 beautiful mandapams adorning the inside and 9 sacred theerthams. There is a Garuda Sthamba, a monolithic pillar 50 ft. tall in the forefront with a miniature Garuda shrine on the top. The sacred waters Haridra Nadhi is only a tank but bigger than Kamalalayam at Thiruvarur. The place is also called Dakshina Dwaraka – Dwaraka of the South. 'Par Pughalum Panguni Triuvizha' will be celebrated every year during the month of March.

Once Jainism seems to have flourished in this part as there are evidences of Jain statues in the vicinity. Mallinathaswami Jinalayam is in the middle of a Jain locality. Meru Parvatham, Padmavathi Amman, Nandiswaradeepam and Trikala Tirthankarar are worth seeing in this Jinalayam.

Jambavanodai Dargah : Located 53 km from Tiruvarur and 25 km from Tiruturaipoondi. This Dargah near Muthupet is also called as Hakkim Sheiku Dawood Kamil Oliyullah Dargah.

Where to Stay?

Tiruvarur (STD : 04366)
• **Hotel Selvies Pvt. Ltd.,** Near Bus Stand, Tiruvarur. ✆ 222080/82, Fax: 04366-222424

- **V.P.K. Lodge.**, Near Bus Stand, Thanjavur Road, Tiruvarur - 610 001. ☏ 222309, 225509
- **Hotel Sudarshan,** 81, South Main Street, (Opp. to R.D.O. Office), Tiruvarur-610 001. ☏ 241536, 244686.
- **The Royal Park.**, By-Pass Road, Tiruvarur. ☏ 251020/21/22
- **Lodge President.**, 33/C10, Thanjavur Road, Opp. Bus Stand, Tiruvarur-610 001. ☏ 222538, 222748

Thanjavur

(Legacy of the later Cholas)

Thanjavur properly situated in the Cauvery delta is the rice - bowl of Tamil Nadu. A fertile land that was also fertile for art, architecture and culture. Though it was a famous city from early times, its importance was fully understood only by the later Cholas (AD 846-1276) who built an empire making it their capital. It was Vijayalaya who founded the later Chola kingdom here and Rajaraja the Great (AD 984-1014) and his son Rajendra I (AD 1012 - 1044) were the real architects of the Chola empire that held sway over India upto the Ganges in the north and held colonies in Myanmar, Malaya and the East Indies. It became the centre of Tamil learning and culture. It became the original home of the Dravidian art and architecture besides being the centre of Tamil classical dance which is now known as Bharatha Natyam all over the world. Even today, the teachers of Bharatha Natyam hail from Thanjavur. Its further glory is the Carnatic music which in essence is nothing but classical Tamil music. The only remains of its glorious past are the beautiful temples that were built by the Cholas known for their amazing architectural wonder, and not less than 74 of them are around Thanjavur itself. The Pandyas, the Nayaks and the Marathas ruled the city after the later Cholas and finally the British made it a district.

How to get there?

Thanjavur is directly connected by rail with Chennai, Nagore, Trichy and Madurai. It is connected to all major cities with road. The local transport system runs buses to all places in and around Thanjavur. Autorickshaws and taxis are also available. Frequent bus services are available to Chennai, Trichy, Madurai, Dindigul. The nearest airport is at Trichy, 58 kms away. The Indian Airlines and Air Lanka operate flights to Sri Lanka. Indian Airlines operates flights to Chennai and Madurai. It is about 350 kms on the meter gauge main line from Chennai.

What to see in Thanjavur?

The Big Temple (or) the Brahadeeswara Temple : This temple, the marvel of Dravidian art and architecture needs several days to go round and enjoy inch by inch, even then one would not go with complete satisfaction. It was built by the Great Rajaraja I the nonpareil of the later Chola dynasty. Begun in A.D. 1003 it was completed in 1010. He was a king of magnificence and his temple also stood magnificent, true to its name Dakshina Meru. Unlike other temples the vimanam (the tower over the sanctum) soars higher than the usual gopuram or portal tower. It soars to a height of 64.8 m (208 ft.). It rises from a square base and shaped like a pyramid with 14 tiers, on the top of which is a higher monolithic cupola carved out from a 81.3 tonne block of granite. It was perched there from the village, 'Saarappallam' by rolling it along a ramp of earth six km long like the way in which the Egyptian pyramids were built. It is set on a spacious prakara of 240m by 125m. The Lingam in the sanctum is 3.70m high. The huge bull (Nandhi) in the outer courtyard is monolithic 3.70m high, 6m long, and 2.50m wide which is the handiwork not of Chola but added by the Vijayanagar rulers. It is the second largest in India, the first being the one at the Lepakshi temple in Andhra Pradesh.

The dwarapalakas flanking the doorways are 5.50m in height. The complex is flanked with various mandapams. There are three gateways with gopurams to enter the temple. The basement is crowded with inscriptions telling the various grants and gifts offered to Brahadeeswara by innumerable kings, chieftains and nobles. The establishment of the temple had 1000 persons, 400 of them were female dancers. The outer side of the exterior wall is divided into 2 storeys with niches filled with images of Saivaite iconography. There are also Vaishnavaite and Buddhist themes in sculptures. One difference here is that even the sculptor's name is engraved.

While the outer walls is ornamented with stone images, the inner wall of the sanctum is covered with Chola murals. They were concealed by the superimposition of Vijayanagar Nayak paintings. It was only in 1930, the originals were brought to light by a special chemical process. Sundaramurthy Nayanar, Cheraman Perumal, Tiripuranthaga, Rajaraja, Karuvur Thevar and Dakshinamurthi were thus discovered to the world manifesting the marvel of Chola painting. With permission from the archaeological department one could see them dazzle in floodlight inside the inner corridor. The outer wall of the upper storey is carved with 81 dance poses of Bharatha Natyam, the classical dance of the Tamils. A look at the inside of the spiralling 14 tiers is quite amazing and the precision of the engineers of the Chola period makes one spellbound. Another wonder is that the shadow of the cupola never falls in the ground – a testimony to the engineering skills of the Chola architecture.

The shrine for the Goddess was added by Pandian rulers in the 13th century A.D. The Subramania shrine was added by Vijayanagar rulers. Sambaji, the Maratha ruler of Thanjavur renovated the Vinayaka shrine.

Nidamba Sudini : This is the earliest image of Kali in Potters Street 1.6 km to the east of the Big Temple. The image of the Goddess is five feet tall wearing a garland of skulls, a snake covering Her breasts, teeth protruding and in unbearable wrath trampling the two demons Chandan and Mundan. This image was installed by Vijayalaya Chola in commemoration of his victory over the Mutharayas which enabled him to found the later Chola kingdom.

The Palace : Not far from the temple and in the heart of the old tower lies the palace with vast labyrinthian buildings, enormous corridors, big halls, watch-towers, moat, fort and courtyards. The palace was built by the Nayak rulers around 1550 A.D. and subsequently renovated and enlarged by the Maratha rulers of Thanjavur. Though a portion is in ruins, much of it is still in its original beauty. Some government offices are located inside besides an art gallery, a library, the hall of music, the audience hall and even today in a portion lives the present legal heirs of the Thanjavur Marathas.

The Rajaraja Chola Art Gallery: It is inside the palace. It has a beautiful collection of granite and bronze idols from the 9th to the 12th centuries. They are fine pieces of workmanship of Chola art. Most of them were brought from the temples in and around Thanjavur and preserved here. The collection holds the onlooker spellbound with their minute details and grace.

The Saraswathi Mahal Library: This is also inside the palace. It was founded in 1700 A.D. by the Maratha kings who ruled Thanjavur. There are over 30,000 palm leaf and paper manuscripts in this library. Books both in Indian languages and European languages are preserved here. In one section on the walls are displayed pictures of Chinese torture of prisoners.

Sangeetha Mahal : It is inside the palace and a specimen of soundproof and acoustically perfect music hall. It is tastefully decorated with fine etchings.

Church : Inside the palace could also be seen a church on the eastern side. It is called Schewartz Church and was built in A.D. 1779 by Raja Serfoji in honour of revered Schewartz of Denmark.

Royal Museum : This is another museum in the palace complex, very interesting to see. It contains a good collection of manuscripts, weapons, dresses, utensils and musical instruments used by the members of the royal family of Thanjavur.

Rajagopala Beerangi : On the eastern rampart of the fort is this big Beerangi (cannon). It is called Beerangi Medu or Dasmedu.

Sharja Madi : It is also located in the palace complex. It is a storeyed building opened for tourists to have a panoramic view of Thanjavur city. There are beautiful wooden carvings and sculptures inside the Sharja Madi.

Rajarajan Manimandapam : This was built during the 8th World Tamil Conference. There is a small garden with children's play materials in it.

Rajarajan Museum : It is in the ground floor of the Manimandapam and under the control of the State Archaeological Department containing interesting exhibits, charts, maps etc. on the history of the Chola empire.

Tolkappiyar Sadukkam : During the 8th World Tamil Conference the Sadukkam (square) was built to commemorate the memory of the ancient grammarian Tolkappiyar who was the author of Tolkappiyam, the oldest Tamil grammar available now in full form in print. From this tower, one can have a panoramic view of Thanjavur.

Sivaganga Park : It is a beautifully laid-out park with a tank known for its sweet water and children's play materials are also kept there.

Timings

Art Gallery	: 9 a.m. to 1 p.m.
	2 p.m. to 6 p.m.
	Entrance Fee: Adult Rs.3/- & Child Re.1/-.
	Holidays : National Holidays only.
Saraswathi Mahal Library	: 10 a.m. to 1 p.m.
	1.30 p.m. to 5.30 p.m.
	Holidays : Wednesdays & National Holidays
	✆ 334107 Fax: 91-4362-333568
Royal Museum	9 a.m. to 6 p.m.
	Entrance Fee : Adult Re.1, Child–Re.0.50.
	Holidays : Govt. Holidays
	✆ 231486

Sharja Madi	:	10 a.m. to 1 p.m.
		2 p.m. to 5 p.m.
		Entrance Fee: Re.1.
Rajarajan Manimandapam		
	:	10.00 a.m. to 8.00 p.m.
		Entrance Free
Rajarajan	:	10 a.m. to 5 p.m.
Museum		Entrance Fee : Adult Re.1/- and Child Re.0.50.
Tolkappiyar		
Sadukkam	:	9 a.m. to 7 p.m.
		Entrance Free

Tamil University : Founded in 1981, this University specialises in research and advanced study of the Tamil language. It is 7 km away and located in a vast area with beautiful buildings. A very good library with a good collection of English and Tamil books is functioning in the University complex. ℂ 226720

Places around Thanjavur

All the places mentioned hereunder can be reached mostly by town buses or by hired vehicles without any difficulty.

Mariamman Temple : It is at Punnainallur 6 kms away from Thanjavur. It is one of the local temples of Thanjavur and attracts enormous crowd.

Thiruvaiyaru Temple : 13 kms from Thanjavur on the banks of the river Cauvery lies this ancient temple dedicated to Panchanadiswara (Lord of 5 rivers). Cauvery, Vennaru, Vettaru, Kudamurutti and Vadavaru form a network like garland to this Lord. Thiruchattruruthurai, Thiru-vedikkudi, Kandiyur, Thiruppoon-thuruthi and Thiruneithanam are Saptha Stalas to which the Deity of Ayyaru proceed during Chitthirai (April-May) festival which attracts great crowd. On the way to Thiruvaiyaru at Kandiyur one can see the beautiful image of Brahma and at Thiruppoonthuruthi the superb panel of Ravana lifting Kailas, Siva mounted on the bull with Uma, Ardhanari and Dakshinamurthi with veena in His hands are fine pieces of art that should not be missed. In Panchanadiswara temple that contains spacious halls and corridors, the idol of Lord Brahma is very exquisitely executed. Some sculptures here are of Chalukyan style having been brought as war trophy.

One of the musical trinity, Thyagaraja's samadhi is on the banks of the river. Near the Siva temple is a one-roomed house where Thyagaraja composed some of his greatest works. The samadhi itself is a fitting tribute to the saint and one can see almost all the scenes of Ramayana as they appear in his songs beautifully sculptured in black marble by Bangalore Nagarathinammal, a devotee of Thyagaraja. There is also the samadhi temple with the saint's statue. The Thyagaraja Aradhana festival is held in the tamil month of 'Thai' on the 'Magula Panjami' day, when most of the leading exponents of Carnatic music come to perform and are listened to by lakhs of ardent fans of classical music. A huge complex is under construction here to accommodate the ever increasing number of devotees.

Grand Anicut (Kallanai) : This barrage was built at the delta head of Thanjavur by Karikal Chola of the Sangam Age and serves even today. This was built by slave labour, the slaves being the prisoners of war from Ceylon. Stones were piled up across the river for 1080 ft. It was 60ft. wide and about 20 ft. high. That it stood the ravages of time and floods for over 1500 years is a testimony for the skills of ancient engineering. It is fully made of stones and earth. In 1805, the dam was repaired by Captain Caldwell. It is the overhead regulator of the water of Cauvery for irrigation. Excessive flood waters were left in Kollidam. There is a park and it is a nice picnic spot. Buses are operated from Tiruchirapalli, Thanjavur and Kumbakonam. It is about 48 km from Thanjavur.

Thingalur : This Siva temple is about 18 kms from Thanjavur. There is a separate shrine for **Chandra (Moon God)** in this temple and it is one of the nine places of Navagrahas. It attracts pilgrims on all days.

Ganapathi Agraharam : It is about 5 kms east of Thingalur. A famous Vinayaka temple is here. Next to it is a Vishnu temple. The Vinayaka Chathurthi festival (August-September) is very famous and thousands of people gather here at that time.

Alangudi : This famous Siva temple is 43 kms from Thanjavur and near Kumbakonam on the Mannargudi Road. It is one of the temples of Navagraha (Nine Planets) and this place has the shrine of **Guru (Jupiter)**. On all days, pilgrims throng this temple from all over India. The temple is of the Chola period and exposes Chola architecture.

Papanasam : It is 30 kms from Thanjavur. It is a historic town. There are two temples here, one Pallavanatha Swamy temple constructed by Chola king and the other is called 108 Sivalingam. There is a granary here of 80 ft. breadth and 36 ft. height for storing 3,000 'kalams' of paddy. It was constructed by the Nayak kings in A.D. 1600-1634. It has been declared as a monument by the state archaeological department. The 108 Sivalingams in one temple is in the Papanasam town.

There is also a famous temple at Thirukkarukavur nearby dedicated to Mullaivananathaswamy.

Thiruvalanchuzhi : This place near Swamimalai has a shrine for Vinayaga. The temple is an architectural marvel. As the river Cauvery changed the course to the right (valam) the place came to be known as *Thiruvalanchuzhi*. The image of Vinayaga is in the form of a sea foam. It is named Swetha (white) Vinayaga. Beautifully chiselled stone pillars and stone lattice work of intricate design could be seen here.

Poondi Madha Shrine : This village is about 3.5 kms from Thanjavur. The nearest railway station is Budalur. It is a Roman Catholic pilgrim centre like Velankanni and people from all over India visit this place. The church authorities provide accommodation to pilgrims.

Manora : It is 65 kms on the way to Kodikkarai in Saluva-nayakkappattinam. A 11 storeyed tower stands here built by Raja Serfoji in 1814 to commemorate the victory of the British over Napoleon in the battle of Waterloo. It served as an observatory and a lighthouse for some time. The tall tower could be seen from a distance of 5 kms. It was utilised to keep books on shipbuilding, by the king.

Kumbakonam : It is 36 kms from Thanjavur linked by road and rail. It is the biggest town in Thanjavur district and a commercial centre for silk, utensils and trade. It is the treasure-house of art and architecture, because almost all the important temples are in and around Kumbakonam. It is a focal point from where all the Chola temples could easily be visited.

Mahamagam, the Kumba Mela of the south which occurs once in 12 years when the planet Jupiter enters the constellation Leo and the Sun in Aquarius is famous here, and lakhs of people from all over India throng here to have a holy dip in the Mahamagam tank which is located in the middle of the town. It is believed that the holy Ganges flows into this tank on that day. Bordered by exquisite mandapams, the tank bears an imposing look with stone-cut steps leading to water level. There are umpteen spring wells in the bed of the tank, called 'Theerthams' or holy waters.

Temples in Kumbakonam

Adikumbeswara Temple : It is an ancient temple, very huge spreading over 4 acres with a gopuram 125 ft. high. The Mahamagam tank itself is its Theertham (holy water). The Navarathri Mandapam with 27 'Stars' and '12 Rasis' (constellations) carved in a single block, the idol of Shanmuga with only six hands instead of usual 12, two stone Nadaswarams and Kiratamurti are the main attractions in this temple. They speak volumes of the artistic attainment of Chola sculptures.

Sarangapani Temple : It is the Vaishnavaite shrine equally famous as the Adikumbeswara temple. The temple has Hema Pushkarani as its holy tank. The inner shrine has a unique feature is being fashioned like a chariot with galloping horses; besides, it has two entrances – Uttara Vasal in the north and Dakshina Vasal in the south. The northern gate is opened for entering the sanctum when Sun reaches the Tropic of Capricorn and the other one closed, until the Sun reaches the Tropic of Cancer. Afterwards, it is repeated vice versa. The gopuram with 12 tiers (150 ft. high) has the dancing poses of Siva

— a strange feature in a Vaishnavaite shrine.

The deity Aravamudhan in the sanctum inside the temple is in the act of rising from His Snake-couch to give darshan to His ardent devotee Thirumazhisai Alwar. The Komalavalli Thayar image is very charming, true to the name of 'Komalam'. The Vaishnavaite literary work Divya Prabhandham 4000 in number was brought to light in this temple just like the Thevaram of Saivism brought to light at Chidambaram temple.

Ramaswami Temple : It is near the Adikumbeswara temple. The Mahamandapam has exquisite sculptures, each a class in itself, the noted ones being Vibhishana Coronation, Trivikrama, a dancer with Veena and Manmatha. The idol in the sanctum installed by Ragunatha Naik of Thanjavur had been found from a tank. Lord Hanuman image in this temple can be seen playing a Veena. The corridor walls are painted with sequences of Ramayana.

Chakrapani Temple : The temple is noted for its exquisite pillars. The presiding deity Chakrapani has eight arms. There is a bronze image of Raja Serfoji worshipping the Lord as he is said to have been cured of an illness by the grace of this God. A panchamukha (five-faced) Hanuman is erected in the prakaram.

Brahma Shrine : The Brahma temple is very rare in India and the Brahma temple here is in the place where He performed a penance.

Nageswaraswami Temple: The temple is so aligned that the rays of the Sun falls for 3 days on the Lingam in the sanctum in the first Tamil month (April-May). The Nrithya Sabha (dance hall) is a typical example of the Chola art.

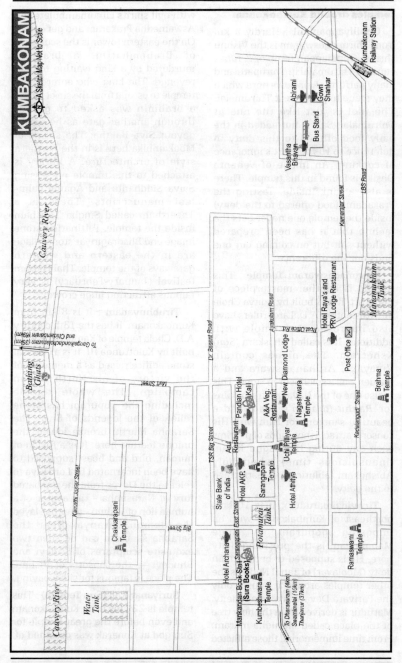

KUMBAKONAM

A Sketch Map Not to Scale

Cauvery River

Cauvery River

Water Tank

Bathing Ghats

To Gangaikondacholapuram (35km)
and Chidambaram (63km)

Kamala Josier Street

Kamadi Josier Street

Chakkarapani Temple

Big Street

Potramurai Tank

Hotel Archana

Mankandan Book Stall
(Sura Books)

Kumbeshwara Temple

To Dharasuram (4km)
Swamimalai (10km)
Thanjavur (37km)

TSR Big Street

Sarangapani East Street

State Bank of India

Hotel AKF

Adul Restaurant

Sarangapani Temple

Hotel Athithya

Uchi Pilliyar Temple

Pandian Hotel

A&A Veg. Restaurant

Kali

Nageshwara Temple

Dr. Basant Road

Mutt Street

Ayakulam Road

New Diamond Lodge

Post Office Rd.

Hotel Raya's and PRV Lodge Restaurant

Post Office

Kardarangudi Street

Brahma Temple

Ramaswami Temple

Mahamakham Tank

Kamarajar Street

L&S Road

Vasantha Bhavan

Bus Stand

Abirami

Gowri Shankar

Kumbakonam Railway Station

Temples around Kumbakonam

Uppiliyappankoil : Hardly a km from Thirunageswaram is the Vishnu shrine, Oppiliappan temple. It ranks equal to Thirumalai in Thirupathi and many perform their vows here which they made to perform at Thirumalai. The idol is just like the one at Thirumalai. Salt is not added in the daily food offered to this deity in deference to His consort's ignorance of cooking. An image of Vedanta Desika is found in this temple. There is also a tank inside. Tasting the Prasadam (food offered to the deity) inside the temple one never gets the feeling that it has been prepared without salt but on coming out one finds out the difference.

Thirunageswaram Temple : This temple is another masterpiece of Chola art. It was built by Aditya Chola in 10th century A.D. Later rulers have also improved the temple with additions. It is called Bhaskara (Sun) Kshetram. The niches contain Vinayaka, Ardhanariswara and a maiden – all a splendour in stone. This is also one of the Navagraha sthalams for *Raghu (dragon's head)* and a beautiful sanctum for Him with His consorts attracts thousands of pilgrims each day during the Raghu Kalam (inauspicious time) when holy Abishekam (ablutions) is performed to the deity.

Tiruvidaimarudur : It is 10 kms northeast of Kumbakonam with an imposing gopuram. A huge Mahalingam is the presiding deity here. He is supposed to be the main deity (Moolavar) of Tamil Nadu as the other temples around it houses only the Parivara Devathas as main deity. Marudur is derived from the holy tree of the place called Marudha maram. From time immemorial, those afflicted with evil spirits circumambulate the Aswamedha Prakaram and get cured. On the eastern tower is the sculpture of Brahmahatthi, a brahmin murdered by a king waiting to take revenge. The king who entered the temple to escape from the sin of killing a brahmin was asked to go out through another gate as he was a devout Siva Baktha. The shrine of Mookambika here is in the northern style of architecture. A library is attached to this temple possessing Saiva Siddhanta and Agama palm-leaf manuscripts. There is a Theertham called Singha Thirtham inside the temple. Pattinathar stone image and Bhadragiriyar stone image are in the eastern and western gateways of the temple. Thai Poosam festival (January-February) is very famous attracting huge crowds.

Tirubhuvanam : It is 8 km from Kumbakonam. It has the 13th century A.D. Chola temple of Kambahareswara built by Kulottunga III. It is a colossal stone edifice raised as a memorial of the victory of his North Indian campaign. The whole temple including the gopuram has stone relief, of the legends of Siva. The Sarabha Murthi bronze idol is the unique feature here. It is a fusion of human, bird and beast supposed to have been incarnated by Lord Siva to release the Devas from the unabated fury of Narasimha - the avatar of a human lion of Vishnu - after he slayed the demon Hiranya. Near the Sarabha sanctum can be seen two exquisite sculptures of Sridevi and Bhudevi — the consorts of Vishnu. The place is famous for silk weaving.

Suriyanar Koil (Sun Temple) : This temple is 22 kms from Kumbakonam and even before the great temple for Sun god at Konarak was dreamed of,

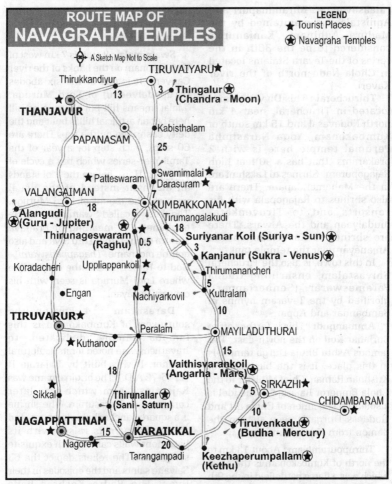

ROUTE MAP OF NAVAGRAHA TEMPLES

A Sketch Map Not to Scale

LEGEND
★ Tourist Places
✪ Navagraha Temples

a temple for Sun and the planets that move around Him was built here. It was built by Kulottungan I. A fifty feet gopuram stands here and passing through it the image of a horse and the chariot of Surya appears into view. The planets have different shrines around the Sun's sanctum which is in the centre. This is one of the Navagraha sthalams and people pour here daily to propitiate Sun God, the chief of the planets according to Indian Astrology. Ratha Sapthami (January – February) is the day of the change of Sun's course (Starting His northern course from Capricorn) and that day is celebrated as a festival day.

Kanjanur : Located near Suriyanar Koil, this Shivastalam is associated with **Sukran** - representing the **planet Venus** and is - regarded one of the nine temples in the Thanjavur area linked with the Navagrahas. This shrine is also referred to as

85 >

Palaasavanam, Bhrammapuri and Agnistalam is maintained by the Madurai Adhinam. Kanjanur is considered to be the 36th in the series of the Tevara Stalams located in Chola Nadu north of the river Kaveri.

Thirucherai : This Divyadesam is located in Tirucherai, near 4 km north Kodavasal and 15 km south of Kumbakonam. Yoga Narasimha Perumal temple here is with 2 prakarams that has a 90 feet high Rajagopuram. Shrines to Lakshmi are in the Mahamandapam. There are also shrines to Rajagopala with his consorts and to Tiruvenkata-mudaiyaan and the Alwars. There are shrines to Kaveriamman and Anjaneyar near the temple tank.

In this town, is also the Tirucherai Shivastalam, enshrining Gnana Parameswarar (Senneriappar), glorified by the Tevaram hymns of Sambandar and Appar.

Ammangudi : This is farther off to Surianar Koil on the north-east. The famous Ashta Bhuja Durga temple is in this place. It is the birthplace of Krishnan Raman, Chief Minister to the Chola Emperor Rajaraja I. The idol is a splendid specimen of Chola art and Goddess Durga is seen slaying the demon from Her lion mount.

Thiruppurambiam : About 13 km to the north of Kumbakonam is the place which was a fierce battlefield in the 9th century deciding the bright future of the Cholas. Chola king Aditya built a temple in sweet remembrance of the turn of tide in his favour and named it Aditeswaram. The present name of the presiding deity is Sakshinatheswarar and the consort bears the beautiful name Kuraivila Azhagi (Beauty Unsurpassed). The sanctum for the Devi was built by Rajaraja I. The sanctum wall contains beautiful sculptures of Parivara Devatas. Lord Ganesa here is performed honey ablutions on the Vinayaka Chathurthi day and all the honey passed on Him is absorbed by Him.

Swamimalai : It stands 7 km west of Kumbakonam on the banks of the river Cauvery. It is one of the six abodes (Arupadaiveedu) of Lord Muruga. 'Malai' means hill but there is no hill here but an artificial hill is built and the deity enshrined on the top. There are 60 steps, each step for a year of the Tamil Year-series which has a cycle of 60 years. Here, before the idol stands an elephant instead of the usual peacock, the mount of Lord Muruga. The deity is called Swaminatha as He explained the meaning of Pranava Mantra to His father Lord Siva and also got the nickname 'Thagappanswami' – God to Father. This is the only shrine where Lord Muruga is seen with his consort Devayani.

Darasuram : 4 km on the southwest of Kumbakonam is this famous temple dedicated to Iravatheeswara noted for its sculptural wonder. It was built by Rajaraja II (1146-72 A.D.). The original name was Rajarajeswaram which was later corrupted as Darasuram. The shrine is a square panchadhala vimanam, and the mandapam is raised with its basement walls carved with exquisite sculptures. The reliefs depict the 63 Saivaite saints and the episodes in their lives. The Badra Koshtas have Dakshina-murthi, Lingodhbhavar, Brahma and Vishnu carved beautifully. Different forms of Siva adorn the Karna Devakoshtas. In the north wall, Mahishasura - the buffalo demon is shown in full human form, not to be seen anywhere else. Even narrow spaces are filled with Kiritarjuna and Ravana lifting Kailas. The cell in the second floor contains Umamaheswara with king Rajendra II. The king wanted to make this temple unique in every respect, so he has lavished it with intricate artwork, even paid attention in the choice of stones for carving the images.

The balustrades of steps reaching the mandapam too are wrought with elaborate sculptures. The middle Ghoshta in the south wall has an awe-inspiring image of Sarabha pacifying Narasimha. In the north-east mandapam, the pillars contain Natya poses and the ceiling with dancers. Even the Balipeetam facing the temple is an ornate structure with a flight of steps (9 nos.) each producing a musical note when struck. The Dwarapalakas that adorn the temple were brought from the western Chalukya capital Kalyanapuri as trophy of victory.

Pazhayarai : About 7 kms from Kumbakonam is this old Chola capital. Rajarajan II has built a temple here for Somanadiswarar. Formerly it had a palace where the Chola kings resided. It was called Cholan Maligai but now no trace of it is left. Life-size image of Durga, chariot-like mandapam drawn by galloping horses, Ardhanariswara (half Parvathi, half Siva form), and Narasimha (human-lion avatar of Vishnu) are most exquisitely carved here.

Kizha-Pazhayarai: On the eastern side of Pazhayarai was a Kailasanathar sculpture. Ravana is seen lifting Mount Kailas, the abode of Siva only to be trapped under its weight when Lord Siva presses it down with the thumb of His right foot - a remarkable sculpture. Saint Appar one of the 63 Nayanmars of the Siva cult is said to have observed a hunger strike here to establish it as a Siva temple.

Patteswaram : This temple is 8 km from Kumbakonam. The presiding deity is Dhenupuriswarar. The right

of this temple is imposing with five gopurams piercing the sky. A life-like statue of the great scholar and minister Govinda Dikshithar of the Thanjavur Naick kings is in this temple. The important idol here is the Kattaivasal Durga at the entrance of the northern gopuram. It was the guardian deity of the palace of the Cholas and after the disintegration was brought with Bhairavar and installed here. Vishnu Durgai is very famous here and pilgrims throng here every day. A little to the west is Ramanathar temple dedicated to Vishnu, which contains niches on the walls housing images of fine artistic skill.

Where to stay?

Thanjavur (STD : 04362)
- Hotel Parisutham, 55, G.A. Canal Road. ✆ 231801, 231844 (10 lines) Email: hotel. parisudham@vsnl.com
- Hotel Oriental Towers, 2889, Srinivasam Pillai Road. ✆ 330724, 331467, Fax: 04362-330770, Email: hotowers@tr.dot.net.in
- Pandiyan Residency, Cutcheri Road. ✆ 230514
- Ashok Lodge, Abraham Pandithar Rd. ✆ 230022
- Kasi Lodge, Ezhadi (seven feet) Rd. ✆ 231721
- Hotel Valli, N.K.M.Road. ✆ 231580/231584
- Hotel Karthik, South Rampart St. ✆ 230116
- Hotel Sangam; Trichy Road, ✆ 339451, Fax: 04362-236695, Email:hotelsangam@vsnl.com
- Hotel Ganesh, 2905/3 & 4, Srinivasanpillai Road, Railway Station, ✆ 231113, 232861, 272518, Fax: 04362-272517, Email: hotelganesh-97@ hotmail.com
- Yagappa Lodge, Trichy Road. ✆ 330421
- Hotel Tamil Nadu I (TTDC), Gandhi Road, Thanjavur. ✆ 331421
- Hotel Tamil Nadu II (TTDC), ✆ 230365
- Rajasekar Lodge, South Rampart St. ✆ 230496
- Tamil Nadu Lodge, Trichy Road. ✆ 331088
- Rajarajan Lodge, Gandhi Road. ✆ 231730
- Raja's Rest House, Gandhi Road. ✆ 230515
- Ajanta Lodge, South Rampart St. ✆ 230736
- Eswari Lodge, South Rampart St. ✆ 230488
- Safire Lodge, South Rampart St. ✆ 230970
- Youth Hostel, Medical College Road. ✆ 223591
- Ganesh Lodge, Gandhi Road. ✆ 230789

Kumbakonam (STD : 0435)
- Hotel Raya's, 18, Head Post Office Road, Kumbakonam - 612 001. ✆ 2423170-172 Fax : 0435 - 2422479

- **Hotel Green Park**, 10, Lakshmi Vilas Street, Kumbakonam - 612 001. ✆ 2403912 Fax : 0435 - 2421956
- **Hotel ARK International**, 21, T.S.R. Big Street, Kumbakonam - 612 001. ✆ 2421234, 2421152
- **Paradise Resort**, 3/1216, Thanjavur Main Road, Darasuram, Kumbakonam - 612103. ✆ 3291354, Fax : 0435-2416469
- **Gemini Towers (Lodge)**, ✆ 2431559
- **PRV (Lodge)**, ✆ 2421820

What to buy?

Thanjavur is famous for repousse (metal work with raised relief) and copper work inlaid with brass and silver. The Thanjavur plates are noteworthy. Bronze images are made by traditional craftsmen at Swamimalai.

The Poompuhar Emporium on the Gandhi Road is ideal for buying them. Besides repousse, wood carvings like temple cars and pith models of Thanjavur temple etc. are stocked here. Ancient brass betal boxes, cutters and Chola bronze pots are also available.

RECREATION

Cultural Programme : South Zone Cultural Centre (Phone : 240072) organises cultural programmes in Big Temple premises on every second and fourth Saturday. Admission free.

Clubs : Cosmopolitan club. Rotary and Union club (On Trichy Road).

Library : District Central Library near State Bank, Opp. to Government Hospital. Phone : 230397.

Municipal Library is situated inside the Sivaganga Park.

Bookshop: Appar Book Stall – situated in South Main street. New Century Book House - Rajarajan Vaniga Maiyam, South Rampart Street, Thanjavur. Higginbothams Book House, inside Railway Junction, Thanjavur.

Swimming Pool: (1) Government Stadium, Thanjavur, (2) Hotel Parisutham, (3) Hotel Oriental Towers.

FESTIVALS:

Saint Thyagaraja Aradhana Music Festival - Thiruvaiyaru - January.

Pongal (Tourist) Festival - Thanjavur - 14th to 16th January.

Mahamagam Festival at Kumbakonam - February & March once in 12 years. Last held in 1992.

Annai Velankanni Festival - August-September.

Arulmigu Thyagarajaswamy Car Festival at Thiruvarur - March and April.

Muthu Pallakku Thiruvizha, Thanjavur - May.

Rajaraja Chola's Birthday - Sathaya Thiruvizha - October every year at Thanjavur.

Places of Worship

Temple - Sri Brahadeeswarar Temple, Mariamman Koil, Bangaru Kamakshi Koil, etc.

Church - Sacred Hearts Church, St. Mary's Church etc.

Mosque - Durgah near old bus stand and Irwin Bridge.

Tourist Information

● Government of Tamilnadu, Tourist Office, Jawan's Bhavan, Opp. Head Post Office, Thanjavur - 1. ✆ : 239084

● Tourist Information Centre, Hotel Tamil Nadu Complex, Gandhiji Road, Thanjavur - 1. ✆ : 231421.

Other Information

Post/Telegraph/STD/ISD/Telex/FAX etc. : Available

Courier Service : Available

P.M.G.H. Raja Mirasdar Govt. Hospital, Thanjavur - 1.

Medical College Hospital, Thanjavur-7.

Chemists and Druggists : Available

Important Telephone Numbers
Tamil University ✆ : 227143, 226518
Art Gallery, Palace Complex ✆ 239823
Public Relations Office ✆ 222645
State Bank of India ✆ 231572/ 236207
Town Police Station ✆ 237666
Rural Police Station ✆ 222711
Railway Station ✆ : 231216
TNSTC ✆ : 221999
SETC., Kumbakonam ✆ : 2431251

Thiruchirappalli
(The Rockfort City)

Thiruchirappalli derived its name due to Jain association with this place. Buddhism and Jainism thrived in Tamil Nadu before the renaissance of Hinduism in the form of the Bhakti cult which popularised Saivism and Vaishnavism and exterminated these anti-Hindu religions. So, we find numerous Jain and Buddhist traces scattered in remote and unapproachable spots throughout Tamil Nadu. 'Chira' is actually the name of a Jain monk and once in this rock was his 'palli' (abode). Therefore, it came to be known as Chirappalli and Thiru was added to it as it is an adjective of reverence in the Tamil language. Now nobody takes pain to pronounce its full name and reduced the beautiful name to 'Trichy' properly pronounced as 'Trichy'–these popular shortening of place names is a peculiar character of the Tamils, e.g. Kovai for Coimbatore, Mayilai for Mylapore, Tharai for Dharapuram, Thanjai for Thanjavur etc. There is a special rule in the Tamil grammar for shortening names like this – it is called "Maruvu".

Even before its association with Jains, it was a famous place in the Sangam Age and the capital city of Cholas, called 'Uraiyur'. It has a prime place in the history of Tamil Nadu. The Cheras, the Cholas and the Pandyas have all held sway and after them, the Pallavas, the later Pandyas, the later Cholas, the Vijayanagar rulers, the Marathas, the Nawabs, the French and finally the British–all of them coveted to possess this strategic place which is more or less centrally located place in Tamil Nadu. This was the scene of the decisive Carnatic War which enabled the British to emerge as the future undisputed masters of the Indian sub-continent. It is at present the fourth major city of Tamil Nadu and the headquarters of Trichy district.

How to get there?

Trichy is very well connected by a good network of roads to all the important places in Tamilnadu. Umpteen bus services with high frequencies ply buses to all major places in Tamilnadu. Town buses ply to the nearby places of tourist importance. It is also a major junction for both metre gauge and broad gauge lines of the Southern Railway and is linked to Chennai, Madurai, Thanjavur, Bangalore, Mysore, Tirupathi, Rameswaram, Thiruvananthapuram and Kochi. The Trichi airport has flights to Chennai, Sharjah, Kuwait and Colombo.

Places to See

Rock Fort : This is the important landmark of Trichy. It is an 83 metre (237 ft.) high rock that is the only outcrop in the otherwise flat land of the city. This is perhaps the oldest rock in the world as old as the rocks of Greenland. The Himalayas are infant rocks compared to its age. There are fascinating temples with brilliant architecture in it: Thayumanavar temple, a Siva shrine in the middle and a Ganesa temple at the top called *'Uchipillaiar Koil'*. Two Pallava cave temples, one on the way to the Pillaiar Koil and the other in the northwest end of the street around the hill. A flight of steps leads to the Thayumanava Swami temple the presiding deity of which is a projection of the rock itself. There are on the whole 437 steps cut into a tunnel through the rock. There is a 100-pillared wall and a vimanam covered with gold in the Thayumanavaswami temple. The cave temple belongs to the Pallava period and Pallava king Mahendra Varman (6th century A.D.) built this cave temple inside which is a beautiful carving of Gangadhara. The image must have been the first one fashioned by the Pallavas. From the Uchipillaiar Koil one can have a panoramic view of the city on all the four sides.

The winding river Cauvery and the temples of Srirangam and Thiruvanaikaval can be seen from the northern side. The view is spectacular and a fitting reward for the painstaking ascend. The Teppakulam built by Viswanatha Nayak is another landmark. This tank with the background of the fort is vey imposing. Teppakulam is the float festival tank.

Nadirshah Mosque : To the west of the city is this mosque containing the remains of Nawabs Mohammed Ali and the headless body of Chanda Sahib who were the principal cause for the Carnatic Wars. The tomb of saint Babbayya Nadir Shah attracts devotees of all faiths in large number.

Srirangam : 'Rangam' means island and Srirangam is the island between Cauvery and Kollidam (Coleroon) where Sri Ranganatha is lying on His Adi Sesha (snake) couch. The main sanctum of Sri Ranganatha is surrounded by 7 large enclosures and 21 majestic gopurams. On the south is

Ranga Vilasam and Seshagiri Royal Mandapam with marvellous sculptural splendour. The main deity is enshrined within the first Corridor. The vimanam shaped like Omkara is plated with gold. The temple was constructed by the Chola King Dharmavarman and even before that, it is said that the temple existed buried under the sand. Almost all the kings who held sway in Tamil Nadu have spent lavishly to embellish the temple and even the British King Edward VII has presented a gold plate. Saint Ramanuja, the author of Vishistad-vaitham tenet functioned from here to spread Vaishnavism and His mortal remains are entombed in a sanctum here.

The unfinished tower started by Krishna Devaraya has now been completed (1987). It is the tallest in India rising 73 m high with 13 tiers. The other gopurams were built between the 14th and 17th centuries by various kings.

The artistical splendour of this temple excels beyond description. The east-facing Krishna shrine is a display of feminine grace in stone. The Seshagiri Rayar Mandapam opposite the 1000-pillared mandapam is unique with its equestrian statues. The tiger hunt sculpture is a marvel in stone. The hall is a living testimony to the dexterity of the Vijayanagar craftsmen. The Amirta Kalasa Garuda is a superb carving in the vehicle mandapam. The eight-armed Venugopala and Lakshminarayana on Garuda are inimitable.

Vaikunda Ekadasi festival is very famous in this temple. At that time, the Paramapada Vasal (Paradise Gate) is opened and lakhs of pilgrims rush to enter it as it is believed that one who enters here will reach Vaikunta after death.

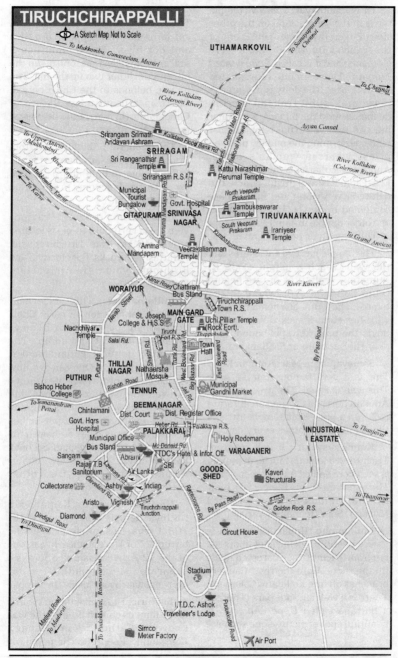

TIRUCHCHIRAPPALLI

A Sketch Map Not to Scale

To Mukkombu, Gunaseelam, Musuri

UTHAMARKOVIL

To Samayapuram Chennai

To Chennai

River Kollidam
(Coleroon River)

Ayyan Cannal

Srirangam Srimath
Andavan Ashram

Kollidam Flood Bank Rd.

National Highway 45

Trichy - Chennai Main Road

SRIRAGAM

Sri Ranganathar
Temple

Srirangam R.S.

Kattu Narashimar
Perumal Temple

River Kollidam
(Coleroon River)

To Upper Anicut
(Mukkombu)

River Kaveri

To Mukkombu, Karur

To Karur

Municipal
Tourist
Bungalow

Govt. Hospital

North Veeputhi
Prakaram

Jambukeswarar
Temple

GITAPURAM

SRINIVASA
NAGAR

South Veeputhi
Prakaram

TIRUVANAIKKAVAL

Mandamana Mandapam Rd.

Kumbakonam Road

Iraniyeer
Temple

To Grand Anicut

Amma
Mandapam

Veerakaliamman
Temple

River Kaveri

Karur Road

Chattiram
Bus Stand

WORAIYUR

Navai Street

Tiruchchirappalli
Town R.S.

St. Joseph
College & H.S.S

MAIN GARD
GATE

Tiruchi
Fort R.S.

Uchi Pillar Temple
(Rock Fort).

By Pass Road

Nachchiyar
Temple

Salai Rd.

Shastri Rd.

Tiruchi
Fort Rd.

Track Rd.

Theppakulam

Town
Hall

East Boulevard
Road

THILLAI
NAGAR

Bishop. Road

Nathaersha
Mosque

West Boulevard Rd.

Big Bazaar Rd.

PUTHUR

Puthur Rd.

TENNUR

Municipal
Gandhi Market

Bishop Heber
College

BEEMA NAGAR

Dist. Court

Dist. Registar Office

To Somasundram
Pettai

Chintamani

Govt. Hqrs
Hospital

Heber Rd.

Palakkarai R.S.

PALAKKARAI

Holy Redemars

INDUSTRIAL
EASTATE

To Thanjavur

Municipal Office

Mc.Donald Rd.

TTDC's Hotel & Infor. Off.

VARAGANERI

Bus Stand

Sangam

Rajaji T.B
Sanitorium

Abrami

Air Lanka

SBI

Cleveland Rd.

Lawsons Rd.

Indian

GOODS
SHED

Kaveri
Structurals

Collectorate

Ashby

To Thanjavur

Aristo

Vighesh

Tiruchirappalli
Junction.

Railway Rd.

By Pass Road

Golden Rock R.S.

Diamond

To Dindigul

Dindigul
Road

Circut House

Madurai Road

To Madurai

To Pudukkottai, Rameswaram

Stadium

Pudukkottai Road

I.T.D.C. Ashok
Travelleer's Lodge

Simco
Meter Factory

Air Port

Tiruvanaikkaval : This Siva temple too is in the same island on the other side of the railway line. This is one of the Pancha Bootha Sthalam (five elements) and it is called *Appu (water) Lingam*. The element represented here is water. The deity is in water. A perennial subterranean spring gushes around the lingam. A peculiar practice observed in this temple is that while performing the midday puja the priest wears a woman's dress. Another peculiarity is the presence of Eka-Pada-Tirumurthi in which the trinity Siva, Vishnu and Brahma are combined in one. It is not found in any other temple in Tamil Nadu except in Thiruvottriyur near Chennai.

The temple has five enclosures and the walls reach a height of 35 ft. Numerous sculptures of rare beauty could be found everywhere in the temple. The figure of a nomadic gypsy with her palm-leaves woven basket holds the onlooker spellbound. It is near the sanctum of Sri Sankara.

Samayapuram Mari Amman Koil : This is a very famous temple near Thiruvanaikkaval. The grace of Mari Amman here, has turned an illiterate fool into a poet. This temple attracts thousands of devotees every day.

Kumaravayalur : It is 8 km from Trichy and a famous Murugan temple is seen here amidst bushy green fields. The gopuram of this temple was built by the famous devotee of Lord Muruga, Sri Kripananda Variar.

Mukkombu (Upper Anicut) : It is a very beautiful picnic spot about 18 km from Trichy. Green carpeted fields fill the route. Here the river Cauvery branches off into Kollidam (Coleroon). There is a well laid-out park. There is a barrage called *Upper Anaicut*. A beautiful spot of picturesque scenery.

Thiruverumbur : 10 km from Trichy is the famous place where an ant (erumbu) worshipped Lord Siva and got bliss. The temple has 3 prakaras or enclosures, one down the hill and the other two up the hill. The temple belongs to the Chola period. There is a beautiful sculpture of Gangalamurthi here not to be missed by any lover of art.

Thiruvellarai : About 15 km from Trichy is Thiruvellarai, famous for its Pallava cave temple and a strange swastika well belonging to the period of Dantivarman.

Gunaseelam : Arulmigu Prasanna Venkatesa Perumal Temple is located around 16 km from Tiruchirappalli. Purattasi Saturdays, float festival and Brahmotsavam are important festivals here.

Pullamangai : This place near Trichy is famous for an early Chola temple built by Parantaka I known for its sculptural splendour. The presiding deity of Pullamangai is Brahmapuriswara. One can see how the Chola sculpture gave life to stone as even the ganas or demons that worship Siva are carved with minute details – expressive faces, pot-bellied in fantastic poses. They embellish the roof of the Ardha Mandapam. Brahma, Lingodhbhava, Dancing Siva, Eight-Armed Durga are the other entrancing sculptures here.

Uraiyur : Uraiyur Kamalavalli Nachiyar temple here is one of the 108 Divya Desam. It is also the birthplace of Thiruppanaazhvaar, one of the 12 Azhvaar saints. There is a separate Samadhi for Thiruppanaazhvaar inside the temple.

Elakurichi : At Elakurichi nearby is the famous church built by the well known Catholic missionary, Constantine Joseph Beschi, popularly known as *Veeramamunivar*. He has done yeoman service to Tamil and even the first modern Tamil dictionary called 'Chathur Agarathi' was compiled by him.

Besides, there are several other churches, colleges and missions dating back to 1760's. As excellent infrastructural facilities are available in Trichy, it can be a convenient place to see east-central Tamilnadu.

Some Important Festivals

Mohini Alangaram, Vaikunda Ekadasi, Garuda Sevai, Flower Festival and Car Festival at Srirangam - (December-January).

The float festival at Teppakulam - (March-April).

Samayapuram Mari Amman flower festival - (April).

Where to Stay?

Tiruchirappalli (STD : 0431)
* **Hotel Tamil Nadu (TTDC),** MC Donald Road. ℂ 2460383
* **Hotel Sangam, (4 Star),** Collector's Office Road, ℂ 2414700, 2414480, Fax: 0431-2415779 Email: hotelsangam@vsnl.com
* **Vignesh,** Dindigul Road. ℂ 2461991
* **Hotel Aristo,** Dindigul Road. ℂ 2461818
* **Hotel Madura,** Rochin Road. ℂ 2463737
* **Hotel Ajanta,** Junction Road. ℂ 2460501
* **Gajapriya,** Royal Road. ℂ 2461144
* **Hotel Anand,** Racquet Court Lane.
* **Vijaya Lodge,** Royal Road. ℂ 2460512
* **Hotel Arun,** State Bank Road. ℂ 2461421
* **Hotel Rajasugam,** Royal Road. ℂ 2460636
* **Hotel Raja,** Junction Road. ℂ 2461023
* **Jenneys Residency,** 3/14, Macdonalds Road, Tiruchirappalli - 620 001. ℂ 2414414, Fax: 0431-2461451, Email: jenneys@satyam.net.in
* **Royal Southern Hotels,** Race Course Road, Khajamalai, Tiruchirappalli - 620 023. ℂ 2421303 Fax: 0431-2421307, Email: royalsouthern@eth.net
* **Abbirami Hotel,** No. 10, McDonalds Road, Contonment, Trichy - 620 001. ℂ 2415001, Fax: 0431-2412819

* **Femina Hotels,** 14-C, Williams Road, Contonment, Tiruchirappalli - 620 001. ℂ 2414501, Fax: 0431 - 2410615, Email: femina@tr.dot.net.in
* **Hotel Aanand,** No.1, V.O.C. Street, Tiruchirappalli - 620 001. ℂ 2415545 Fax: 0431-2415219, Email: hotelaanand@hotmail.com
* **Ramyas Hotel,** 13/D-2, Williams Road, Trichy - 620 001. ℂ 2415128 Fax: 0431-2414852 Email: ramyas@ramyashotel.com
* **Ashby Hotel,** 17-A, Rockins Road, Tiruchirappalli - 620 001. ℂ 2460652, 2460653 Email: chinoor@ yahoo.com
* **Sri Raajaali Hotel,** 8/6, 3A, Tanjore Road, Near Chennai Byepass Road, Tiruchirappalli - 620 008. ℂ 2200470, 2200439 Fax: 2200470

Pudukkottai

(Archaeological Treasure-house of Tamil Civilization)

Pudukkottai, the former princely state that was the first to join the Indian Union after breaking away from foreign yoke, is indeed the archaeological treasure-house of Tamil civilization. Pre-historic and proto-historic finds like megalithic burials, dolmens stone circles etc. in the district blaze forth the civilization of the Tamils of the past. Sangam classics mention this tract as a notable place of highly cultured elites. The rich cultural heritage of this district is also evidenced by the archaeological and cultural remains of Kodumbalur, Narthamalai, Kudumiyanmalai, Kunnandar Koil, Sittanna Vasal, Thirumayam and Avudayar Koil. Its emergence as a princely state occurred in the 17th century and even before that, from time immemorial, it has been a centre of culture, civilization, art, architecture, fine arts and polity. It is therefore no wonder that historians, anthropologists, archeologists and lovers of art have an absorbing interest in Pudukkottai.

This town lies on Chennai-Rameswaram line, 390 kms away from Chennai, 53 kms from

Thiruchirappalli and 57 kms from Thanjavur. The rulers of Pudukkottai have left historical landmarks like buildings, temples, tanks, canals, forts and palaces.

How to get there?

Air : Nearest airport–Trichy 53 kms, from where flights are available to Chennai, Sri Lanka, Sharjah and Kuwait.

Rail : Chennai-Rameswaram railway line will take you to Chennai, Trichy, Thanjavur, Madurai and Rameswaram.

Road : It is well connected to Chennai, Thanjavur, Trichy, Madurai and Rameswaram by road. Town buses are available to all tourist centres in and around Pudukkottai. Besides, taxis, private vehicles and contract carriages are also available.

Shopping

* **Poompuhar Handicrafts,**
  851, North Road.
  Working Hours : 9 a.m. to 1 p.m. & 2 p.m. to 8 p.m.
  Handicrafts, handlooms, silk, paper-mache, cane articles, mats made from korai grass etc. are available.
* **Karpagam Palm-leaf Products** near Anna Statue, Pudukkottai.
  Working Hours: 9.30 a.m. to 1.30 p.m. & 4 p.m. to 8 p.m.

Places to See

Sri Kokarneswar Temple : This temple of Pallava period is a rock-cut cave temple of Mahendravarma Pallava. The presiding deity is Kokarneswarar and His consort Brahadambal. Some later additions have also been made. The idols of Ganesa, Gangadhara, Saptha Kannikas are artistic creations of perennial value. An image of the saint Sadasiva Brahmendra is seen at the foot of a Bikula tree. The deity is the family deity of the Raja and in reverence of Brahadambal, coins called 'Amman Kasu' were released by the king. The place is called Thirukkokarnam and is about 5 kms from the railway station.

Government Museum : It is also located in Thirukkokarnam. It contains a wide range of collections in the sections of Geology, Zoology, Paintings, Anthropology, Epigraphy, Historical Records etc. which are very interesting. Fine sculptures and bronzes of various periods exhibited here are the main attraction.

Timings	: 9 a.m. to 5 p.m.
Admission	: Free
Holiday	: Friday
Phone	: 236247

Places of tourist interest around Pudukkottai

Sittannavasal : 16 kms from Pudukkottai is this ancient abode of Jains dating back to the 2nd century B.C. The main attractions are the rock-cut cave temple with its beautiful paintings in natural colours akin to the ones at Ajanta and stone beds called Eladipattam and a cave where the Jain monks sought refuge in those days. An Ardha Mandapam and inner shrines of the cave temple contain images of Jain Tirtankaras in the niches. But the ceilings and walls contain frescoes that resemble Ajanta paintings. Though partially damaged they are quite absorbing. Flowers, calves, elephants, geese — all executed in inimitable poses and all relate to the Jains. They were believed to be a Pallava creation, but later discovery of inscriptions proved it to be the work of Pandyas.

As this place has been developed under the District Excursion Project, it is easily approachable by road and frequent bus services are available. In places around Sittannavasal, there can be sighted many pre-historic burial sites consisting of Kurangup-pattarai, cairns, burial urns, cists etc.

Kudumiyanmalai : 20 kms from Pudukkottai. There are exquisite sculptures and a 1000-pillared hall in the temple of Sikharagireeswarar. Inscriptions abound in this temple and the quite interesting one is that of Mahendra Varma Pallavan who has actually made a treatise on music here - especially on the seven notes called Saptha Swara. He is a versatile man and calls himself 'Vichitra Chittan', 'Chitthirakkarappuli' (Man of Wonderful Mind and Adept Painter). He has also done research in music especially on the saptha swaras in a veena called 'Parivadhini' with 8 strings. There is also a rock-cut temple above called 'Melakkoil' which too was scooped by Mahendra Varma Pallavan. The Anna Agricultural Farm and Agricultural Research Institute located here indicates that even today the place is not bereft of research - the former was a cultural research though the present one is on agriculture.

Kodumbalur: 36 kms from Pudukkottai, this place is also known as Moovar Koil. Irukku Velirs, an illustrious warrior clan related to the Cholas once ruled over this place. Of the Moovar Koil (Three temples) only two exist now. They were built by Boodhi Vikrama Kesari, a general of the Chola army in the 10th century A.D. One of the Irukku Velirs who ruled this place, named Idangazhi Nayanar is included in the canons of the 63 Nayanmars. This place was also a stage of fierce battles between the Pandyas and the Pallavas. The architecture of this temple is unique

among the temples of south India. The sculptures of Kalarimurthi, Gaja (Elephant) Samharamurthi, Gangadaramurthi etc. are unique masterpieces. Nearby is the temple dedicated to Muchukun-deswarar of the early Chola period.

Viralimalai : The temple of Lord Muruga is built here on a hillock. It has been existing from the 15th century. The presiding deity is seated on a peacock mount with His two consorts Valli and Deivayanai. There is also a peacock sanctuary. It is 30 kms from Trichy and 40 kms from Pudukkottai.

Narthamalai : It is 17 kms from Pudukkottai. It contains several Jain monasteries on the hill sides. Rare medicinal plants and herbs such as black gooseberry (Karunelli), Jathi tree etc. could be seen in the forest. This is also a place of historical importance and the capital of Mutharaiyar chieftains who had an upper hand in the polity of Tamil Nadu before the rise of the later Cholas. The earliest structural stone temple, circular in shape built by Mutharaiyars, the Vijayalaya Choleswaram cave temple built by Vijayalaya the first king of the later Cholas and Kadambar Malai temple are worth a visit in this place.

Thirumayam : It is 21 kms from Pudukkottai. The fort, the Siva and the Vishnu temples are the tourist attractions here. The fort played an important role in the history of Tondaiman rulers of Pudukkottai and the British. This 40 acre wide fort was built by Vijaya Ragunatha Sethupathi of Ramanathapuram in 1687 A.D. On the hill, there is a rock-cut Siva temple with inscriptions on music. There are the relics of another fort. At the foot of the hill are the Siva and Vishnu temples. The Vishnu temple houses the largest Anantasayi in India. It is a natural cavern which has been changed into a shrine. It was in this fort that the brother of Kattabomman, Oomaithurai was ensnared and imprisoned. An old chain armour used by him is exhibited here.

Avudaiyarkoil : It is 40 kms from Pudukkottai. It is also called Thiruperunthurai. The presiding deity is Atmanatha. This temple is unique in many ways. There is no Lingam in the sanctum, only the Avudaiyar or its bottom pedestal is worshipped. Even the Goddess is not displayed by any form. No Neivedyam of food is offered to the deity. Even Nandhi the mount of Siva usually in front of the deity is absent. There is deep spiritual significance in the queerness. Hinduism allows idol worship only for the beginners in the initial stage. As the devotee and his devotion mature he has to realise the absolute truth as formless. Simply to illustrate this, this temple has been modelled like this on monistic principles. This is the only Saivaite shrine in the whole of India to portray the supreme truth symbolically. Since the soul (Atma) has no form, the deity is called Atmanathar. This temple is supposed to have been built by Manicka Vasagar, one of the 63 Saivaite saints who spent all the money he got for purchasing horses for the Pandya king in building this temple. As he was bereft of money, God played one of His Thiruvilaiyadal by transforming foxes into horses and once they were entrusted to the king, they were reconverted into foxes again. Many legends vividly describe this.

Besides the legendary and spiritual fascination, the temple is also unique and unrivalled from the sculptural point of view. The temple is noted for its zephyr (granite roof) work. The ceiling of the Kanaka Sabhai is a grandeur creation in stone – the rope, rafters and nails are all in granite. The bow wielding Muruga, Kali and Siva's Rudra Thandavam are the finest specimens in sculptural art.

Avur : 28 kms from Pudukkottai lies this place famous for churches. The old chapel was constructed in 1547 A.D. by Fr. John Venatius Bachet and the new Roman Catholic Church was built in 1747 A.D. The renowned Tamil scholar Rev. Father Joseph Beschi (Veeramamunivar) also served in this church. The Easter passion play followed by car festival in summer attracts people of all faiths.

Kumaramalai : About 10 kms from Pudukkottai is located a temple for Lord Muruga at a small hill. Kumaran is another name for Lord Muruga, hence the name Kumaramalai. The tank water of this hill is considered to be holy.

Kattubava Pallivasal : 30 kms from Pudukkottai is this important Islamic pilgrim centre. Located on the Thirumayam-Madurai highway, it is visited by devotees of all faiths. The annual 'Urs' occurs in the month of Rabiyul Ahir.

Vendanpatti : It is 40 kms from Pudukkottai on the way to Ponnamaravathi. The Nandhi known as Nei Nandhi (Ghee Bull) in the Meenakshi Chokkeswarar temple is very famous. Though made of black granite, it shines like marble due to frequent ablutions with pure ghee. One more astonishing feature is the absence of flies and ants despite the Nandhi being showered with pure ghee daily. Every day large number of devotees visit this temple.

Arantangi : It is the second largest town in Pudukkottai district after the headquarters. There is a ruined fort here that attracts people, the walls of which are not constructed with bricks or stones. Large interstices are filled with mud. Inside the fort, there are no ruins of palaces or any striking building. The date of the fort is not known. But a line of Tondaimans who had no connections with those of Pudukkottai were in power during the 16 and 17th centuries. They are believed to have constructed it. There is also a eleventh century A.D. temple built by Rajendra Chola Varman.

With this we have covered all the important places for tourists in mid-east Tamil Nadu and we now move to the mid-west part of Tamil Nadu which contains Salem, Dharmapuri, Erode, Coimbatore and Nilgiri districts.

Where to Stay?

Pudukkottai (STD : 04322)

* **Balaji Woodlands** ✆ 223845
* **Gnanam Lodge** ✆ 222237
* **Hotel Maaris**, 2382, West Main Street, Pudukkottai - 622 001. ✆ 221874, 226874
* **Hotel Royal Park**, 5840, Santhanathapuram 4th Street, Pudukkottai - 622 001. ✆ 227783, 224259
* **Iyya Tower** ✆ 222296
* **Shivalaya** ✆ 221864
* **Siva Sakthi Ganesh** ✆ 220956
* **Nandhini Hotel** ✆ 220823

Salem

(The Steel City of Tamil Nadu)

Salem got its name from the Sanskrit word 'Sailam' which means mountain. As this area is surrounded by hills, it is apt to be called Salem. It is a land of minerals. The hills around Salem has iron ore, bauxite, limestone, precious stones etc. Salem is the fifth largest city of Tamilnadu. It was originally got by the British from Tipu Sultan as Bara Mahal which contained 12 localities. This district was later divided into three: Dharmapuri, Namakkal and Salem. Another speciality of the name is that it is made up of the initial letters of its dominant specialities: S - for steel, A - for aluminium, L - for limestone, E - for electricity (There is hydro-electric power generation in Mettur) and M - for mango (Salem mangoes are famous). Yercaud, a beautiful hill station, is located here. Since Salem is a city with infrastructures well developed, tourists can stay in this place and visit the places in the neighbouring districts of Namakkal and Dharmapuri.

How to get there?

Salem is on the Chennai broad gauge line, 335 kms from Chennai. The train services are available from here to Chennai, Kochi, Coimbatore, Ooty, Thiruvananthapuram and Bangalore. It is well connected by road with all the major towns in Tamil Nadu. Local buses are available to all the places of tourist interest from here.

Nearest airport is at Coimbatore, 162 kms from Salem. Flights are available from here to Madurai, Chennai, Bangalore, Kochi and Mumbai.

Places to see in and around Salem

Yercaud : This charming hill station is about 8 kms from Salem at an altitude of 5000 ft. The temperature never rises beyond 29°C and never falls below 13°C. There is neither a biting winter nor a scorching summer. An ideal place to visit throughout the year. It is on the Shevaroy range of the Eastern ghats. It was brought to light by Sir Thomas Munroe, the erstwhile Governor of Madras in 1824. A fine motorable ghat road with several hair-pin bends links the top after a 23 kms ride through coffee plantations. Fruit plantations like apple, cherry, orange also abound. 'Yer' means beauty in Tamil, 'Kadu' means forest. Hence, Yercaud in Tamil means 'beautiful forest'. Some say that the word was a corruption for Erikadu which means forest full of lakes and true to it there are a number of lakes big and small and waterfalls on this hill. A beautiful lake with boating facilities adorns the centre. Yercaud is also ideal for trekking.

How to get there?

Frequent bus services are available from Salem to Yercaud. Private carriages like taxis, vans and buses are also available from Salem.

What to see in Yercaud?

Yercaud Lake : The lake is centrally located and is the centre of attraction. It is a cool clean sheet of water surrounded by well laid-out gardens and woods. Boats are available and boating in the chill water is an enchanting and refreshing experience.

Anna Park : It is a beautiful, well laid-out garden near the lake and a dream land of fragrance and colour with buzzing bees busily seeking honey in the flowers.

Lady's Seat : It overhangs on the winding ghat road and is a spectacular viewpoint. The panoramic view of the plains down the mountain is breath-taking and dizzy if you look down the steep gorge. At night with the twinkling lights, Salem city looks like a far-off dream land — an unforgettable spectacle. The telescope mounted at Lady's Seat gives a picturesque view of the valley below.

The Pagoda Point, Prospect Point and Arthur's Seat are the other vantageous viewpoints to look and enjoy the magnificent thrilling sights.

The Kulliar Falls : This 3000 ft high waterfalls among sylvan surroundings is a beautiful sight for spending hours together without boredom.

Bear Cave : It is formed of two huge boulders and is situated near Nation Bungalow — an oldest bungalow here. Special arrangement has to be made to reach this place.

Servaroyan Temple : It is at the top of the Shevaroys. It is said that this is the third highest peak in the range. Special arrangement with local guides have to be made as no regular transport services are available to reach this place. The annual festival is observed in May and all the hill tribes around assemble to celebrate it.

Montfort School : It is a famous public school and the Sacred Heart Convent is another school imparting education to boys and girls respectively.

The Retreat : This institution started by brothers of Don Bosco in 1945 serves as a Novitiate house where students of the religious order stay and study.

Places of Worship

Temples : Servaroyan temple and Sri Rajarajeswari temple.

Churches : Sacred Heart Church, The Retreat Church, St.Joseph's Church, Holy Trinity Church, C.S.G. Church and Lutheran Church.

Mosque : Yercaud Mosque.

Other Places of Interest in Yercaud: Ornamental Plants & Tree House, Orchard cum nursery of rose plants, Silk farm, Horticultural Research Station, Orchidorium, Mettur View, Cauvery Peak and Salem View.

Festivals : Summer festival during middle of May.

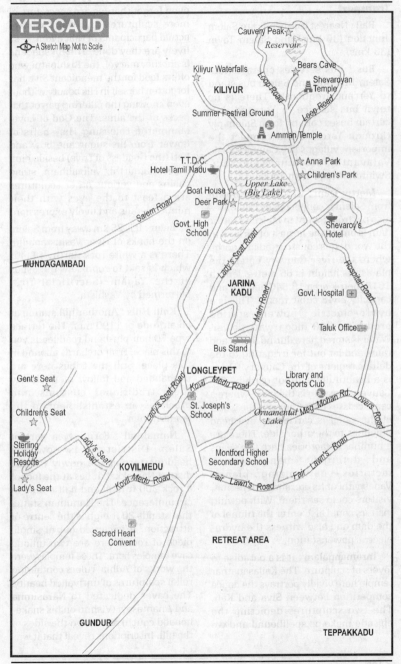

YERCAUD

-N- A Sketch Map Not to Scale

Cauvery Peak ☆
Reservoir
Kiliyur Waterfalls ☆
Bears Cave ☆
Shevaroyan Temple
KILIYUR
Loop Road
Loop Road
Summer Festival Ground
Amman Temple
T.T.D.C.
Hotel Tamil Nadu
Anna Park ☆
Children's Park ☆
Boat House ☆
Upper Lake (Big Lake)
Deer Park ☆
Salem Road
Shevaroy's Hotel
Govt. High School
MUNDAGAMBADI
Lady's Seat Road
JARINA KADU
Govt. Hospital
Main Road
Hospital Road
Taluk Office
Bus Stand
Gent's Seat ☆
LONGLEYPET
Kovil Medu Road
Library and Sports Club
Lady's Seat Road
Children's Seat ☆
St. Joseph's School
Ornamental Lake
Meg. Mohan Rd.
Lovers Road
Sterling Holiday Resorts
Lady's Seat ☆
Lady's Seat Road
KOVILMEDU
Kovil Medu Road
Montford Higher Secondary School
Fair Lawn's Road
Fair Lawn's Road
Sacred Heart Convent
RETREAT AREA
GUNDUR
TEPPAKKADU

Transport

Rail : Nearest rail-heads are Salem Junction (36 kms) and Salem Town (33 kms).

Bus : Bus services operate from Salem Junction and Salem bus stand to Yercaud frequently. There is no town bus service in Yercaud, but certain buses coming from Salem ply through Yercaud and connect the important villages like Cauvery Peak, Valavanthi, Nagalur, Velakkadi, Swinton Bridge with Yercaud.

Mettur Dam : Mettur about 30 km from Salem is connected by rail. Buses also ply from Salem to Mettur. Mettur dam is one of the largest of its kind in the world. It is constructed in a gorge where the river Cauvery enters the plains. Its height is 65 metre, length 1616 metre, area 15,540 hectare and capacity 2648 cubic metre. This is a hydro-electric power station producing 240 mega watt power. Water is stored here during floods and rains and let out for irrigating to the deltaic regions of the Cauvery. There is a beautifully laid-out garden. The Cauvery crossing is the place where a canal crosses over Cauvery–the water of the canal is carried by overhead pipelines to the other side. There are a number of factories here like soaps and detergent manufacturing factories, galvanizing plants, Vanaspathi units etc. and with permit, visitors could see them. With permit, visitors could also enter the tunnel of the dam and also witness the hydro-electric power station.

Taramangalam : It is a paradise to lovers of sculpture. The Kailasanathar temple here vividly portrays the dance competition between Siva and Kali. The two sculptures depicting the episode make us spellbound and we even forget that we are spectators of mere sculptures and think we are actual participants of that event — so lively are they done. The Bikshadana is another marvel, the Rishipatni who offers food for the mendicant Siva has forgotten herself in His beauty without even knowing the pilfering parrot that pecks at the alms. The God of Love, Manmatha releasing His shafts of flower from his sugarcane bow and Rati (the Goddess of Love) beside him, Dakshinamurthi, Valivadham, stone chains and various other sculptures are a feast to the eyes with their minute details and lively expression.

Belur : It is 25 km away from Salem on the banks of river Vashistanadhi. There is a white rock north of Belur which is said to represent the ashes of the Yagam (Sacrificial fire) performed by Vashista.

Kolli Hills : Another hill station at an altitude of 1190 mts. The terrace type 70 hair pin-bend road leads you to this place. Fruit orchards abound in this place. Still the tribes here are unchanged and follow meticulously their traditional customs and practices–an astonishment to the modern men.

Namakkal : Formerly a part of Salem District, it is now the headquarters of the newly formed district Namakkal. It lies at the foot of a rock 200 ft high and half a mile in circumference. The Hanuman statue that stands 20 ft high is the centre of attraction. It is carved out of single piece of rock.There are two unique cave temples here. These temples were the works of 'Adhia' rulers containing relief sculptures of unrivalled beauty. The caves dedicated to Narasimha and Anantasayi (Vishnu on his snake-hooded couch) are cut on the sides of the hill. Inscriptions reveal that it was built by Gunaseelan of the Adhiakula (Adhia clan) (784 A.D.). The Narasimha cave has an enormous rock with the image of Lord Narasimha tearing the entrails of Hiranya the demon - a splendid sculpture that chills the heart of the beholder. The mandapa of the side of the cave reveals three forms: Narasimha Avatar, Vamana Avatar, Varaha Avatar. The images of Vaikunta Narayanan, Bala Narasimha, Brahma, Chandra, all reveal the dexterity of master hands. The two Vamana Avatar idols in Narasimha cave and Anantasayee cave differ from each other in that the former has a parasol and a sacrificial horse which is absent with the latter. The hollows in the rock have become sacred pools, one of them is named Kamalalayam.

Thiruchengodu : In the southwest of the district is an important shrine dedicated to Ardhanariswarar (Siva and Uma in one form) situated at a height of 2000 feet. Flights of winding steps lead to the temple. Along the steps by the side is a huge hooded serpent-sculptured so real that it creates awe in our face. A huge Nandhi faces the hill presuming it to be Lord Siva. Mr. Davis, a former collector has renovated the partially damaged Ganesa Mandapam of this temple and his relief portrait adorns a pillar. Climbing still further one can reach Maladi (a barren woman) hills, where a huge boulder is precariously perched on the tip of an edge of an abyss of 800 ft threatening each moment. Barren women crawl around it three times to be blessed with pregnancy. The famous Gandhi Ashram founded by Rajaji is still functioning actively at Thiruchengodu.

Sankakiri : The **fort** here is one of the important historical places in Salem district. The **Someswar temple** attracts large crowds. Here too we can see a boulder akin to one at Maladi hills. It is about 40ft. high and almost equally broad. There is a well known cement factory since limestone is enormously found here.

Dharmapuri : This was once part of Salem district but now its headquarters. During the Sangam Age it was called Thagadur. It was the capital of Adiaman Neduman Anji. The 7 ft. high Hanuman in the temple of Anna Sagaram is the main attraction here. The curious feature about Him is that He has no tail at all.

Hogenakkal : The main picnic spot in Dharmapuri is Hogenakkal, the place where the Cauvery enters Tamil Nadu. It is one of the most beautiful places in the state with picturesque scenes. The broad stream of the river Cauvery gets forked at this point, forming an island from where one stream continues and plunges into a deep chasm to create a lovely waterfalls. As the spray of this waterfall raises clouds of droplets resembling smoke this place is known as Hogenakkal (Hoge means smoke, Kal - rock) – smoking rock. Earlier above, the river Cauvery flows in a particular narrow gorge so narrow that it could be easily leapt by a goat and hence the name of that place is Meka Dhattu (Goat's leap). Since the water of Cauvery flows through a herbal forest before it reaches Hogenakkal, bathing in the falls here is considered good for health. A large number of people gather here daily to have bath in river. A bath after a malish with oil (smearing of oil) is very refreshing. One can find malish experts are busy here minting money. If one wants to taste the thrill of adventure one can hire a 'parisal' (round basket-like boats) to ply in the river. Hogenakkal offers a quiet holiday in comfort. The magnificent, rugged mountain scenery around the falls can be better enjoyed by long walks and treks.

Hosur : Though this place located in the Krishnagiri district is very well known as a centre of industries, it does not lack the charms of being a tourist centre. Thali located nearby is known as 'Little England' to the British because of its beautiful green downs and salubrious climate.

The Tamil Nadu Tourism Development Corporation arranges for student package tours–

For details, contact: Ph : 0427-2316449. email : ttdc@vsnl.com

Where to Stay?

Salem (STD : 0427)
• **Hotel Salem Castle**, A/4, Bharathi Street, Swarnapuri, Salem - 636 004. ✆ 2448702, 2444774, Fax: 0427-2446996, Email: salemcastle@eth.net
• **Hotel LRN Excellency**, No. 7, Sarada College Road, Salem-636 007. ✆ 2414411/66, 2412383-86
• **Hotel Shevaroys**, Hospital Rd., Yercaud Hills. ✆ 222288, 222383, 222386, Fax: 04281-222387
• **National Hotel**, 132/18E, Bangalore Road, Salem - 636 009. ✆ 2353800, 2353900
• **Hotel Sri Chandra**, 231, Cherry Road, Salem - 636 001. ✆ 2415775, Email: cafechandra@yahoo.com
• **Hotel Tamil Nadu**, ✆ 222273 Fax : 04281-222745
• **Sterling Holiday Resorts**, (Near Lady's Seat). ✆ 222700-222707. Fax : 04281-222537
• **Hotel Shevaroys**, Hospital Road, Yercaud. ✆ 222001
• **Hotel Select**, Near Bus-Stand, Yercaud. ✆ 222525
• **Hotel Juhu Regency**, Meyyanur, Salem-4. ✆ 0427-2441444
• **Township Rest House**, ✆ 222223

Erode
(Paradise of Handloom Textiles)

Erode occupies the 5th place for handloom textiles in India. It is a business centre and the birthplace of Thanthai Periyar, the greatest social reformer and father of the self-respect movement in Tamil Nadu. It was formerly part of the Coimbatore district and became a separate district in 1979. The river Cauvery flows through Erode. Erode got its name from the famous Arthra Kapaleeswarar. Arthra means wet. The Tamil word is 'Iram' (ஈரம்) and 'odu' means kapala or the skull. So, the word Ira-Ottu-Isar in due course was corrupted to be pronounced as Erode. This district contains some important temples and places of tourist importance.

How to get there?

Erode is on the broad gauge railway line and can easily be reached by numerous trains that pass through this important junction. It is 398 kms from Chennai. Almost all the trains to the west coast pass through this junction. It is connected to Chennai, Arakkonam, Salem, Coimbatore and Nilgris by rail. The town is connected to all important towns in Tamil Nadu by good roads. Umpteen town buses also ply to places of tourist importance. Private vehicles and taxis are also available to any place in the district.

Bannari : A Mariamman Koil is on the western side of Erode about 10 km from Bhavani Sagar. Goddess Mariamman is famous here and attracts thousands of pilgrims. The festival at this temple during the month of Adi (August-September) is attended by large number of people. The fire walk by the devotees is very thrilling.

Bhavani Sagar : Bhavani town is situated at the confluence of the river Cauvery and Bhavani one of its major tributaries. The Sangameswarar temple is at this confluence. This place is also known as the *'Thriveni of South*

India'. It is an important pilgrim centre and also an important picnic centre. Lord Sangameswara with His consort Vedanayaki is the presiding deity. Legend goes that once the collector of the Coimbatore and Salem districts of the colonial period, William Garraw was directed by the Goddess Vedanayaki to immediately vacate the building in which he was staying. The collecter obeyed and immediately after vacating, the building collapsed. In reverence of this miracle, the collector presented an ivory cradle to the temple which even today can be seen there with the collector's signature on it. People also visit the Bhavani Sagar Dam which presents a beautiful feast to the eyes. There is a swimming pool and a park. Bhavani is known the world over for its blankets with floral designs.

Kodumudi : It is situated 40 km from Erode. A special feature of this place is that the Trinity of the Hindu faith Siva, Vishnu and Brahma all have their shrines in a single temple complex. Muchukundeswarar is the name of Siva and Veera Narayana Perumal is that of Vishnu here. This is an important temple in Erode district.

Chennimalai : It is located 30 km from Erode. There is a famous temple dedicated to Lord Muruga on the top of Chennimalai (Mountain). Rare forms of Muruga – Agni Jather - with two faces and eight arms; Gourapeyar - with four faces and eight arms, as hunter with a single face and six arms – can be seen here. Originally the presiding deity had the idol of Subramanya with six faces. As it was damaged, a Dandayuthapani idol like the one at Palani has been installed as the presiding deity. Chennimalai is an important handloom weaving centre.

Kangeyam : It is 40 km from Erode. A famous Muruga temple is located here. It was once famous for bullocks called Kangeyam Kalai. From here, on the Muthur Road about 10kms is situated Kuttappalayam where a modern Dhyana Mandapam (Meditation hall) is built dedicated to Sri Aurobindo and the Mother of Pondicherry. The mandapam is located amidst a spacious 5 acre land which is being developed as a beautiful garden. Inside the mandapam is an exact replica of the Sri Aurobindo and Mother samadhi found in Pondicherry. The relics of Sri Aurobindo and the Mother have been enshrined in the samadhi here. Every month on the 2nd Sunday, group meditation is conducted from 9.00 a.m. to 12.00 noon which attracts large gathering from far and near.

Dharapuram : About 70 km from Erode, an old Siva temple is located here on the northern banks of river Amaravathi. The temple has Lingam and Devi shrines. There is a separate shrine for Bhairava. A flight of steps lead to the river. On the southern side also there is a Siva temple quite older than this one containing several inscriptions. The Dhakshinamurthi in the niche here is different from the usual one. The idols are beautifully carved in this temple.

Thindal Malai Murugan temple, Pariyur Amman temple, Sivanmalai Arthra Kapaleeswarar temple, Kooduthurai, Kodiveri, Varattuppallam, Kunderippallam and upper dams are the other places of tourist attraction in this district. Bus services are available to all the places. The Thalavadi hills and Andhiyur forests border this district.

Where to Stay?

Erode (STD : 0424)

* **Brindhavan Hotels,** 1499, E.V.N. Road, Erode - 638 011. ✆ 2222355/56/57
* **Hotel Meridien,** Brough Road, Erode. ✆ 2259362, 2259367
* **Hotel Oxford,** 120, Park Approach Road, Erode - 638 003. ✆ 2226611, Fax: 0424 - 2226618, Email: oxford-mohan@yahoo.com
* **Hotel Sivaranjani,** 177, Brovgh Road, Erode - 638 001. ✆ 2257880, Fax: 0424-2253106

Coimbatore

(The Manchester of Tamil Nadu)

Coimbatore is the 3rd largest city of Tamil Nadu. It is the district headquarters and the most industrialised and commercialised city in Tamil Nadu. It is the textile capital of the south and called the *Manchester of Tamil Nadu.* It is on the banks of Noyyal, a tributary of the river Cauvery. The hinterland with black cotton soil and the ideal climate are suitable for the development of textile industry. It was in existence even before 2nd century as the capital of Kongu kings. It came under the reign of Karikal Chola of the 2nd century A.D., the Rastrakutas, Chalukyas, Pandyas, Hoysalas and Vijayanagar rulers, and Mysore Wodeyars too held sway in this region. When it finally fell into the hands of the British, its name was perpetuated as Coimbatore. As it is located in the shadows of the western ghats, it enjoys a very pleasant climate throughout the year with the fresh breeze that blows through the 25 km wide Palakkad gap which is the main link to the neighbouring state Kerala. The first textile mills came up here as far back as 1888 but now there are over hundred mills in Coimbatore. Mettuppalayam (35 km from Coimbatore) that borders the Nilgiris district, is the disembarking point to board the mountain train that goes to the 'Queen of Hill Stations' - Ooty.

How to get there?

Coimbatore is 497 kms from Chennai. It is connected by road to all major places in South India. There are regular bus services from Chennai, Madurai, Trichy, Salem, Erode, Udagamandalam etc. Inter-state buses also run from Palakkad, Ernakulam, Thrissur, Bengalooru and Mysooru. It is a major railway junction on the Southern Railways and has trains to Chennai, Rameswaram, Madurai, Bengalooru, Mumbai, Kanyakumari, Kozhikode, Mettupalayam, Kochi and Delhi.

There is an airport here at Sulurpet and flights go to Chennai, Mumbai, Madurai, Kochi and Bengalooru.

Local bus transport and private vehicles and taxis are also available to go to all the places of tourist importance in the district.

Places to see

Perur : This place 7 km from Coimbatore junction is the most important place to be visited for its sculptural splendour. It is often called the *Mecca of Art Lovers.* The other name of this place is Mel-Chidambaram. The Perur temple was built by Karikal Cholan of 2nd century A.D. There are shrines to the presiding deity Patteeswarar and his consort Pachainayaki. The Kanaga Sabha pillars are chiselled with images of unsurpassing beauty. The images of Gajasamhara, Veerabadra, Bikshadana, Oorthuva Thandava, Veena Pani Saraswathi, all rival with one another in artistic perfection. Imposing corridors with numerous carvings is a feast to the eyes. The Panguni.Uthiram festival in March-April attracts thousands of people every year. Nearby flows the Noyyal river with green lushy banks. One can also visit the Santhalinga Adigalar

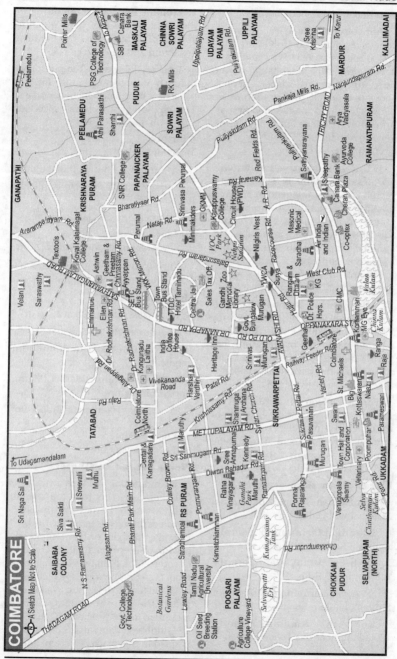

COIMBATORE

A Sketch Map Not to Scale

Mutt and Tamil College here.

Agricultural University : The most famous Agricultural University, the best in South East Asia, is located here. It was originally established as an agricultural farm in Saidapet, Chennai and later moved to Coimbatore in 1907. The name got changed first as Agricultural College and it developed into the Agricultural University. It is 5 km from railway station.

G.D.Naidu Industrial Exhibition : G.D. Naidu the famous technocrat of yester-years was a legend in his own time. His contribution to automobile, electronics, mechanical and agricultural sectors are invaluable. He founded a technical institute and the Industrial Exhibition is located here. It is a splendid exposure to science, technology and modern industry.

V.O.C. Park : Named after the eminent freedom fighter and patriot V.O.Chidambaram Pillai, this huge park is maintained by the Municipal Corporation. There is a mini zoo, and a joy train in this park amuses children as well as the grown-ups.

Forest College : It is just 3.5 km from the railway station. It is one of the oldest institutes of its kind in India. It trains forest rangers. The college museum has wonderful collections and demands a visit.

Places of Worship

Koniamman Temple, Big Bazaar Street, Town Hall.

Thandu Mariamman Temple, Avinashi Road, Uppilippalayam.

Rathina Vinayagar Temple, R.S.Puram, D.B.Road.

Sri Ayyappan Temple, Sithapudur, Satyamangalam Road.

Kamatchi Amman Temple, Ukkadam, near B-2 Police Station.

Mundhi Vinayagar Temple is in the heart of the city. This gigantic statue of Vinayagar is a modern attraction and landmark.

Ichanari Vinayagar Temple : This modern Vinayagar temple on the outskirts is becoming famous nowadays. The temple is kept spotlessly spick and span with modern facilities.

Churches

St. Michael's Cathedral, Big Bazaar.

St. Antony's Church, Puliakulam.

Christ King Church, Dr. Nanjappa Road.

Fathima Church, Gandhipuram.

Mosques

Big Mosque, Oppanakkara Street.

Big Mosque, Kottaimedu.

Mosque, 1st Street, Gandhipuram.

Shopping

Big Bazaar, Oppanakkara Street,

Raja Street, Ranga Gounder Street,

Sukravarpettai (for handloom goods)

Chintamani Super Market (Main), North Coimbatore

Poompuhar Handicrafts Emporium
Co-optex
Khadi Crafts
TANSI Sales Centre

Places around Coimbatore

Marudamalai : 12 kms away from Coimbatore is this hill- top temple dedicated to Lord Subramanya. Devotees throng this temple as the Lord Dhandayuthapani of this temple has performed several miracles to devotees. The temple is reached by a flight of steps. There is also a motorable road and temple buses are available to reach the top. Marudamalai is a mountain full of rare herbs. One of the 18 siddhars, Pampatti Siddhar has resided in this place. The cave where he resided is now a shrine of worship. Thai Poosam (January-February) and Thirukarthigai (November-December) festivals are very famous here. They are celebrated with pomp and gaiety. The greenery of this mountain is pleasing to the eyes and the chill breeze atop is quite refreshing.

Vaideki Waterfalls : It is 30 km from Coimbatore via Narsipuram village. A beautiful picnic spot and a heaven for trekkers. A perennial waterfalls is the chief attraction of this place.

Sengupathi Waterfalls : The Sengupathi waterfalls are located 35 km from Coimbatore on the Coimbatore-Siruvani main road. It is a nice picnic spot and people come in large number to bathe in the falls.

The Siruvani Waterfalls and Dam: The dam and waterfalls are at a distance of 37 km from Coimbatore on the western side. The water of Siruvani river is known for its taste and mineral properties. The panoramic view from the dam and the falls enchant the visitors.

Parambikulam-Aliyar Dam : This dam is a multi-purpose project. It consists of a series of dams interconnected by tunnels and canals for harnessing waters of Parambikulam, Aliyar, Nirar, Sholaiar, Thunnakadavu, Thekkadi and Palar rivers, lying at various elevations, for irrigation and power generation. The scheme is an outstanding example of engineering skill and inter-state relationship. It is in the Anaimalai range at the foot of the entrance to Valparai. It is about 64 km from Coimbatore. There is a park and boating can also be done. The early morning mist that hangs over the Aliyar Dam is an enchanting dreamy sight.

Monkey Falls : This falls is ideal even for children to bathe. It is located on the Pollachi-Valparai High Road just on entering the ghat section after passing the Aliyar-Parambikulam multi-purpose project. An entrance fee of Rs.2/- is collected.

Valparai : It is 102 km from Coimbatore in the Western ghats of the Anaimalai range. A ride in ghat road that passes through the Indra Gandhi Wildlife Sanctuary is fantastic. The flora of this place is quite interesting and a paradise for botanists. All along the road one can see innumerable tea plantations. The Kadambarai power project is on the way and could be visited with permit. On the top is a Balaji temple built by the Birlas. A beautiful and neatly kept temple with an enchanting idol. One can also see plantation workers busily picking tea leaves and smoking the area to ward off insects and flies. It is a nice place and a developing hill station. The scenery and the murky sky with intermittent drizzle is quite enjoyable. Valparai is really the *Princess of Hills* as it is called.

Mazani Amman Temple : This is near the highway to Anaimalai Topslip from Pollachi. It stands on the banks of river Amaravathi. It is a renowned local temple. The main feature in this temple is the grinding of red chillies by devotees. It is said that the deity here is Goddess of revenge and would punish severely the enemies of Her devotees if they grind the chilly on a stone grinder kept here for that purpose. The devotee chants the name of the deity and prays for the ruin of his enemy while grinding the chillies. The chillies to be ground are available in the temple.

Topslip : It is a picturesque spot in the Anaimalai Hills about 37 km from Pollachi. There is a waterfalls on the top, an ideal picnic location. Arrangements are made at Topslip to take tourists around the sanctuary on elephant's back or in a van.

Thirumurthy Swamy Temple & Waterfalls: It is about 96 km from Coimbatore and 20km from Udumalaipet at the foot of the Thirumoorthy hills. The presiding deity is called Ammanalinges-warar. True to the name, the main deity is left nude (Ammanam) without any clothes on. It is an old temple with beautiful setting and some rare sculptures with a spacious front hall. There are some inscriptions too. A perennial stream flows by the side of the temple. Just a km from the temple on the hill is a beautiful waterfalls. There are bathing arrangements and one can hold the iron chain fastened to the walk beneath the waterfalls and enjoy the thrill of a chill water massage. Above, after a strenuous climb lies another waterfalls which is more vigorous and refreshing. It is an ideal place for trekking too. At the foot of the hills lie the Thirumoorthy dam with boating facilities. There is also a swimming pool and a well laid-out garden. Local buses ply from Udumalaipet to this place. There is rail link to Udumalaipet from Coimbatore on the metre gauge line.

Amaravathi Dam : The steep Amaravathi dam across the river Amaravathi is just 25 km from Thirumoorthy Dam. Buses from here and Udumalaipet ply to this place. There is a well laid-out park and on climbing the steep dam on steps, one can have a picturesque view. There is a crocodile farm nearby and umpteen crocodiles of all sizes basking in the sun and suddenly making a stride or piled up on one another could be seen.

The Anaimalai Wildlife Sanctuary: The Indira Gandhi Natural Park and Anaimalai Wildlife Sanctuary is at an altitude of 1400 metres in the western ghats near Pollachi about 90 km from Coimbatore. The area of this vast sanctuary is 958 sq. kms. The flora and fauna of this place is very unique and rare varieties which are fast disappearing could also be seen here. The fauna consists of elephant, gaur, tiger, panther, sloth-bear, deer, wild boar, wild dog, porcupine, flying squirrel, jackal, pangolin, civet cat, snakes and birds like rocket-tailed drango, red-whiskered bulbul, black-headed oriole, tree pie, spotted dove and green pigeon. A large number of crocodiles are seen in the Amaravathi reservoir in Anaimalai. Places of scenic beauty are Karainshola, Anaikunthishola, grass hills, waterfalls, groves, teak forests, estates, dams and reservoirs. Rest houses and safari sightseeing are available at Topslip, Vanagaliar and Mount Stuart. The sanctuary can be visited any time of the year but the best time is to go in the very early morning or late evening. Transport through the sanctuary is arranged by the forest department. The reception centre is at Parambikulam dam.

Black Thunder : A water theme park named Black Thunder is located at 8 km from Mettupalayam (35 km from Coimbatore) - Udagamandalam ghat road at the foot of the Nilgiris. It is a fine amusement park and said to be Asia's number one theme park. Numerous tourists visit daily. The entrance fee is Rs.150/-.

Timings : 10.00 a.m. to 07.00 p.m. on all days.

Tiruppur : It is 50 kms from Coimbatore and is associated with the illustrious freedom fighter Kumar called 'Kodi Katha Kumaran' (Kumaran who saved the honour of the flag). A statue is erected for him in this place. It is an important textile centre and famous the world over for hosiery products.

Where to stay?

Coimbatore (STD : 0422)

- **Cag Pride,** 312, Bharathiar Road, Coimbatore - 641 044. ℂ 2527777
- **Heritage Inn,** 38, Sivasamy Road, Ram Nagar, Coimbatore - 641 009. ℂ 2231451
- **Hotel Surya International** 105, Race Course Road, Coimbatore - 638 452 ℂ 2217751-55 Fax:0422-2216110 Email: suryaint@md2.vsnl.net.in
- **Resort Black Thunder,** Ooty Main Road, Mettupalayam, Coimbatore - 641 305. ℂ 226632-40, 225739 Fax: 04254-225740
- **Sree Annapoorna Lodging** 75, East Arockiasamy Road, R.S.Puram, Coimbatore - 641 002. ℂ 2547621/2547722 Fax: 0422-2547322 Email: apoorna@md2.vsnl.net.in
- **The Residency** Avinashi Road, Coimbatore - 641 018. ℂ 2201234 Fax: 0422-2201414 Email: rescbe@vsnl.com
- **Nilgiri's Nest** 739A, Avinashi Road, Coimbatore - 641 018. ℂ 2217247, 2214309, 2217130 Fax: 0422-2217131 Email: nilgiris@md3. vsnl.net.in
- **Hotel Seetharam** 67, Malaviya Street, Ram Nagar, Coimbatore - 641 009. ℂ 2230724-25, 2231086 Fax: 0422-2233328
- **Hotel Indrapuri** K.V.K. Complex, 91, S.S. Kovil St., Pollachi, Coimbatore Dist., ℂ 04259-225550, 226550
- **Howard Johnson The Monarch Resort,** 286, Off Ponnuthu Road, Pannimadai, Coimbatore - 17. ℂ 2858413, 2858416 Fax: 0422-2858411 Email: themonarch@vsnl.com
- **Annalakshmi Foods,** 106, Race Course Road, Coimbatore - 641 018. ℂ 2212142, 2217770-72 Fax: 0422-2217810
- **Bombay Anand Bhavan,** 293, Big Bazaar Street, Coimbatore - 641 001. ℂ 0422-2397949
- **Dakshin The South** Sree Annapoorna Annexe, 75, East Arokiasamy Road, R.S. Puram, Coimbatore - 641 002. ℂ 2437722, 2431722 Fax: 0422-2437322
- **Sree Annapoorna Park Restautant** 75, East Arokiasamy Road, II Floor, R.S. Puram, Coimbatore - 641 002. ℂ 2547722, 2541722 Fax: 0422-2547322
- **Sri Krishna Sweets** 137, D.B. Road, R.S. Puram, Coimbatore - 641 002. ℂ 2472458 Fax: 0422-2473416
- **Hotel Tamil Nadu (TTDC),** 2, Nanjappa Road, Opp. Bus Stand, Coimbatore. ℂ : 2302176/78 Fax : 0422-2302185
- **Hotel City Tower** ℂ : 2230641
- **Hotel Alankar** ℂ : 2238888
- **Hotel Thaai** ℂ : 2302736
- **Hotel Diana** ℂ 2230982
- **Hotel Meena** ℂ : 2235420

- **Jyothi Hotel** ℂ : 2300077
- **Ambika Lodge** ℂ : 2231660
- **Sahri Hotels** ℂ : 2232866
- **Park Inn** ℂ : 2301284
- **Mangala International** ℂ : 2232012
- **Hotel Devi** ℂ : 2301667
- **Hotel Vishnupriya** ℂ : 2233652
- **Hotel Pushpam** ℂ : 2234366
- **Hotel Maruthi** ℂ : 2471270
- **Elite Tourist Home** ℂ : 2303607
- **Cheran Palace** ℂ : 2300211

The Nilgiris (Udagamandalam)
(The Queen of Hill Stations)

Udhagamandalam or Ooty is rightly called the *'Queen of Hill Stations'* on account of its unrivalled beauty and everlasting charm. It is in the Nilgiris where the western and eastern ghats meet. The mystic beauty of Ooty lied unknown to the rest of India until it was discovered by the British in the early 1800s. Though the whole area was inhabited by hill tribes like the Todas, the Kotas, the Kurumbas, the Badagas, the Panias and the Irulas, it was only after the first railway line was constructed that much of its enchantment was revealed. Its popularity grew because of the gold hunt pursued by early colonialists in the Nilgiris. Though the gold hunt was given up in the early 20th century, its rich endowments of nature came to the limelight and Europeans and the well-to-do natives settled there. It became the summer capital of the then Madras Presidency. It is known as 'Nilagiri' meaning 'blue mountain' because of the blue haze that prevailed to look at from a distance. It is at a height of 2240m, and is the headquarters of the Nilgiris district. Besides coffee and tea plantations, eucalyptus, pine and wattle dot the hill sides of Udagamandalam. The summer temperature is rarely higher than 25°C with a minimum of 10°C and winter with a high of 21°C and a low of 5°C, rarely it touches 0°C.

Settlement in Udagamandalam began in 1822 with the construction of the Stone House by John Sullivan the erstwhile collector of Coimbatore. It was locally called 'Kal Bangala' and is now the chamber of the Principal of Govt. Arts College. Following this, several English cottages with pretty gardens sprang up. Even today, the atmosphere of the British Raj lingers in places like the club where snooker was invented by a subaltern Neville Chamberlain, the Nilgiris library with rare and invaluable collection of books on Udagamandalam and St. Stephen's Church which was Ooty's first church.

How to get there?

Rail : Ooty is on the narrow gauge railway connected to Mettupalayam which is directly connected to Coimbatore and Chennai. Mettupalayam 89 kms from Coimbatore is the downhill railway station.

Road : It is also connected by good motorable road. It is 535 kms from Chennai via Salem and Mettupalayam. From Coimbatore (89kms) road link is available to Mettupalayam and umpteen buses ply from there to Ooty and the surrounding places in Ooty. Private vehicles and taxis are also available. There is also a road link from Mysore.

Air : The nearest airport is at Coimbatore (100 kms) and flights connect you from there to Chennai, Mumbai and Bengalooru.

Places of Worship

Temples : Murugan temple, Elk Hill, Venkateswara Perumal temple, Sri Mariamman temple, Subramania-swamy temple, Vittobha temple, Muniswara temple.

Churches : St. Stephen's Church, Union Church, Holy Trinity Church, Sacred Heart Church, St. Mary's Church, St. Thomas Church and Kandal shrine.

Mosques : A few mosques are also available.

Places to see in and around Udagamandalam

The Botanical Garden : The Botanical Garden maintained by the Horticulture Department is a unique place containing a wide range of plants that include different kinds of roses, important shrubs, rare flowering plants, eucalyptus trees, several old trees and even a fossilised tree trunk that has become a hard stone in about 20 million years. A beautiful Italian garden, green carpets of well maintained lawns attract the visitors inclined to relax. The summer festival is held here annually in the month of May, surely an added attraction to tourists. The annual flower show is the pride of this festival, besides, cultural programmes are also organised to bring to light traditional classical arts. Adventurous sports like trekking also form part of the festival.

Entry Fee	: Rs. 10.00 (Adult)
	Rs. 5.00 (Child)
Camera	: Rs.30.00
Video Permit	: Rs.500.00
Phone	: 0423-2442545

Mini Garden : It is about 1 km from the railway station. This mini garden also called 'Children's Lake Garden' is on the way to Boat House. There is a children's amusement park here. A snack bar is also available. Maintained neatly by the Tamil Nadu Tourism Development Corporation, the garden is open from 8 a.m. to 6 p.m.

Entrance fee Rs.2/-, Camera fee Rs.5/-, Video Camera fee Rs. 100/-.

Ooty Lake : It is an artificial lake created by Sullivans. It has boating

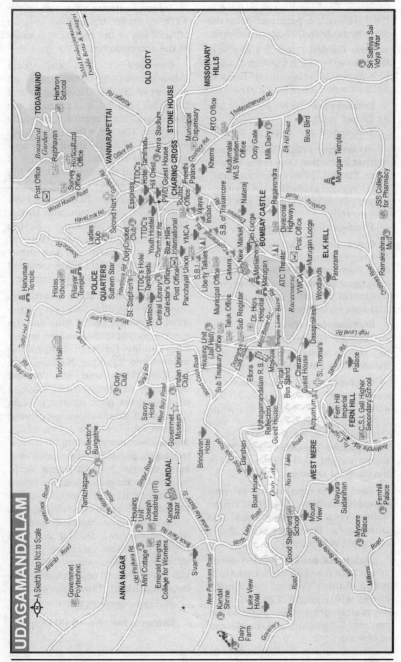

UDAGAMANDALAM

A Sketch Map Not to Scale

facilities. Even fishing can be done in the lake with a permission by the office of the Asst. Director of Fisheries.

Rose Garden : Just 3/4 km from the Railway Station is the Rose Garden. It is about 10 acres full of roses of 1419 varieties–a real feast for the eyes.

Entrance fee : Rs.5/- per adult and Rs.2/- per child.

Timings : 8 a.m. to 6 p.m.

Art Gallery : Lalitha Kala Academy is about 2 km from Ooty in the Mysore Road. The Art Gallery is located here. It has various collections of contemporary paintings and sculptures from all over India.

Timings : 9.30 a.m. to 5 p.m.

Government Museum : The government museum is on the Mysore road. Items of tribal objects, district's ecological details and representative sculptural arts and crafts of Tamil Nadu are on display.

Entrance fee : Nil

Timings : 10 a.m. to 1 p.m. & 2 p.m. to 5 p.m. It is closed on Fridays, 2nd Saturdays & national holidays.

Wenlock Downs : It is a heaven for nature lovers, sprawling over 20,000 acres. It was the famous erstwhile Udagamandalam Hunt. The Gymkhana Club, the Hindustan Photo Films Factory, The Government Sheep Farms and the Golf Course are all in the Wenlock Downs.

The Viewpoints around Udagamandalam : Elk Hills, Green Valley View, Snowden Peak and Dodabetta Peak are the most important viewpoints.

Dodabetta peak : Located about 10 km from the main town, Dodabetta is the highest peak of the Nilgiris district with a height of 2637m. If the day is clear, one can see as far as the plains of Coimbatore and the plateau of Mysore.

Telecopic House : It is run by the TTDC to enable the tourists to get a better view of the charming scenary of the surroundings.

Coonoor : 17 km from Udagamandalam, Coonoor is at an altitude of 2000 ft and is the first of these hill stations. It is a small town with an equable climate that has made it popular. The Sim's Park is the major attraction, though small it is well maintained and contains varieties of plants not to be found in other hill stations. Lamb's Rock, Lady Canning's Seat, Dolphin's Nose, St Catherine Falls, Law's Falls, Rallia Dam, The Droog, Pomological Station, Kallan Agricultural Farm, and Burliar Agricultural Farm are the other important view points, picnic spots and places of tourist interest in Coonoor.

Mudumalai Wildlife Sanctuary: Mudumalai Wildlife Sanctuary is the most prominent in the state and the most important in the southern region. The thickly forested Mudumalai borders the Bandipur National Park in Karnataka and the Wynad Sanctuary in Kerala. Tiger, spotted deer, elephant, gaur, sambar, barking deer, wild boar, civet cat, flying squirrel, four-horned antelope, bison, mouse deer, common langur, bonnet macaque, pangolin, the scaled anteater, panther, leopard, hyena, slothbear and jackal roam about the forest. The birds of the forest include peacock, woodpeckers, several species of owls, vultures, buzzards and the grey jungle fowl. During the April nights, the whole sanctuary is lit up by millions of glow-worms which look like a dream world of illumined quiet. Best time to visit : Feb - May, Sep - Oct

✆ 0423 - 2526235

Entrance fee : Rs. 15.00 (Adult)

Theppakadu is an elephant camp within the sanctuary. There is a rest-house here — besides, accommodation is also available in TTDC youth hostel and rest-houses in Masinagudi, Abhayaranyam, Kargudi and Bamboo Banks Farm. The best season is between January-March and September-October. The Wildlife Warden at Coonoor Road, Udhagamandalam can be contacted for further information.

Ketti Valley Viewpoint : Located on the road to Coonoor, this idyllic spot is a cluster of tiny villages that extend to the plains of Coimbatore and Mysore plateau.

Glenmorgan : It is about 17 km from Ooty. Ecologically it is a rich forestry spot. From here, the Electricity Board winch carries staff from Glenmorgan Viewpoint to power house at Singara. All the 4 km of the winch track passes through undisturbed sholas and wildlife habitats. Prior permission of the E.B. is necessary to enter the viewpoint zone.

Upper Bhavani : It is about 10 km from Korakundha and 20 km from Avalanche. This spot is a naturalists' paradise. This is also a rich and undisturbed wildlife habitat. From Bangithapal via Sirpura one can trek to Silent Valley. The permission of the forest department is necessary to go there.

Kalhatty Falls : It is on the Kalhatty slopes, 13 kms from Udhagamandalam on the Mysore-Kalhatty ghat road. The height of the waterfalls is 100 ft. Kalhatty- Masinagudi slope is rich in wildlife such as panthers, bisons, wild buffaloes, wild dogs, spotted deer, sambars and different varieties of hill birds.

Cairn Hill : It is about 3 km on the road to Avalanche and is one of the few surviving original walks. The entrance road to the hill is flanked by dense cypress trees. The clearing underneath them make good picnic spots. The quietitude and silence of the cypress woods is broken by the chirping of birds in the shrubs –an experience unforgettable.

Kandal Cross Shrine : This Roman Catholic church is to the Nilgiris Catholics 'The Calvary of Tamilnadu'. It is about 3 km from Ooty railway station on the western side. A relic of the true cross is here and it cures the sick, bestows peace and joy to the visitors. Special prayers and holy masses are offered every Friday. The annual feast falls on 3rd May each year.

Kamaraj Sagar (Sandynallah Reservoir): The Kamaraj Sagar dam is a nice picnic spot. It can be reached via Kandal amidst old trees and green shrubs of various terrains via the Hindustan Photo Films in Gudalur road. Apart from studying nature and the environment, fishing provides excellent game in the dam. Upper Bhavani and Avalanche are also good places for fishing. The trout fish abounds in them.

The Mukurthi Peak and Mukurthi National Park : It is about 40 km from Ooty. It is located on the south-eastern corner of the Nilgiris. The area contains a large number of Nilgiri trees (Hamitragus hilverius). The Silent Valley is located on the western side of these ranges. The main feature of Mukurthi Sanctuary is its variety and similarities to Himalayan flora and fauna.

Pykara : It is 21 km on the Ooty-Mysore road. Pykara has a well protected fenced sholas, Toda settlements, undisturbed grassy meadows and wildlife habitat. The

Pykara dam, Pykara falls and Pykara reservoir attract many tourists. T.T.D.C. maintains a boat house and restaurant here. The Pykara power station to which water is carried through pipelines along the slope is a fascinating sight.

Avalanche : It is 28 km from Ooty. A beautiful lake teeming with a thick shoal where even sunlight cannot penetrate and abundant with a wide variety of avifauna – really a paradise for nature lovers.

Western Catchment : It is 28 km from Ooty. It contains rolling grassy downs interspersed with temperate shoals occupying depressions and valleys.

Kotagiri : It is 31 km from Ooty. It is 6503 feet above sea level. The climate here is very salubrious. It is shielded by the Doddabetta ranges which receives much of its rain from the north-west monsoon. One can enjoy a pleasure ride on roads flanked by green tea beds on either side.

Kodanadu Viewpoint : It is about 16 km on the eastern edges of the Nilgiris. On either side is a panoramic view of tea estates and the river Moyar is breathtaking. A watch-tower is there to view the panoramic view of Rangasamy peak and pillar. Bus services are available for Kotagiri.

St. Catherine Waterfalls : From Dolphin's Nose, Coonoor, one can have a magnificent view of St. Catherine waterfalls which is about 250 feet high. But it can't be reached from Kotagiri which is 8 km from here. To reach the top of the hills, tourists should take a diversion at Araveni on the Kotagiri-Mettupalayam road.

Gudalur : It is 51 km from Udagamandalam. It is the gateway to Nilgiris from Kerala and Karnataka.

Udagamandalam, Coonoor and Kotagiri lie in the upper plateau of Nilgiris while Gudalur lies in the lower plateau. The Ooty-Calicut road and the Ooty-Mysore road meet at Gudalur town. Most of this area is a green carpet.

Frog Hill Viewpoint : It is 14 km from Gudalur on the way to Udagamandalam. From here, one can see the gigantic frog shape of a hill view.

Needle Point Rock View : It is 12 km on the way to Udagamandalam from Gudalur. From here, one can enjoy panoramic views of Mudhumalai wildlife sanctuary and Gudalur town.

Numbal Kattah : 8 km from Gudalur. A shrine of Battarayaswamy (Lord of the hunts) with sub-shrine built in Kerala style is situated here. Wynad scenes are visible from here.

Nellakotta : 15 km from Gudalur. A dilapidated old fort is seen here.

Nellialayam : 20 km from Gudalur. Ruins of the historical Ummathur dynasty can be seen here.

Cherambadi : 35 km from Gudalur. It is the extreme western corner having plantations and mica mines. Sultan Bathery is very near this place.

Hanging Bridges : It is 14 km from Gudalur on the way to Mudhumalai wildlife sanctuary. A Siva temple at Baro Wood Valley, Marava Kandy Dam at Masinagudi and Moyar waterfalls are the other places of tourist attraction here.

Summer Festival : The Summer Festival in Udagamandalam is the best event during the season in May. Regular cultural programmes, fashion shows, flower and fruit shows, boat races, boat pageantry, dog shows etc. are held during the festival. It is a gay occasion of fun and frolic and enjoyment of never - forgettable experiences.

Where to stay?

Coonoor (STD : 0423)

• **Taj Garden Retreat,** Church Road, Upper Coonoor, Coonoor - 643 101. ℰ 2230021, 2230042 Fax: 0423-2232775
• **Velan Hotel Ritz,** Ritz Road, Bedford, Upper Coonoor, The Nilgiris - 643 101. ℰ 2230484, 2230084, 2230632 Fax: 91(95) 423-2230606
• **Hotel Tamil Nadu Youth Hostel** Mount Pleasant ℰ 2232813
• **Sri Lakshmi Tourist Home,** Kamaraj Ngr. ℰ 2231022
• **Hotel Blue Hills,** ℰ 2231348
• **Vivek Tourist Home,** ℰ 2231292
• **Venkateswara Lodge,** ℰ 2234309

Udagamandalam (STD : 0423)

• **Savoy Hotel** 77, Sylks Road, The Nilgiris, Udagamandalam - 643 001. ℰ 2444142, 2444147 Fax:0423-2443318 Email:savoy.ooty@tajhotels.com
• **Holiday Inn Gem Park Ooty,** Sheddon Road, Udagamandalam - 643 001. ℰ 2442955, 2443066, 2441761, 2441762 Fax: 0423-2444302 Email: higp@vsnl.com
• **Hotel Sinclairs Ooty,** 153, Gorishola Road, Udagamandalam - 643 001. ℰ 2441376-80, 2444309 Fax: 0423-2444229 Email: sinooty@sancharnet.in
• **Howard Johnson The Monarch,** Church Hill, Off Havelock Rd., Udagamandalam - 643 001. ℰ 2444306, 2443655 Fax: 0423-2442455 Email: themonarch@vsnl.com
• **Nahar Hotels (Nilgiris),** 52 A, Charing Cross, Ooty, The Nilgiris - 643 001. ℰ 2443685, 2442173 Fax: 0423-244751, 2445173
• **Welcomgroup Sullivan Court,** 123, Selbourne Road, Udagamandalam - 643 001. (2441415-16 Fax:0423-2441417 Email: wgsull@md5.vsnl.net.in
• **The Willow Hill,** 58/1, Havelock Road, Udagamandalam - 643 001. ℰ 2442686, 2444037, 2444758 Fax: 0423-2442686
• **Merit Inn Southern Star,** 22, Havelock Road, Udagamandalam - 643 001. ℰ 2443601-06, 2440240 Fax: 0423-2440202, 2441098 Email: dean@md3. vsnl.net.in
• **Fernhill Palace Hotel,** Fernhill Post, Udagamandalam - 643 004. ℰ 0423-2443910-15
• **Hotel KHEMS,** Ettines Road, Udagamandalam - 643 001. ℒ 2444188, 2441265/66, 2441635/36 Fax: 0423-2442461 Email: khems999@yahoo.co.in
• **Hotel Lakeview,** West Lake Road, Udagamandalam - 643 004. ℰ 2443580-82, 2443904, 2440978-83 Fax: 0423-2443579 Email: lakeview@md3. vsnl. net.in
• **Howard Johnson The Monarch,** Safari Park, Bokkapuram, Masinagudi - 643 223. ℰ 2526250,

2526343 Fax: 0423-2526326 Email: themonarch@vsnl.com
• **Regency Villa,** Fernhill Palace, Fernhill Post, Udagamandalam - 643 004. ℰ 2442555, 2443098 Fax: 0423-243097
• **Sterling Holiday Resorts (India) Ltd.,** P.B. No. 73, Kundah House Rd., Fernhill, Ooty - 643 004. ℰ 2441073, 2450948, 2450949 Fax: 0423-2445890 Email: sterling@md4.vsnl.net.in
• **Sterling Holiday Resorts,** ELK Hill P.B. No. 25, Ramakrishna Mutt Road, Ramakrishna-Puram, Udagamandalam - 643 001. ℰ 2441395 Fax: 0423-2444265 Emal: sanjeevfernhill@rediffmail.com
• **The Nilgiri Woodlands,** Ettiness Road, Udagamandalam - 643 001. ℰ 2442551, 2442451 Fax: 0423-2442530
• **Charring Cross Dasaprakash,** 343/1, Garden Road, Charing Cross, Udagamandalam - 643 001. ℰ 244803, 240184
• **Hotel Tamil Nadu, Youth Hostel,** Botanical Garden Road, ℰ 2443665
• **Hotel Impala Lodge,** Commercial Road, Udagamandalam, ℰ 0423-2443313
• **Hotel Vinayaga,** Udagamandalam, ℰ 0423-2443313
• **Hotel Sowbagya,** ℰ 2443353
• **Railway Retiring Rooms,** ℰ 2442246
• **Central Park Guest House,** ℰ 2444046
• **Seetalakshmi Lodge,** ℰ 2442846

With this, we complete the places of tourist interest in Mid-Tamil Nadu and move to the south Tamil Nadu consisting of Dindigul, Madurai, Theni, Tirunelveli, Tuticorin, Ramanathapuram, Virudhunagar and Kanyakumari districts.

Dindigul
(The City of Locks)

Dindigul is the district headquarters now. Formerly it was part of Madurai district. Dindigul played a strategic role during the colonial period. Tipu Sultan wielded this fort under Wodeyar period, he strengthened the Dindigul fort and trained an excellent army which stood him in good stead during the Carnatic War. The fort on the Dindigul hills was built by Muthu Krishnappa Nayaka who hailed from the Madurai Nayaka clan. This district is number one in the production of flowers and grapes in Tamil Nadu. The Dindigul locks are world famous. It is also famous for tobacco and silk sarees especially the

Chinnalappatti (artificial) silk saree. Kodaikanal, the 2nd important hill station and Palani temple which is next to Tirupathi in generating revenue are other highlights of this district. It was originally a Jain settlement and the Jains who stayed on the mountain had beds made of rock for their use. Hence, the place came to be known as (dindu - bed, kal - rock) Dindigul .

How to get there?

Dindigul is very well connected by national highways to all the important towns of India. It is 430 km from Chennai. Buses are available from Chennai, Madurai, and Trichirappalli to Dindigul. It is also having a rail link in the Chennai-Madurai chord line and can be easily reached. Besides, many omnibuses and private transport go to Dindigul from Chennai and other places. Local transport is available to all the places in and around Dindigul. The nearest airport is at Madurai (62 km), from where Indian Airlines operate flights to Trichy, Chennai and Coimbatore. Recently, it has been linked to the broad gauge line from Chennai to Kanyakumari via Erode and Karur.

Places to see in and around Dindigul

Dindigul : There is a fort on the hills visible from the town. It was built by the Nayaks of Madurai and strengthened by Tipu Sultan. It is now in heavy ruins and practically there is nothing left in the fort except a magazine built with mud and bricks which remains unplastered. Even the stone beds of the Jains could not be found now. Only heaps of rubble could be seen exposing the fury and revenge of the colonial rulers who vowed to destroy all the forts in the southern part of Tamil Nadu which did not bow down to them posing a stiff resistance. The ruins of a temple also could be seen. The Mariamman temple that was on the hill has been shifted down. Even today, people throng there to worship the Goddess. The Abirami Amman Temple is also famous.

Sirumalai : Sirumalai is a small hill station 20 km away from Dindigul on the Natham Road. The place is cheap and convenient compared to other hill stations. It is 1200 m high and spreads over 60,000 acres. The place has lot of birds and animals and is suitable for trekking and mountaineering.

Tadikombu : It is about 8 km north of Dindigul. There is a temple here dedicated to Sundararaja Perumal possessing exquisite sculptures, monolithic pillars 12 ft high – all of excellent workmanship. Though carved in one stone, they present several designs. Garuda, Rudhrathandava, Kali, Chakkarathalwar, Vaikuntanatha, Rama mounted on Hanuman – all make the onlooker spellbound. The hill of 250 ft height 'called Anaimalai' looks like a recumbent elephant (Elephant Hill). At the bottom is the temple of Narasimha Perumal built by Paranthaka Chola I. South-west of this shrine is a cave temple. The deities and other figures are cut out of solid rock. Farther off are relics of a Jain monastery with Tirthankaras on a boulder. The boulder is quite astonishing—precariously over-heading and forming a cave. Besides several Tirthankara figures vatteluthu inscriptions are also found here. A pool filled with water is pointed out as the eye of the reclining elephant.

Gandhigram University : It is a rural university 15 km from Dindigul near Ambathurai railway station. Named after the father of the nation

Mahatma Gandhi, it was inaugurated by Pandit Jawaharlal Nehru. The university is located in a spacious area covering 300 acres. Rural demography, rural development, foreign and Indian languages and rural upliftment are the main subjects taught. It is a central university and the Vice President of India is the ex-officio Chancellor of this university.

Rajakaliamman Temple : This famous temple is located 22 km from Dindigul on the Palani-Dindigul-Madurai road near Kannivadi. The place is called Thethuppatti. The story goes that the guardian-deity of Madurai named Madurapathi shifted here from Madurai after it was partially burnt by Kannagi's curse who lost her husband as the king gave him capital punishment without proper enquiry, deciding him to be a thief. It is also said that one of the 18 siddhars Bogar did penance here before making the idol of Palani Andavar in 'Navapashanam'. The presiding deity Rajakaliamman is seen with a sceptre in Her hand. Besides the principal deity, there are sanctums for Bogar, Anjaneya, Navagrahas, Ayyanar and eight-headed serpent called Ashta Nagu. The peculiarity of this temple is, there are two sanctums of Navagrahas, one in the usual way and the other in the Kochara style i.e. the Navagrahas are placed in the constellations they are at present staying on date. With the result we can see two or three planets of the zodiac in one 'House' or 'Graha' (constellation) according to their wandering positions. Navagraha Santhi Yagam is performed here. Sri Chakra which wards off the evil eye is also available here. On Tamil New Year Day (April), there is a flower festival. The Siddhar festival is celebrated on 18th of Adi (August). Besides,

Navarathri is also celebrated here. People throng this temple in large numbers. Town buses ply from Dindigul to this place.

Gopinathaswamy Temple : Popularly known as Kopanaswamy Koil, this temple is also at Kannivadi about a km from Rajakali Amman temple. It is on the top of a hill called Varahagiri. It is also called Harikesa Parvatham or Kannivadi hills. A flight of steps leads to the temple. There is a beautiful idol of Lord Krishna called Gopinatha in the sanctum. Though the idol is about 2½ ft., its grace and beauty can't be described by words. This temple is considerably older than the other one.

Palani : Palani the most important temple of Tamil Nadu which is second only to Balaji temple of Tirupati is about 68 km from Dindigul. It is dedicated to Lord Muruga here called Dhandayuthapani as He just has a staff in His hand. The idol installed by Bogar one of the 18 siddhars is made of Navapashana - 9 medicinal herbs that have curative powers and together a panacea. Hence the abluted water of this idol is supposed to be a cure for all diseases. The temple is on a steep rocky hill 450 ft high at the mouth of the Vaiyapuri valley. It is a major pilgrim centre and each day is a festive day here. A winding flight of steps leads to the Palani Andavar shrine. There is also the elephant path through which elephants go up, which is easier to climb than the steps. An electrically operated winch is also available to go up. Palani Andavar is known as Palani Babha to the Muslims since the deity here is an Andi (Fakir). There is a shrine for Bogar who installed the idol here. *'Panchamirtham'* a mixture of Sirumalai plantains, honey, sugar, dates etc. is offered to Lord Muruga and after ablution, the 'Panchamirtham' is distributed. Another important Abhisekam is the pouring of sacred ash. The deity looks beautiful with the ash covering His body. Tonsure and carrying of Kavadi (a balance held on the shoulder with hanging basket filled with offerings like milk, rose water, flowers and sandal etc.) are performed as vows by devotees. One can find the place full of tonsured heads smeared on with sandal paste.

Nearby are its constituent temples Avinankudi where Lord Muruga as a child is seated on His mount Peacock. The place is also known as *Thiru Avinankudi*. It is one of the six abodes of Lord Muruga called Arupadai Veedu. Perianayaki temple is also nearby where one can witness rare pieces of sculpture especially that of Uchchimakali. Since Palani is a pilgrim centre one can always find enormous crowd of devotees from all over India.

Where to Stay?

Palani (STD : 04545)

* **Hotel Ganapathi**, Adivaram. ✆ : 242294
* **Rajalakshmi Hotel**, ✆ : 243313
* **S.K.N.Lodge**, Dindigul Road. ✆ : 243237
* **New Thiruppur Lodge**, Adivaram. ✆ : 242303
* **Hotel Subham**, Adivaram Road. ✆ : 242672
* **Sitaram Lodge**, ✆ : 242856
* **Hotel Karpagam**, Adivaram Road, ✆ : 242544
* **Modern Home**, Railway Junction Road. ✆ : 242376
* **Hotel Tamil Nadu (Near the Winch)**, ✆ : 241156

· **Kodaikkanal** : It is Dindigul's pride to have this beautiful hill station – the princess of hill stations – included in the district. It is about 60 km from Dindigul and 120 km from Madurai. Of all the three major hill stations of Tamil Nadu — Ooty, Kodaikkanal and Yercaud–it is definitely the most beautiful and unlike Ooty does not warrant heavy woollen clothes during winter. It is located on the western crest of the Palani hills amidst thickly wooded slopes, precipitous rocky outcrops, waterfalls, fragrant and colourful flowers with astonishing viewpoints that is incomparable to any place in India. Unlike Ooty where you have to travel long distances to see the places of tourist interest, here you can visit all the places within walking distance. This is a nice place not only to escape the heat of the tropical summer and a perennial place of relaxation.

Kodaikkanal means a cool resting place in summer (Kodai). The hill is of 7000 ft height (2133m) and was discovered by the Madurai American missionary around 1820. The erstwhile collector of Madurai Vere Leving constructed several roads and dug the lake. The climate is quite ideal for blossoms to bloom and the Pambar stream provides excellent water. One of the world's oldest solar observatories (1899) is also located here.

How to get there?

There is no rail link to this hill station. Those who come by rail have to get down at Kodai Road railway station on the Chennai-Madurai line and take buses from there. Umpteen buses ply to Kodaikkanal from Madurai which is 120 km away. From Trichy also buses are available via Dindigul. It is well connected by roads to Palani, Pollachi, Valparai, Dindigul and other places. Private vehicles and taxis are also available.

Places to See

Kodai Lake : The lake skirted by a 6.4 km road is the chief attraction. This artificial lake was dug in 1820 by the erstwhile collector of Madurai, Mr. Vele Leving. It is a star-shaped lake spread over 24 hectares. Boating and fishing are allowed. The lake glitters like sapphire embedded in emerald green. It is nice experience to stroll along the road or to row a pleasure boat.

Bryant Park : It is on the eastern side of the lake. A well laid-out park with exotic and native flowers, hybrid varieties etc. The flowers are even cut and exported. The annual horticultural show is held here in May.

The Solar Observatory : This is one of the oldest observatories in the world that came into being in 1899. The solar observatory is being used to observe sunspots and their behaviour. Solar Physics, Astronomy and Meteorology are the main concerns. It is about 850 ft higher than the lake.

Coaker's Walk : It is about a km from the lake. It runs along a steep slope on the southern side of the hill. It is a semi-circular beautiful path overlooking the plains. The view from here is simply captivating. The distant plains appear to be a dream land.

Kurinji Andavar Temple : Kurinji is the name of a flower of the hills. That is why in Tamil, the mountainous region is called *Kurinji*. It is a small bush and blooms once in 12 years. The flowers are a delicate mauve and during the flowering season the hill sides look completely mauve and look like a mauve-tinted fairy land. Near the Prospect Point is the Kurinji Andavar temple. The presiding deity is Lord Muruga just like Lord Dandayuthapani of Palani. The site for the temple was picked by a Ceylonese named Sri Ponnambalam Ramanathan simply because of the visibility of Palani 60 km away and 6000ft below. One can also get a glimpse of the Vaigai dam which is 3.2 km from here.

Telescope House : Two telescopes are erected in two different viewpoints in Kodaikkanal to have a clear view of the plains and valleys. One is near the Kurinji Andavar temple and the other is at Coaker's Walk. Entrance fee has to be paid to look through them.

Green Valley Viewpoint : It is about 5.5 km from the lake and near the Golf Club. It commands a beautiful view of the entire Vaigai dam.

The Pillar Rocks : 3 massive granite rocks about 400 ft high standing abreast on an edge by the Coaker's Walk are called the Pillar Rocks. The sight is quite enchanting. It is about 7.5 km from the lake and a nice road passing through a charming greenery takes you there.

Waterfalls : Fairy Falls, Silver Cascade, Glen Falls and Bear Shola Falls are the main falls that serve as good picnic spots. Bear Shola Falls is about 1.5 km from the lake and can be reached by a picturesque ragged path. Silver Cascade is on the ghat road to Madurai 8 km from Kodaikanal. The other falls are also within walking distance from the lake. They are beautiful and charming as their names indicate.

Dolphin's Nose : It is 8 km from the lake and is a plateau with steep chasms on either side. The yawning chasms below is quite breathtaking and dizzy. A thrill passes through the veins that makes one tremble for a while.

The Perumal Peak : It is a trekkers' paradise, situated 11 km from Kodaikanal. Its height is 2400 metres. It is a day's trip on foot and one feels little strenuous as the path is quite bewitching and absorbing with beautiful sceneries all through. The actual climb begins at a point called Neutral Saddle.

Berijam Lake : This lake is beyond Pillar Rocks at a distance of 21 km. It supplies drinking water to Periakulam town. It is a fine picnic spot offering picturesque scenery.

Kukkai Cave : About 40 km from Kodaikanal is this natural cave where cavemen dwelt. It is a nice camping centre with ample scope for trekking.

Shenbaganur Museum : Located about 5.5 km from Kodaikanal is this museum devoted to the flora and fauna of the hills. The museum is being run by the Sacred Heart College, a seminary founded in 1895. Some of the archaeological remains are also exhibited here. It is a must for every visitor as it enlightens on subjects very interesting to hilly habitat.

Orchidorium : This is also maintained by the Sacred Heart College. It is one of the best of its kind and contains about 300 species of orchids.

Important Telephone Numbers

- Astrophysical Observatory ✆ 2241336
- Office of the Sub-collector ✆ 2240296
- Govt. Hospital ✆ 2241292
- T.V. Relay Monitor ✆ 2241026
- Police Station ✆ 2240262
- Panchayat Union Office ✆ 2240204

Where to Stay?

Kodaikkanal (STD : 04542)

- **The Carlton**, Lake Road, Kodaikkanal-624 101. ✆ 240056, 240071, Fax: 04542-241170, Email: carlton@krahejahospitality.com
- **Hotel Taj Villa**, Cokor's Walk, Kodaikkanal - 624 101. ✆ 04542-243556.
- **Punjab Hotel**, P.T. Road, Kodaikkanal - 624 101. ✆ 04542-241169.
- **Hotel J's Heritage**, P.T. Road, Near Seven Roads, Kodaikkanal - 624 101. ✆ 241323, Fax: 04542-240693, Email: jaherit@md5.vsnl.net.in
- **Hill Country Holiday Resorts**, Attuvampatti P.O., Kodaikkanal - 624 101. ✆ 240953/240958, Fax: 04542-240947, Email: hillctry@md3.vsnl.net.in
- **Hilltop Towers**, Club Road, Kodaikkanal - 624 101. ✆ 240413, 242253-54, Fax: 04542-240415, Email: httowers@md3.vsnl.net.in
- **Hotel Jewel**, 7, Road Junction, Kodaikkanal - 624 101. ✆ 241029, 241185, Fax: 04542 - 240518, Email: glentravels@vsnl.com

- **Hotel Kodai International**, 17/328, Lawsghat Road, Kodaikkanal - 624 101. ✆ 245190-92, Fax: 04542-240753, Email: hki@vsnl.net
- **Sornam Apartments**, Fernhill Road, Kodaikkanal - 624 101. ✆ 240562, 240731, 240421
- **Hotel Tamil Nadu**, 47, Fern Hills Road. ✆ 241336
- **Valley View**, Post Office Road. ✆ 240181
- **Hotel Astoria**, Near bus stand. ✆ 240624
- **Hotel Sivapriya**, Convent Road. ✆ 241144
- **Hotel Jayaraj Annexe**, Bazaar Road. ✆ 240178
- **Garden Manor**, Lake Road. ✆ 240461
- **Sterling Holiday Resorts**, ✆ 240313

Sivagangai

(The Land of Marudhu Pandyas)

Sivagangai is the land of Marudhu Pandyas who opposed the colonial power with patriotic fervour. They were a nightmare to the British who in the guise of traders grabbed the whole of India and founded an empire here. Had there been many Marudhus, the history of India would have been different from what it turned out to be. Sivagangai is now the headquarters of the district. It was formed out of Ramanathapuram as a separate district in 1985.

How to get there?

It is 531 km from Chennai on Chennai-Rameswaram metre gauge main line and can be reached by train via Chidambaram, Mayiladuthurai, Thanjavur, Trichy, Pudukkottai and Karaikudi. It is connected by road to all the important towns in Tamil Nadu. Bus services are available from Chennai, Thanjavur, Trichy, Madurai and Rameswaram. Private carriages, omnibuses and taxis could also take you there from anywhere in Tamil Nadu. The nearest airport is at Madurai which can be reached by bus. From Madurai, flights are available to Chennai, Coimbatore and Trichy.

Places to see

The Sivaganga Palace : The old

royal palace, besides being magnificent, is full of historical association.

Tondi : Tondi was a maritime trade port several centuries before the first century A.D. It is also an ideal location for sea-bathing and boating.

Karaikudi : This town is 41 km from Sivagangai. Magnificent mansions have been built here by Chettiars — a merchant class known for their wealth and magnificence. Though the owners have left, still these palatial wonders with beautifully carved woodwork, stone and mortar works are amazing and attract visitors. The Alagappa University founded by Dr. Alagappa Chettiar is functioning here.

Pillayarpatti : It is 12 km from Karaikudi on the national highway proceeding to Thiruppathur. There is an old Ganesa or Pillayar temple. It is a beautiful cave temple of the Pandya period exhibiting fine architecture. The presiding deity, Pillayar is a bas-relief sculpture on the wall of the cave and named as Karpaga Vinayagar. It is different from other pillayar idols in having only two hands instead of the usual four, besides there are no weapons in His hands, quite different from the others. It is said to have been the earliest image that would have been made when Pillayar worship was introduced in Tamil Nadu. This is also attested by the inscriptions of this temple. During the 12th century, this temple came under the administration of the Nagarathar community and the temple is still in their hands. Siva is always represented with four arms but queerly in this temple He is found with two arms. There are vatteluthu inscriptions in this temple dating back to 7th century A.D. The mandapam has the sculpture of Ashta Lakshmi.

The Vinayaga Chathurthi day (August-September) and January 1st are very famous in this temple. Lakhs of people visit and worship Lord Pillayar here on these days. A giant size Kozhukkattai (Modhaga) is made weighing several kilos and offered to the deity on the Vinayaka Chathurthi day. It takes 3 or 4 days for steaming the Kozhukkattai.

Kundrakkudi : It is hardly 2 km from Pillayarpatti. This temple dedicated to Lord Muruga is also a rock-cut temple of the Pandya period. It is on a hill called Mayuragiri and the hill is shaped like a peacock. Lord Muruga the presiding deity with six faces and twelve hands is mounted on a peacock atop the hill which could be climbed over a flight of steps. The vibudhi (sacred ash) of this temple is believed to have curative powers. Marudhu Brothers of Siva gangai were patrons of this temple and have done improvements to it. In another cave, the eight-armed dancing Nataraja is sheltered. Another attraction is the very rare image of Gaundaku Vishnu.

Thenithangal : This ancient rock-cut shrine is also near Pillayarpatti. The presiding deity is Veera Narayana Perumal. Inside the sanctum, images of Garuda, Pradyumna, Nila-devi, Usha-devi and Jambaqavathi are beautifully sculptured.

Madurai
(The Athens of the East)

Madurai which is usually called 'Nanmadakkoodal' in Tamil literature is an ancient city more than 4000 years old. Koodal means assembly and as all the 3 Tamil Academies (Sangams) were established in Madurai, it got the name Koodal. Literary evidences prove that the first Madurai was devoured by the sea and what we now see is the second Madurai founded by the Pandya king Kulasekara in 6th century B.C. The culture of Tamil Nadu is woven with the history of Madurai in all aspects— history, religion, art, legend, polity, learning and so on. It was the city of elites and learned men, so it is aptly called the 'Athens of the East.'

The name Madurai is associated with 'Maduram' meaning nectar. The legend is that when Lord Siva came here to marry Devi Meenakshi, few drops of nectar fell from His locks and therefore named as Madurapuri, the land of nectar which was shortened later as Madurai.

From the Sangam Age, it was the capital of the Pandyas and except for a brief spell under the Cholas till the Muslim invasion by Malik Kafur (1290-1320 A.D.), it was ruled by the Pandyas. Afterwards, it came under Vijayanagar rule and their governors, the Nayaks from 1371. The Nayaks ruled for over 200 years and their reign is the golden age when Madurai was at its height in art, architecture and learning. They embellished Madurai with temples and buildings, including the Meenakshi temple, which are landmarks of the city. Madurai now is the 2nd largest city of Tamil Nadu very much modern and progressive.

How to get there?

Madurai has an airport and flights from Chennai, Mumbai, Trichy and Coimbatore arrive here. It is very well connected by roads to all major cities in India. Buses ply from Chennai, Thanjavur, Dindigul, Palani, Rameswaram, Tirunelveli and Kanyakumari to Madurai. It is linked to all the places in Tamil Nadu by both the metre gauge and broad gauge of the Southern Railway. Bus services are available to all the places in and around Madurai. Taxis and private carriages are also available in plenty to take you to all the places of tourist importance.

Places to see in Madurai City

Meenakshi Temple : It is in the midst of the city. The entire city is planned keeping the temple as its core like a lotus. The city is planned according to the silpa canons and the other city that has the same basis is Kanchipuram famously known as 'Nagareshu Kanchi' in Sanskrit. The temple is an important landmark and nucleus of the life of the city. The temple has 11 gopurams and the tallest of them is at the southern portal rising to a height of 200 ft. This portion is exclusively dedicated to Goddess Meenakshi. The shrine is usually entered from Vittavasal Street the entrance of which is adorned by the Ashtalakshmi (eight forms of Goddess Lakshmi) Mandapam. Scenes of Kumara Sambhava and the marriage of Goddess Meenakshi with Sundareswara are painted on the ceiling. At the entrance are the statues of Subramanya and Vinayaka and on the passage is the beautiful sculpture of Siva and Meenakshi as a huntress. An exquisite brass-faced doorway gifted by the rulers of Sivaganga is the inlet to the mandapam lined with sculptures of Siva in various poses. It leads to the Pottramarai tank with arcades all around. The corridors of the tank display the 64 Leelas called Thiruvilaiyadalgal of Siva. The doors in the shrine display poses of Bharatha Natyam. The temple having been built in several epochs reveal different styles of architecture. There is a musical pillar near the north tower corridor which emits the seven musical notes when struck.

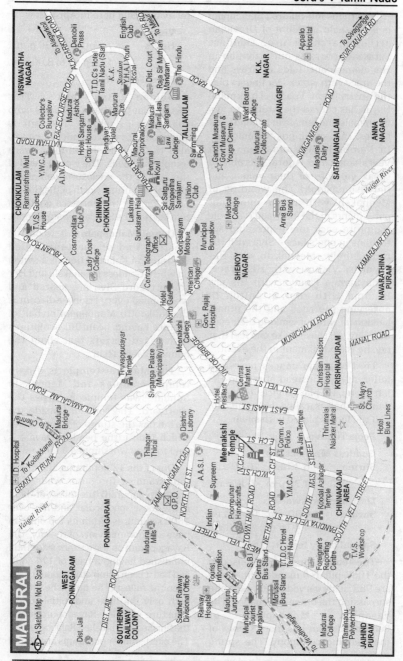

MADURAI

A Sketch Map Not to Scale

The thousand-pillared mandapam is a veritable museum of Dravidian art and architecture. Goddess Saraswathi arrests our attention in Her demeanour, folds of dress and the grace with which Her fingers play the instrument Veena. Thirumalai Nayak has carved the Ardhanari idol (both male and female in left and right halves) that spellbinds the onlooker. In Kambathadi Mandapam, Agni Veerabadra and Agora Veerabadra speak volumes of their valour and fiercesome look. The wedding of Meenakshi with all the important participants in the marriage is a lively sculpture each one expressing apt feelings in one's face – Siva with His magnanimity, Meenakshi with Her coyness, Vishnu with His grace, Malayatwaja Pandya with His joy, Brahma with rapt attention in observing the rites and the others looking on without winking their eyes in gaiety. All these make one feel that he/she is a participant in the event.

Lord Nataraja dances here in a different style instead of raising His left leg up, He plays it vice versa. The dancing hall is called *Velliambalam* and the idol is plated with silver.

Pooja Timings :

Goddess Meenakshi's Shrine : 6.30 a.m., 10.30 a.m. 4.30 p.m., 7.30 p.m.

Lord Sundareswarar's Shrine : 6.40 a.m., 10.40 a.m. 4.40 p.m., 7.40 p.m.

Special entry fee : Rs. 15/-

The Temple Museum is housed in the 1000-pillared mandapam. There are 985 richly carved pillars each one surpassing the other in elegance. The Vasantha Mandapam or Pudumandapam has more scenes of the wedding ceremony. The spring festival is held here in April-May.

Visiting Hours : 7 a.m. to 12.30 p.m. 4.00 p.m. to 8.00 p.m.

Entry Fee : Rs.5/-

Golden Lotus Tank : This rectangular tank has a tall brass lamp column in its middle. The tank is surrounded by a colonnade, for which, also the Meenakshi Sundareswara temple is famous. The western end of the tank is the enclosure wall of the Meenakshi shrine. North of the Golden Lotus Tank is the entrance gopuram that leads to the Sundareswara Temple.

Oonjal Mandapam : It is on the western end of the tank called Pottramarai Kulam. There is a swing on which Goddess Meenakshi and Her consort Lord Siva are seated and worshipped every Friday. Adjacent is the Kilikoottu Mandapam or hall of parrots having beautiful sculptures with caged parrots that chant the name of Meenakshi.

The Madurai temple is a twin temple complex and Meenakshi Sundareswar temple is across the courtyard. The corridor outside the shrine has the stump of a tree under which Indira (the head of Devas) is said to have worshipped a Lingam.

Out of the 12 gopurams, the tallest four stand at the outer walls. The southern gopuram, the tallest of them is the most spectacular and has over 1500 sculptures. From its top one can have a panoramic view of the city. The Rayagopuram on the eastern side is still unfinished having a base of 174 sq.ft. and had it been completed it would have been the tallest (The unfinished tower with only the base and initial super-structure is called Rayagopuram and the finished one is called Rajagopuram). The eight smaller gopurams are within the compounds of the twin temples. There are few temples in India which share the grandeur of this twin temple complex. It is so huge that newcomers will be upset to find their way proper, hence, it is better to go with a guide or with a person who had already been there several times.

The Mariamman Teppakulam: This tank is also known as *Vandiyur Teppakulam* and is about 5 kms east of Meenakshi temple. It occupies an area equal to the twin-temple complex. This tank was also built by Thirumalai Nayakar. In the middle is an island with a temple for Ganesa. The tank was created due to digging of earth to make bricks for the Thirumalai Nayak palace. It is 1000 ft long and 950 ft wide and four white turrets border the garden of the island. The float festival of the Meenakshi Amman temple is held here in January-February.

The Thirumalai Nayak Mahal: This is the palace of Thirumalai Nayak, just a km away from the temple. This Indo-Saracenic marvel was constructed in 1523A.D. It has pillars of granite cased with mortar and supporting arches which present a majestic view. The corner of the east face has towers. On three sides of a quadrangle 250 ft. by 180 ft. are corridors with arches supporting roof. The most remarkable part of the structure is the Swarga Vilasam or the audience hall. Its dome is 60 ft in diameter and 70 ft in height. Such a lofty dome stands firm without any support revealing the engineering skill of its builders. Circling this is the zenana from where the royal ladies witnessed the durbar. It is a fine example of the architectural style of the Nayaks.

It is open to public from 9 a.m. to 1 p.m. and from 2 p.m. to 5 p.m.

Entry Fee : Rs. 10.00 (Adult)

Rs. 5.00 (Child)

Sound and light shows on the life of Thirumalai Nayak and the story of Silappathikaram (one of the 5 major epics of Tamil) are held every day.

Timings: English – 18.45 hrs

Tamil – 20.15 hrs

Fee :   Rs.5, Rs.3 & Rs.2

Koodal Azhagar Temple : Lord Vishnu in Madurai is called Koodal Azhagar and His temple is as ancient as the Meenakshi temple. Though tall Gopurams are absent, the Vimana called Ashtanga stands in the centre with diminishing tiers under which is the sanctum. Ferguson, the connoisseur of arts, estimates that it surpasses anything of its kind to be found in South India. The base has excellent carvings. There are three sanctums where the deities are seen in sitting, standing and recumbent postures one above the other.

The Tamakam : It is a beautiful relic of Thirumalai Nayak resembling his palace, the Mahal. The Lotus Hall here has a dome with ceiling, shaped like an inverted lotus. It was the Nayak's summer palace.

Alanganallur : This small town is very popular for the 'Jallikattu', the wild bull taming sport played in Tamil Nadu as a part of Pongal celebration. The term Jallikattu comes from the term 'Salli' kaasu (Coins) and 'kattu' (meaning a package) tied to the horns of the bulls as the prize money.

Goripalayam Mosque : There is a large mosque in Goripalayam containing two tombs of two Delhi Sultans of the Madurai sultanate. The amazing thing about it is that the dome which is 70 ft. in diameter and 20 ft. in height is made of a single block of stone. It is said that it was built by Thirumalai Nayak for his muslim subjects.

The Gandhi Museum : It contains a picture gallery, a gallery of relics, a Khadi and Village Industries section and a South Indian handicrafts section. It is located in an old palace.

Timings : 10 a.m to 1 p.m &
2 p.m to 5.30 p.m.

Phone : 0452 - 2531060

Places around Madurai

Tirupparankundram : One of the abodes of Lord Subramanya is located 8 km south of Madurai. The six abodes are known as Arupadai Veedu. Out of the six, two are near Madurai, the other Padaiveedu is **Pazhamuthircholai**. It is a cave temple. It is known from the Sangam times and one of the Sangam poets Nakkiran has sung a long poem about this temple called *Thirumurugatrupadai*. As in the case of other temples, new structures have been added later on. There are a series of mandapams one above the other in elevation in this temple. There is a shrine dedicated to Nakkirar. The front mandapam contains the marriage of Deivayanai and the sculptures of Thirumalai Nayak and Mangammal. In the descent from the mandapam are caves with images of Annapoorna, Varaha Avataram, Narasimha Avataram, Mahalakshmi etc. The Sivathandavam is a masterpiece sculpture of the group and Uma is witnessing it reclining on the bull. The Kudarmugha drum is also seen being beaten by a celestial attendant. The important feature is that Siva is holding the flag of Rishaba in His hand while dancing — a rarity, not to be found elsewhere. Separated by a wall is another group of sculptures with Nandhi standing in bull-head and human-body form beside some sages. About 7 km away is another cave with images of Nataraja, Sivakami,

Heramba Ganapathi, dancing Sambandar etc.

Azhagarkoil : 21 km from Madurai is this important Vishnu temple at the foot of a wooded hill. 'Azhagu' in Tamil means beauty and true to its meaning, everything here is a thing of beauty and a joy forever. The main deity is Paramaswami and the itinerant idol is Kallazhagar. It is a beautiful idol made of pure gold. The other temple having a gold idol is at Thiruvananthapuram. Barring these two, no other temple has an idol made of pure gold. The ablution water for this idol is brought from Noobura Gangai - a perennial waterfall 3 km up on the hill the water of which contains copper and iron minerals. The Vimanam of this temple is called Somaskanda Vimanam (tower over the sanctum) and a unique one of its kind. The Kalyana Mandapam contains sculptures that rival the one at Madurai—the images of Krishna, Rathi, Manmatha, Garuda Vahana, Trivikrama, Lakshmi and Varaha Avatar are really masterpieces in stone. The British contemplated to shift the temple in toto like the one they wanted to shift at Vellore to one of the museums in England, but anyhow the attempt was failed.

Pazhamuthircholai : It is about 4 km above on the hill. Beautifully situated amidst sylvan surroundings, the temple has to be climbed through thickly shaded woods through which the rays of sun rarely peep in. On the way, there are several perennial springs and beyond the Muruga temple is the Noobura Gangai. It is one of the 6 abodes of Muruga. Lord Muruga stands with His 'Vél' (spear) in His hand. The ruins of a fort built by Thirumalai Nayak can also be seen here.

Thiruvedagam : About 15 km northwest of Madurai on the left bank of the river Vaigai is the place where Saivite supremacy over the Jains was established by performing Punal Vadam i.e. each contestant will put into the stream sacred palm leaves on which are written hymns and if the palm leaves do not sink or get carried by the running stream but sail upstream the one who set it sail is the winner. The palm leaves of the Jains were carried away by the stream and the palm leaves of Gnanasambandar sailed upstream thus proving Saivite supremacy over the Jains.

Thiruvadhavur : This place is about 9 km from Melur near Madurai. One of the Saivaite saint Manickavasagar was born here. He was the minister to a Pandya king. He built a temple for Siva with the money he was entrusted to buy horses for the king. A miracle was performed by Siva in which foxes were transformed into horses and after they were taken by the king and sent to the stables they again turned into foxes. The site of the house of His birth is pointed out to visitors.

Madappuram Badrakali Amman Temple : This famous temple visited often by V.I.Ps, cine stars and I.A.S. officers is at Madappuram about 20 km from Madurai near Thiruppuvanam. It stands on the banks of the river Vaigai on the northern side of Esanar Koil. It is amidst a cool coconut grove. The first idols that greet the visitor here are that of Lord Ayyanar and His horse. The horse with its protruding teeth and bulging eyes and Lord Ayyanar with fierce looks really make one tremble. The horse is of a height of 30 ft which wears a garland of lemons. The devotees pray to the Goddess, the presiding deity of this temple, for creative comforts, promotions in job and for the ruin of their enemies. One curious practice in this temple is to cut a coin and offer it to the deity to get relief from being bullied by the mighty. A gunny bag full of cut coins can be seen here. The presiding deity Badrakali Amman is armed to the teeth and seen standing at the breast of a horse with fierce looks amidst a group of demons-really awe-inspiring.

Periyar Wildlife Sanctuary (Thekkady) : It is on the verge of Kerala about 155 km from Madurai. The sanctuary is between Tamil Nadu and Kerala. It is formed around Periar reservoir and dam spread over 729.29 sq.km. The animal watchers have to go by a motor boat along the Periar lake and watch them on the hills surrounding the lake. Many animals come for drinking water at various places. Boats can be hired from which the animals could be watched in their natural habitat basking in the sun, adult elephant helping elephant calves to climb the slopes, bathing in the water, preying, frolicking etc. Tigers, elephants, bisons, deers and boars could all be seen by lucky tourists. The most common sight is the elephant herd with elephants of all sizes. The route from Madurai to Kumily is itself a picturesque ride through the slopes of western ghats. On entering Kumizhi one can breathe the fragrance of cardamom and other spices that emanates from the estates around. Kumizhi is the border line and from there Thekkady can be reached by a short walk amidst sylvan surroundings.

Buses are available to visit all the places mentioned here from Madurai. Staying at Madurai all these places could be visited.

FESTIVALS

Avani Moolam Festival – August-September.

Float Festival – January-February.

Chitthirai Festival – April-May.

Government Chitthirai Exhibition – April-May.

The dates in each year will vary as the festivals are observed based on the lunar months and not as per the Gregorian calender which is universally followed.

Important Telephone Numbers

- Arulmigu Meenakshi Sundareswarar Temple
  ✆ : 2344360
- Tourist Office, Madurai ✆ : 2334757
- Tourist Information Office Railway Junction
  ✆ : 2342888
- TN State Transport Corporation - Mattuthavani Bus Stand ✆ : 2380112
- TN State Express Transport Corporation - Mattuthavani Bus Stand ✆ : 2585838
- Railway Enquiry ✆ : 2343131
- Indian Airlines ✆ : 2341234 - 6
- Indian Airport ✆ : 2690333

Where to Stay?

Madurai (STD : 0452)

- **Hotel Aryas,** Melur Main Road, ✆ 2587088
- **Taj Garden Retreat,** No. 40. T.P.K. Road, Pasumalai, Madurai - 625 004. ✆ 2371601, Fax: 2371636, Email: retreat.madurai@tajhotels.com
- **Hotel Madurai Ashok,** Alagarkoil Road, Madurai - 625 002. ✆ 2537531, 2537675, Fax: 2537530 Email: ashokmadu@vsnl.com
- **Hotel North Gate,** Goripalayam. ✆ 2523030, Fax: 2537727
- **Hotel JK Residency,** 14, Dhanappa Mudali Street, ✆ 2340314/54
- **Hotel International,** 46, West Permaul Maistry St., Madurai - 625 001. ✆ 2341552-55, Fax: 2340372
- **Hotel Supreme,** 110, West Perumal Maistry St., Madurai - 625 001. ✆ 2343151, Fax: 2342637
- **New Arya Bhavan,** 241-A, West Masi Street, Madurai - 625 001. ✆ 2340577, 2340345, Fax:2344481
- **Hotel Tamil Nadu-I,** West Veli Street, ✆ 2337471 - 75. Fax : 2331945
- **Hotel Tamil Nadu-II,** Azhagar Koil Road. ✆ 2537461-66. Fax : 2533203
- **Hotel Blue King,** Near airport. ✆ 2620511
- **Railway Retiring Rooms,** Railway Station, Rani Mangammal Choultry, (Opp. Railway Station).

- **T.M.Lodge,** 50, West Perumal Maistry St., ✆ 2341651
- **Jupiter Rest-house.** ✆ 23543786
- **New College House,** Town Hall Road. ✆ 2342971
- **Hotel Prem Nivas,** 102, West Perumal Maistry St.. ✆ 2342532
- **Hotel Grands Central,** 47-48, West Perumal Maistry Street. ✆ 2343940
- **Pandyan Hotel,** Race Course, ✆ 2356789 Fax: 2533424
- **Hotel Empee,** 253, Nethaji Road. ✆ 2341525/26
- **Hotel Aarathy,** 9, Perumal Koil West Mada Street, ✆ 23331571
- **Hotel Sulochna Palace,** 96, West Perumal Maistry Street, ✆ 2341071-3
- **Hotel Dhanamani,** Sunnambukara Street. ✆ 2342703
- **Hotel Chentoor,** 106, West Perumal Maistry Street. ✆ 2347022
- **Hotel Park Plaza,** 114-115, West Perumal Maistry Street. ✆ 3011111
- **Hotel Vijay,** 122, Tirupparankundram Road. ✆ 2336321
- **Hotel K.P.S.,** 8-9, West Marret Street. ✆ 2341541
- **New Modern Lodge,** 10, Perumal Tank East. ✆ 2342797
- **Laxmi Towers,** 40A, Koodalazhagar Perumal Koil South Mada Street. ✆ 2332069
- **Hotel Boopathi International,** 16-17, Perumal Tank (E). ✆ 2343627
- **Hotel Thilaga,** 111, West Perumal Maistry Street. ✆ 2343383
- **Classic Residency,** 14-15, West Marret Street. ✆ 2343140
- **Hotel Ramson,** 9, Perumal Tank East. ✆ 2343406
- **Ashoka Lodge,** 12, Perumal Theppakulam East, Town Hall Road. ✆ 2340282
- **Hotel Gangai,** 41, West Perumal Maistry Street. ✆ 2342180
- **Prabhat & Co Lodging,** 15, Perumal Theppakulam. ✆ 2340810
- **Kavery Mahal Annexe,** 35-37, Pachai Nachiyamman Koil Street. ✆ 2342368
- **Hotel Keerthi (P) Ltd.,** 40, West Perumal Maistry Street. ✆ 2341501
- **Hotel Blue King,** Near Airport, ✆ 620511

Besides, there are umpteen lodges and boarding houses in Madurai. Madurai is also famous for open-air catering stalls on pavements after 6 p.m.

Theni
(The Land of Spices)

As a result of bifurcation of Madurai district, Theni district has come into existence. Three taluks namely Uttamapalayam, Periyakulam and Andipatti of the erstwhile Madurai district were separated from its parent district to form this new district.

Places around Theni

Vaigai Dam : The dam across the river Vaigai is 69 km from Madurai. In order to augment water supply, a dam has been constructed across Periar of Kerala state and the water from there is diverted through tunnels to flow into the river Vaigai. The height of the dam is 106 ft and its breadth is 11,657 ft. Its capacity is 58,000 cubic ft. It irrigates about 2½ lakh hectares of land. There is a beautiful garden laid out here. It is a popular picnic spot.

Kambam Valley : The Kambam Valley located in the newly formed Theni district could easily be reached from Madurai. The Kambam valley offers beautiful scenic spots like Kandamanur, Kadamalai Kundu, Mayiladumparai and various streams like Varaha Nadhi, Mullaiyar etc. and various hills and estates. It is really the catchment area of river Vaigai and a beautiful place with frequent drizzles. There are various barrages across the streams and picturesque sceneries greet us everywhere. The chief attractions are the Suruli Falls and Thekkady on the verge of Kerala.

Suruli Falls : It is 128 km from Madurai on the way to Thekkadi. It is a sacred spot visited by pilgrims on specific days. Of late, it is becoming a picnic spot. Though of lesser height than the Courtallam Falls, the water gushes with great force out of caves. It is a fine place for bathing and

arrangements are made for the safety of the bathers. There is a rope rail from Suruli dam to Moonaru for about 50 kms distance for the quick transport of tea leaves from the estates.

Kuchanoor : The temple dedicated for Saneeswarar is located at Kuchanoor near Chinnamanur on the banks of river Surabhi. The chief deity Saneeswaran is the main God and its genesis was its own (Suyambu).

Uthamapalayam : Two ancient temples dedicated to Lord Shiva and Sri Kalahastishwara Swamy are popular pilgrim centres.

Megamalai Falls : Megamalai is located on the slops of the Western Ghats, amidst the lush green tea plantations and cardamom estates. Its altitude is 1500 m above sea level. Best time to visit September to March.

Virudhunagar
(The Grocery Town)

Virudhunagar was formerly part of Ramanathapuram district and now a new district and its headquarters. It was under the Pandyas and passed into the Paligars known as '*Palayakararkal*' in Tamil. They showed stiff opposition to the colonial supremacy and finally were subdued by the British. Now Virudhunagar is a very big grocery centre in Tamil Nadu and plays a vital role in edible oil business too and a number of cement factories are also located here. It is the birthplace of Kamarajar, popularly known as Kala Gandhi (kala–black), who played a vital role in freedom struggle and at one time became the king-maker of India. The house where he lived is preserved as a monument and memorial. It is 44 km from Madurai and 536 km from Chennai. It can be reached by rail or by bus from Chennai and other important towns. The nearest airport is at

Madurai which connects to Coimbatore, Trichy and Chennai.

Aruppukkottai : It is 19 km from Virudhunagar. It is an important weaving centre and grocery trade centre.

Tiruchuli : This place is so-called because it was saved from being sucked into the earth during the deluge. It is 33 km from Virudhunagar. Several sacred pools are scattered here. This is the birthplace of the great saint Ramana Maharishi.

Sivakasi : It is a town of cottage industries engaged in the manufacture of safety matches and fireworks. It is also famous for litho-printing and calendar manufacture. Out of 3932 match factories more than 80% are located here. There are about 120 litho printing presses located here. It is 25 kms from Virudhunagar.

Srivilliputhur : This is the most important tourist attraction because of the ancient Andal temple. It is the birthplace of Andal, one of the twelve Vaishnavaite saints called Alwars. Alwar means one who is immersed and since they are immersed in Vishnu Bhakti they are called Alwars. It is the 60 metre tower of this temple that has been portrayed in the insignia of the Government of Tamil Nadu. The residence of Perialwar, the foster father of Andal, has now become the Nachiar Koil and the other part of the temple is known as Vadabhadra Sayi temple.

The temple has beautiful sculptures and the delicacy of carving is more dominant in the coiffure of feminine images - Andal's hair style and head ornamentation are a speciality of South India and it is this style on which the sculptors have lavished their skill. The images of Rathi, Swan, Parasakthi, a lady playing the Veena, a warrior brandishing his sword are superb examples of embellishments in stones. The scene of the mutilation of Soorpanaga's nose and breast in the Ramayana has so well been captured by the dextrous hands of the sculptor that it should be seen to be believed of its excellence. The temple is one of the biggest and has beautiful wood carvings. It is 71 kms from Madurai and about 48 km from Virudhunagar.

Rajapalayam : It is close to the temple town of Srivilliputhur and the coolest place in the district located almost on the western ghats. Rajapalayam dogs are known for their ferocity. It is an industrial centre and famous for teak industry. The Gandhi Kalai Mandram and Library are very popular here. They are the gift of the late Chief Minister of Madras and the Governor of Orissa, Mr. P.K.Kumaraswamy Raja.

Rameswaram
(The Lifeblood of National Integration)

India is a land of variations and multiplicity, the one chain of integration that binds India together is Hinduism. Though the people speak different languages, eat different kinds of food, clothe differently and differ in habits and customs, still they are united by religion and spiritualism. From Varanasi to Rameswaram, a chain of holy shrines unite the Indians into a single entity. The lifeblood of national integration runs thus. For every Hindu, Varanasi or Kasi in the north and Rameswaram, in the south are indispensable. Those who go to Kasi have to consummate their pilgrimage at Rameswaram. The north Indians and south Indians thus emerge as true Indians by this integration.

Rameswaram the holy island is in the district of Ramanathapuram, the land of Sethupathi who sent Swami Vivekananda to the Parliament of Religions held at Chicago. It is 167 km from Madurai and 666 km from Chennai. It is sacred for both Vaishnavites and Saivaites. Never ending pilgrims from all quarters of India is the greatness of this place. It is also the seaport from where the ferry to Sri Lanka port Thalaimannar is operated throughout the year barring November and December when the sea turns rough.

How to get there?

Rameswaram is connected by train from Madurai and Chennai. It is also connected by road to all towns and bus services from Chennai, Madurai, Coimbatore and Trichy etc. are available. Train services are operated from Rameswaram terminal to Chennai, Madurai, Coimbatore, Trichy and Thanjavur. The main island is connected by the Pamban bridge. The nearest airport is at Madurai (167 km) from where flights are available to Chennai, Coimbatore, Trichy and Sri Lanka.

Places to see in and around Rameswaram

Ramanathaswamy Temple : This temple is the centre of attraction and thousands of pilgrims pour in daily. It is a gem of Dravidian architecture. It is known worldwide for its magnificent corridors running 4000 ft (1220 metres) in length and 30′ in breadth lined by massive sculptured pillars. Figures representing elephants lifting their trunks caught between the paws and fangs of rampant lions, hunters and warriors riding on horses or elephants are favourite themes. The temple was built by Sethupathis, the rulers of

Ramanathapuram district between 1414 A.D. and 1649 A.D.and it has grown in leaps and bounds to the present stage. The statues of Sethupathis line the corridor at the eastern gate before the Nataraja shrine. Some are found in the Kalyana Mandapam too. They are all lifelike in appearance. The gopuram on the east facing the sea front rises to a height of 126 ft. and is 100 metres away from the sea. Devotees bathe in the sea water here which is considered to be sacred and called Agni Theertham. Sacred pools or Theerthams like this are innumerable in Rameswaram and the pilgrims plunge into them with untiring zeal and devotion. The temple is built at the spot where Rama worshipped Lord Siva after slaying the demon Ravana, king of Lanka, who was a great devotee of Siva. In order to worship Siva, Hanuman was sent to Kailas to bring the Lingam. It so happened that Hanuman could not return before the arrival of the auspicious hour; so Sita Herself moulded a Lingam for Rama. When Hanuman arrived later, He was consoled and the Lingam brought by Him was given precedence over Ramanatha and made to worship first before the worship of Ramanatha by the devotees.

Kothandaramaswamy Temple: This Vishnu shrine is located 18 km away on the southern tip of the island called Dhanushkodi. This temple is the only structure that survived the 1964 cyclone which washed away the rest of Dhanushkodi. It can be reached by road from Rameswaram and buses ply to this place. It was the place where Vibishana the brother of Ravana is said to have surrendered to Rama. The temple has beautiful idols of Rama, Sita, Lakshmana, Hanuman and Vishnu. On the very tip of

Dhanushkodi is a sacred pool - a lovely bathing ghat.

The Gandhamathana Parvatham (Hillock) : It is in the north-west of the island and the most elevated point of the island. It is a two-storeyed structure with a ruined fort. Hanuman is said to have leapt from this point across the sea to reach Lanka. The feet of Rama is in the centre of the lower storey. It is also known as Ekantha Rameswaram and contains handsome idols of Rama, Sita and Lakshmana. Here, Rama is seen raising one of His arms. From this elevated place, one can have an excellent view of the whole island.

Coral Reefs : The coral reefs of Rameswaram is another attraction mainly for marine biologists, who throng these islands for research and observation. There are sandy beaches fringed by coconut palms and swaying tamarind trees. A wide variety of sea creatures live in these reefs. The Kurusadai Islands on the west and the Pamban bridge are ideal places of exploration. The Gulf of Mannar has been declared as a bio-sphere reserve and is being developed as an ecologically sensitive area. It is about 20 km from Rameswaram via Mandapam. The permit of the Fisheries Department is necessary to go there.

Adam's Bridge : It is 26 km at the eastern edge of Rameswaram. It is also called Thiruvanai, Adhisethu, Nalasethu and Rama's bridge. This is formed like a bridge between Dhanushkodi and Thalaimannar. It is said that Rama crossed this way with his Vanara sena (army of monkeys) to Lanka. Till 1480 A.D. this was a land route to Lanka. Series of cyclones have washed away the continuous stretch and broken them into islands. Most of them are submerged under 3 to 4 ft water. The sandy banks of these islands quickly change and some may even vanish. There are at present about 19 islands on the route interspersed with gaps the longest of them being 19 km in length. They are called 'Theedai' by the local fishermen. In some of them shrubs can be seen. The depth of the sea here is between 7 ft and 11 ft only. Hence, big boats cannot reach there. Swift sea currents flow in the canals between the islands. This place is full of different varieties of fish and they are being caught only by using small country boats. A lot of birds also can be found here and some varieties of migratory birds too throng here.

Mandapam : It is the end of the mainland from where people have to proceed for the island of Rameswaram either by road, rail or by boat. A boat-ride to Kurusadai Island can be arranged from here. The Indo–Norwegian Fisheries Project is located here. During the colonial period, this was the quarantine camp for passengers proceeding to Ceylon.

Thiruppullani : It is 14 km from Rameswaram. It is a Vishnu shrine. It is also called *Dharbasayanam* as here Rama took rest on a couch of grass. Lord Rama here is seen lying on a couch of grass. Thiruvadanai, Pularanyam, Adhisethu and Ratnaharam are the other names of this place. The presiding deity is Adhi Jagannatha Perumal who was worshipped by Rama before launching His Lanka expedition. The temple has a gopuram and after crossing it one reaches the sanctum of Goddess Padmasini Thayar. A pipal tree is the tree of this place and we can see it behind the sanctum. There are over hundred Nagas (serpents) in stones

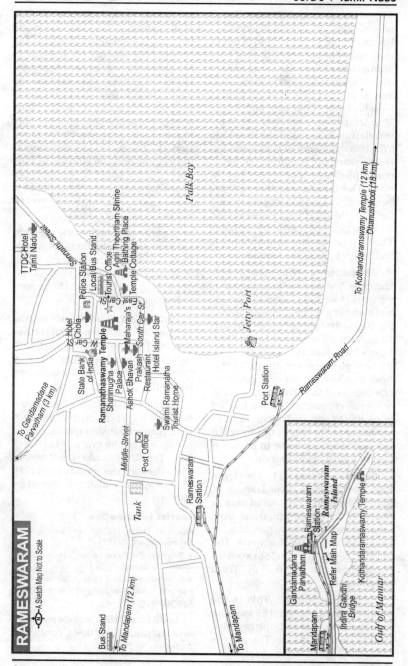

RAMESWARAM

A Sketch Map Not to Scale

Palk Bay

Jetty Port

Port Station

Rameswaram Road

To Kothandaramaswamy Temple (12 km)
Dhanushkodi (18 km)

TTDC Hotel Tamil Nadu

Samiratti Street

Police Station
Local Bus Stand
Tourist Office
Agni Theertham Shrine
Bathing Place
Temple Cottage
East Car St.

Hotel Chola

W Car St.

Maharaja's
South Car St.

Ramanathaswamy Temple
Sharmugha Palace

Ashok Bhavan
Prakash Restaurant

Hotel Island Star

State Bank of-India

To Gandamadana Parvatham (3 km)

Swami Ramanatha Tourist Home

Middle Street

Post Office

Tank

Rameswaram Station

To Mandapam (12 km)

Bus Stand
To Mandapam

To Mandapam

Rameswaram Island

Rameswaram Station

Gandamadana Parvatham

Refer Main Map

Rameswaram Station

Kothandaramaswamy Temple

Mandapam

Indira Gandhi Bridge

Gulf of Mannar

around the tree. After this, one has to go to the sanctum of Adhi Jagannatha. Following this is the sanctum of Rama lying on the grass couch, three stems of lotus branch from His naval and on each of them are seated Brahma, Siva and Moon. At the feet of Rama, Sugabrahmar, Charapar and Brigu Maharishis are seated. In the mandapam is a sculpture in which Vibishana, the king of Lanka and his Devi worship Vishnu. It is a masterpiece which no tourist should miss. The temple was built by the Pandyas, Vanadhirayas and Sethupathis. Life-size statues of Sethupathis could also been seen here. Those who do the pilgrimage to Rameswaram visit the temple too.

Devipattinam : This place is also known as *Navapashanam*. This coastal village is 15 km from Ramanathapuram and there is a temple here dedicated to Devi. It is the place where Mahishasura was slayed by Goddess Durga Devi. Rama is said to have set up stones here for the planets. Besides, there are two temples here, one dedicated to Thilakesava and the other to Jagannatha. The beach is full of multicoloured shells and corals of varied forms thrown by the waves of the sea. Hence, it came to be called also as Ratnakara Kshetram.

Ervadi : It is 21 km from Ramanathapuram. The Dargah of Ibrahim Syed Aulia is located here. It is visited by Muslim pilgrims from other states and countries like Sri Lanka, Malaysia and Singapore. The annual festival is celebrated in December. It is 8 km from Keezhakarai.

Ramanathapuram : This is the district headquarters and 55 km from Rameswaram. The Sethupathis ruled their territory from here. This place is

also known as Sethupeetam. A fort is at the centre of this town and inside the fort is Ramalinga Vilasam, the palace of the Sethupathis. It is built in Moorish style with Byzantine arches. Murals of historic scenes adorn the walls. Inside is a crude platform surrounded by a square block of stone on which the first Sethupathi is said to have been crowned by Sri Rama Himself. The successors sat there as the viceroys of Rama. The tomb of the philosopher-saint Thayumanava Swamigal is also in the town. Both the palace and the tomb are worth visiting.

Kanchirankulam : This is about 44 km from Ramanathapuram. A water-bird sanctuary is located here. Migratory water fowls from far-off places visit this place from November to February.

Valinokkam : It is a seaside village, around 30 km from Ramanatha-puram. The beach is verdant with natural scenery. The sea here is very calm. It is an ideal location for sea bathing.

Nayinar Koil : It is 46 km from Ramanathapuram on the western side. A dumb Muslim girl recovered her speech by the grace of Lord Siva here. The Muslims call Him Nayinar–'Father', hence the name Nayinar Koil. This temple is hailed and visited by Muslims.

Tourist Information

● Tourist Office (TTDC), 14 East Car St, Rameswaram. ✆: 221371

● Tourism Information Centre (TTDC), Railway Station Compound. ✆ : 221373

● Temple Information Centre, inside the temple, east side, Ramanathaswamy temple. ✆ : 221246

SHOPPING

Local handicrafts include sea-shell articles, palm leaf articles, corals and conches.

Where to stay?

Rameswaram (STD : 04573)

* **Shriram Hotel Island Star**, 41-A, South Car Street ✆ 221472 Fax : 04573- 239932
* **Hotel Shanmuga Paradise**, 10/98, Middle Street ✆ 222984 / 222945
* **Hotel Tamil Nadu**, Agnitheertham, Rameswaram. ✆ 221064 - 67. Fax : 04573-221070
* **Hotel Aishwarya,** ✆ 225457
* **Hotel Blue Diamond,** ✆ 220671
* **Hotel Royal Park**, Semma Madam ✆ 221680 Fax : 04573 - 221680

Festivals in Rameswaram

Thai Amavasai - January

Maha Shivarathri - February-March

Thirukalyanam - (July-August)

Mahalaya Amavasai - (September)

Thoothukudi
(The Gateway of Tamil Nadu)

Tuticorin is properly called Thoothukudi in Tamil. As Mumbai is the Gateway of India, Thoothukudi is the Gateway of Tamil Nadu. It is a major seaport in India. It is also called *Pearl City* as pearl fishing is a major occupation and the oysters yield a fine quality of pearl. It is a major industrial centre too. SPIC fertilizer plant, a heavy water plant, a thermal power station, chemical factories etc. are all located here. It is also a major salt producing centre in Tamil Nadu. It was made into a new district from Tirunelveli and is the district headquarters. It is 48 km from Tirunelveli.

How to get there?

It is linked to Tirunelveli by road and rail. From Chennai you can reach by train directly to Thoothukudi. Thoothukudi is also linked to other places by road. It will be convenient to visit all the places in this district by making Tirunelveli as the headquarters and staying there one can visit all the places around Tirunelveli and Thoothukudi.

Tiruchendur : It is around 40 km from Thoothukudi and can be reached by train and by buses. It is the most important tourist attraction in Thoothukudi district. It is one of the six abodes of Lord Muruga called Arupadai Veedu. Of them, this is the only one standing on level ground, the others are on hills or elevated places. It is the place where Lord Muruga offered His thanksgiving prayers to His father Lord Siva for gaining victory over the demon Surapadman by slaying him. The temple is on the edge of the sea and the main deity has been cut on a rock lying on the shores. The idol of the Urchavar or festival-deity is kept in a separate shrine facing the opposite direction. This idol was recovered from the sea by a local chief called Vadamalai and installed there. The silver vessels presented to the shrine by the erstwhile collector of this district, Lushington expose the devotion of foreigners too. Kumarakuruparar (17th century A.D.) the famous saint and poet who was originally dumb got his power of speech in this temple and sung hymns on the deity.

Srivaikuntam and Alwar Tiru-nagari : These two Vaishnavite shrines are on the way to Tiruchendur from Tirunelveli. Srivaikuntam is also known as Kailasapuram and has in the Nataraja shrine, 8 artistically carved pillars. The most famous is the Kallapiran, the festival- deity and the presiding deity is called Vaikuntanatha. On the 6th day of the Tamil month Chitthirai (April), the sun rays fall on the main deity as token of worship. The idol is most exquisitely carved with club in hand. Lions, Yalis and Elephants are carved in the pillars of the mandapam. The temple served as a fort during the patriotic war of Kattabomman with the British.

In the north of the town is a mud enclosure of 10 ft high running round with a gate in the middle. The women of this fort never stir beyond the wall. The outside world is sealed for them. Kattai pillaimars as they are called never marry outside their clan.

Nava Tirupatis : The nine holy shrines of Vishnu called Navathiruppatis are in this district. Thiruvaikundam, Thiruvaraguna-mangai, Thiruppulingudi, Thirukkulandai, Thirutholaivilli Mangalam, South Thirupperai, Thirukkolur, Alwar Thirunagari are their names. The Sri Aravinda Lochana sanctum in Thiruvaikuntam is also counted as one Tirupati. Thus, the Nava Tirupatis are near one another in this district.

Panchalamkurichi : It is 54 km from Tirunelveli and 3 km from Ottappidaram. It is the home of the patriot Kattabomman, a 17th century freedom fighter. The original fort of Kattabomman is now in ruins and under the custody of Archaeological Survey of India. The Kattabomman memorial fort was constructed in Panchalamkurichi by the Government of Tamil Nadu in 1974. Near the fort is the temple of Jakkamma, the family deity of Kattabomman. A cemetery of British soldiers too is found near the fort. Ottappidaram is the birthplace of V.O.Chidambaram Pillai, the freedom fighter of the pre-Gandhian era. Kayatharu is the place where Kattabomman was hanged to death by the British. There is a Vishnu temple in this place.

Ettaiyapuram : The birthplace of the national poet Bharathiar. Ettaiyapuram is 71 km from Tirunelveli. Here, Manimandapam is constructed for Bharathiyar. There is also a memorial for Bharathiyar. His patriotic songs aroused the Tamilians from slumber and made them conscious of the evils of foreign dominators and inspired them to fight relentlessly for freedom.

Kazhugumalai : It is 76 km from Tirunelveli and 24 km from Sankaran Koil. A huge rock has been shaped into a shrine here. The unique feature is, the temple instead of rising from the foundations has been chiselled from the top. This temple is called Vettuvar Koil by the local people. Two friezes of ganas (demons) line the front porch. Even the tiniest of them has received full attention from the sculptor. A musical soiree of these ganas is portrayed, one playing a musical instrument, another dancing etc.

The top of the vimana (tower over the sanctum) of any temple could be appreciated from a distance but here it is topsy-turvy. It is octagonal and embellished with lion heads. Four vimana deities, Siva and Parvathi in the east, Dakshinamurthi in the south, Narasimha in the west and Brahma on lotus in the north, are the peaks of art. Lord Dakshinamurthi here is unique playing a mirudangam (drum), which cannot be seen anywhere. The image of Lord Siva holding a Naga displays His 'Vishabarana' aspect. The cobra seems to wriggle out of His hold - so lifelike! Nearby is a big rock containing Jain figures like Tirthankaras, Yakshas and Yakshinis. These Jain temples are among the oldest in the country and the bas-relief sculptures mentioned above are excellent pieces of art.

Manappadu : This place is 71 km from Tirunelveli on the shores of the Bay of Bengal. There is a 400-year-old Holy Cross Church here. Some fragments of the True Cross from

Jerusalem are enshrined here. It is one of the churches connected with St. Francis Xavier.

Where to stay?
Thoothukudi (STD : 0461)
• Danam ✆ 2325382
• Geetha International ✆ 2346174
• Hotel Geetha ✆ 2346174
• Hotel Suma ✆ 2324590

Tirunelveli
(The Cradle of the Dravidian Civilization)

Tirunelveli district in the south is really the cradle of the Dravidian civilization, supported by the excavations of Adichanallur. The burial urns discovered here proclaim the antiquity of this region made fertile by the Thamirabarani river. The Tamil hill called Podiyamalai is on the western border with evergreen vegetation. It is the abode of Agastya who is said to be the father of Tamil Grammar. Even Buddhists make a claim to this hill calling it Bodhi Malai which was later corrupted as Podhiamalai. They argue it was the seat of Avalokideswara and go to the extreme that Potala of Tibet took its name only from Podhikai. It was the land of the Pandyas, so Pandya art and architecture and cave temples abound in this district. The district headquarters is Tirunelveli.

Tirunelveli stands on the banks of Thamirabarani river. Its history goes back to the Sangam Age and beyond it to pre-historic times. It is now the headquarters of the district and the 6th major city of Tamil Nadu.

How to get there?

Tirunelveli is well connected by road with all the towns of Tamil Nadu, Chennai, Madurai, Trichy, Coimbatore and Kanyakumari. It is a major junction on the Southern Railway and has rail connections to all important places in the country. The nearest airport is at Madurai in Tamil Nadu, 157 kms from Tirunelveli. Flights are available to Coimbatore, Trichy and Chennai. Umpteen bus services are available to all the places of tourist importance in the district and the neighbouring district of Thoothukudi which formed part of this district before it was formed as a new district.

Places to see in and around Tirunelveli

Tirunelveli City : The city is situated on the banks of the river Thamirabarani. There is a legend to the name of the place. Vedasarma an ardent devotee of Lord Siva went to bathe in the river after spreading paddy in the open space to dry. As he was bathing, a heavy downpour came and Vedasarma simply prayed Lord Venuvana Nathar and after his bath went back. To his surprise not a drop of rain had fallen on the paddy. All the rain poured avoiding the paddy that was put to dry. As the Lord guarded the paddy like a fence (veli) the place got the name Tirunelveli (nel-paddy) and the God came to be known as Nellaiyappar. The twin temple of Kanthimathi (Goddess) and Nellaiyappar is the main attraction in the city. The gopuram was built in 1606 A.D. The Nandhi idol in stucco is huge as at Rameswaram. There are 46 musical pillars in the mandapam. The sculptures here are delicately carved — Yalis (lion-headed elephant), Purushamirugas (half human and half animal forms), the Pandavas and Anjaneya (Monkey God) are some shining examples. The Thamira (copper) Sabha (hall) is nicely adorned with wood carvings. The beautiful bridge across the river was modelled after the Waterloo bridge on the river Thames and stands on two arches. Dalavai (General) Arianatha Mudaliar designed the town and built a fort at Palayamkottai.

Krishnapuram: The Krishnapuram temple dedicated to Vishnu lies about 13 km from Tirunelveli and should not be missed by lovers of art. As there are Belur and Halebid in Karnataka and Tadpatri and Lepakshi in Andhra to boast of the art and architecture, Tamil Nadu has Krishnapuram to brag. This temple dedicated to Lord Venkatachalapathi is filled with sculptural beauties of excellent workmanship. Krishnappa Nayak (1563-73) a connoisseur of art has built this edifice of beauty. The Ranga Mandapam is a theatre of arts. Mythological scenes are beautifully portrayed with expressions suiting the moods in which they are captured. Even contemporary social life is not left out. A gypsy woman with a child on her back while a toy is held before it by a man to keep it from crying, a Korava kidnapping a princess, being rescued by the prince wounding the Korava in the encounter and the wound profusely bleeding are examples. One wonders how the red tint of the gushing blood was introduced within the sculpture! Unlike Belur with its dwarf-like figures, here the figures are of life-size carved with intricate delicacy.

Sankarankovil : It is 56 km north of Tirunelveli. The Sankara Narayanan temple is famous here. A fusion of two faiths Saivism and Vaishnavism is aimed at in this temple by presenting an image combining both aspects. The right half has all the symbols of Siva, deer, cobra, moon etc. while the left half has all the symbols of Vishnu like Chakra, conch etc. There are fine paintings in the 'Prakarams' (corridors). Goddess Gomathi's penance called 'Adi Thapasu Vizha' and the car festival celebrated in June-July attract nearly 3 lakhs people to this place. Sankarankovil is connected by road and rail to important places in the state. The nearest places are Tirunelveli, Thoothukudi, Tenkasi, Kovilpatti, Srivilliputhur and Madurai.

Kuttalam Waterfalls : Kuttalam 59 km from Tirunelveli is the *"spa of the south,"* situated at an elevation of 170 metres, on the western ghats. Besides being a tourist spot, this is also a health resort. The waters of Courtallam has therapeutic value to cure physical ailments as the water flows through a herbal forest. During the season (June to September) thousands of tourists from far and near visit this place. There are nine waterfalls here: 1) Main falls, 2) Chitraruvi, 3) Shenbagadevi falls, 4) Thenaruvi (thèn–honey, aruvi– waterfalls), 5) Aindharuvi (five falls), 6) orchard falls, 7) New falls, 8) Tiger falls and 9) Old Kuttalam falls.

The place itself is picturesque with a mountainous backdrop (6000 ft). The main fall is formed by Chithra Nadhi dropping 300 ft down a precipice, a trough called Pangimangodal, then falls out into beautiful cascades for the visitors to bathe. Cloud capped peaks, inspiring temples, evergreen and lush verdure, salubrious climate, snow-white waterfalls and their gurgling noise with the chirping of birds, rare fruits mangosteen and durian make this place a paradise on earth. The rain too is not torrential here but a soothing drizzle called 'saral'. Drenching in saral combined with the cool breeze braces the body.

The deity of the temple is called 'Kutralanathar' and the stunted jackfruit tree is the tree of the temple. Therefore, he is also called "Kurumpala Easar". The Lingam of this temple is carved on the face of a rock. The temple is called *Chitra Sabha* - 'Chitram' means paintings – and the Chitra Sabha (hall) contains a number of mural paintings of rural deities and episodes from epics. The sabha is one of the five sabhas where

Nataraja performed His cosmic dance. Chitra Sabha is made of medicinal herbs. The wooden carved door itself is a wonder. The painting of Lord Nataraja is another marvel.

Tenkasi : Tenkasi means Dakshina Kasi – Varanasi of the south. Pandya king Paranthaga Pandiyan after his return from the Benaras created this temple dedicated to Viswanatha and called it Tenkasi. The inscriptions of this king reveal his spiritual ardour and his concern for future maintenance. The temple for a very long time had its gopuram damaged by lightning but now it has been completely renovated. There are beautiful sculptures in the temple besides a flag staff 400 years old. It is 53 kms from Tirunelveli and 7 kms from Kuttalam.

Thirumalaiappan Pozhil : 15 km from Courtallam is this beautiful temple dedicated to Lord Muruga atop of a hill rock.

Thirumalaipuram : It is 6.4 km from Kadayanallur (16 kms from Tenkasi). There is a rock-cut temple here with Ganesa, Vishnu and dancing Siva. The dance of Siva here is different from the usual types - in chatura pose, with His right hand thrown in a 'Mirgasirsha' attitude. A dwarf near His feet plays the instrument called Chandala Vallaki (something like veena). Murals in the ceiling are badly damaged.

Kalakadu Wildlife Sanctuary: It is around 42 km from Tirunelveli. This is renowned for its flora and fauna. Botanists and ornithologists throng this area. Tiger, panther, jackal, wild dogs, cobra, python and several snakes and other reptiles, the lion-tailed monkey—all could be sighted in the thick forest. The best season is between March and September. The temple near Kalakadu has 16 musical pillars.

Shengaltheri : It is located in the Kalakadu mountain area. It is 20km from Kalakadu village and 68km from Tirunelveli. It is in the area of wildlife sanctuary. It is an important picnic spot and also popular for its natural scenery and salubrious climate. There is also a perennial waterfalls. There is a rest house and a watch-tower. Manimutharu originates from this place. There is also a P.W.D. inspection bungalow near the bus stop. This place is connected to all important pilgrim and tourist centres by road. The nearest railway station is Valliyur. For going there, prior permission of the Deputy Director of Wildlife, Ambasamudram, Mundanthurai and Kalakadu Wildlife Sanctuary is necessary.

Pattamadai : This hamlet 13 km from Tirunelveli is renowned for weaving mats of korai grass. One can see the beautiful korai mat manufacturing unit here. Some of the mats can be folded like cloth. This is also the birthplace of Swami Sivanandha.

Thirukkurungudi : It is located in the western ghats about 52 km south of Tirunelveli. It is one of the 108 divine Vishnu shrines. It is also known as *Vamana Kshetram*. The temple is spread over 18 acres. It is dedicated to Azhagiya Nambi and shelters splendid sculptures. The images of Varuna, Dakshinamurthi, Vamana, and Gajendra Moksha are best specimens. A lady's horror at seeing a scorpion makes the heart flutter. Generally, Lord Vishnu in any shrine can be seen only in one of the forms, standing, sitting or lying. But here, He is seen in five forms as Standing Nambi, Sitting Nambi, Lying Nambi, Parkadal Nambi and Thirumalai Nambi. There is a sanctum for Siva also in the temple exposing the Saivaite-Vaishnavaite unity. There are more than 90 vatteluthu inscriptions in this temple. The temple is surrounded by tall granite walls. It has been sanctified by four Alwars in Nalayira Divya Prapandham.

Koonthankulam Bird Sanctuary: It is situated 33 km south of Tirunelveli in Nanguneri taluk. It is a small and beautiful village of natural scenery. It is covered with natural forests and ponds. During the season from January to April, more than 10,000 birds from various countries like Pakistan, Myanmar, Sri Lanka, U.S.A. and Australia migrate to this place. Daily over 5000 people come here to watch them. Ariyankulam is another bird sanctuary 13 km east of Tirunelveli.

Shenbagaramanallur : It is near Nanguneri and the temple here has a stone pillar with a conical bore in the centre about a foot long. When blown from one end which is bigger the sound of a conch and from the smaller end the sound of an ekkalam (a long pipe-like musical instrument) is produced. The sculpture in the Vishnu temple is marvellous, each image producing a musical note when struck. The sculptor's dexterity is revealed in the nerves and nails of the sculpture. It is astonishing that even these things could be produced in stone.

Thiruvalliswaram : It is on the Tirunelveli-Ambasamudram (35 km) road and contains many exquisite images. On the upper tier, the figure of Nataraja is a feast for the eyes. The sway of His dress in the whirl of His dance, the locks crowning His head, His slender waist of a dancer are all brought out skilfully by the sculptor. Gangadhara, Dakshinamurthi and Ardhanari images too enchant us.

Cheranmadevi : It is 22 km from Tirunelveli on the Tiruchendur M.G. railway line. There are eight beautiful shrines here. Of them, the Milagupillayar shrine is the most famous and unique too. When the water level in the village channel

drops, pepper paste is plastered over the idol and lo! miraculously enough, the water overflows.

Papanasam : It is located 49 km from Tirunelveli. The famous Siva temple is located at the bottom of the western ghats and also very near to the origin of river Thamirabarani. Every year, the Chitthirai Vishu festival is celebrated in the month of April and another festival Adi Amavasai is celebrated in July. About 2 lakhs people congregate at these festivals. It is also a picnic spot.

Kalyana Theertham : It is reached after a strenuous trek of 24 km through the wilds. The river cascades into a drop of 125 feet vertically. This falls is the Papanasam waterfalls. There is a pool of the falls. This is called Kalyana Theertham. Near the pool is a temple dedicated to Lord Siva.

Pana Theertham : The river Thamirabarani originates and commences its course from Pana Theertham. It is located just opposite to the upper dam. One has to reach this place crossing the dam by boat. During festival days, local tourists around Papanasam will visit this place.

Agasthiyar Temple and Falls : This temple adjoining the falls named Agasthiyar Falls is located half way to the Pana Theertham which is 4 km from Papanasam Siva temple. One can reach the falls and the temple by trekking 3 km. Regular buses are available to these temples.

Upper Kodaiyar and Manjolai: This is a quiet hill station in the western ghats about 6000 ft. above sea level. Manjolai is the nearby town and an ideal summer resort. It is 50 km from Ambasamudram (35 km from Tirunelveli). The hill station may also be reached from Nagercoil. One can reach lower Kodaiyar by winch. There is also a road from Balmore to upper Kodaiyar. The hill resort with panoramic views is a tourist's heaven. Oothu and Kuthiraivetti are excellent viewpoints. The guest-house of the Travancore royal family located here is called "Muthukuzhi Vayal". The approach road begins from Manimutharu and Ambasamudram to Kodaiyar Manjolai. Regular bus services are available from Manimutharu and Ambasamudram.

Mundanthurai Wildlife Sanctuary : This sanctuary is situated 42 km from Tirunelveli. It is mainly a tiger reserve forest. Anyhow one is likely to see other animals like leopard, sambar, sloth bear, cheetah and a wide variety of Indian primates including bonnet macaque, common langur, Nilgiri langur and lion-tailed macaque. The best time to visit is between October and January. The sanctuary lies on the mountains verging Kerala. The nearest railway station is Ambasamudram from where regular bus services are operated. Since, tigers are likely to be seen only in the very early morning or late evening, a stay for the night is essential. The forest department will arrange to take tourists round the sanctuary. There is a forest rest house for accommodation that could be reserved earlier.

Ovari Paravnattam : It is a village on the shores of the Bay of Bengal on the way to Tiruchendur from Kanyakumari in Tirunelveli district, 45 km from Kanyakumari, around 38 km from Tiruchendur and 72 km from Tirunelveli. Nadar Uvari is famous for Swayambulingaswamy Siva temple. 3 important festivals are held here every year. Bharatha Uvari is a Roman Catholic Centre where one can see an ancient church as well as a modern church. The structure of the modern church is like that of an aeroplane. The annual festival falls in mid-January attracting over 2 lakh pilgrims.

Aathankarai Pallivasal : This pallivasal is between Tiruchendur and Kanyakumari coastal road in Tirunelveli district. It is 30 km from Valliyur. There are two tombs belonging to 2 sufi saints Syed Ali Fathima and Hazarath Sheik Mohammed. It is a pilgrim centre for all faiths. More than 50,000 visit during the festival held in September.

Places of worship

Temples: Kanthimathi Nellaiyappar temple, Tirunelveli; Salaikumaraswamy temple, Tirunelveli Junction; Subramanyaswamy temple, Kurukkuthurai.

Churches : C.S.I. Church and Roman Catholic Church.

Mosque : One in the town and the other near Tirunelveli Junction.

Shopping Centres in Tirunelveli and Thoothukudi Districts

Poompuhar Handicrafts Emporium, S.N.High Road, Tirunelveli Junction.

Khadi and Village Bamboo Industries, Sengottai.

Bell Metal Industries, Vagaikulam, Ambasamudram taluk.

Mat Knitting Industries, Pattamadai and Kayathar.

Terracotta Industries, Thenpothai in Tenkasi taluk.

Nellai Super Market, S.N.High Road, Tirunelveli Junction.

Important Private Travel Agencies
• Standard Cabs, S.N. High Road, Tirunelveli. ✆: 2337666
• Ambika Cabs, Trivandrum Road, Vannarapettai, Palayamkottai. ✆: 576664
• Regaul Travels, Madurai Road, Tirunelveli Junction. ✆: 2339172
• Air King Travels, S.N.High Road, Tirunelveli Jn. ✆: 2334846
• Southern Cars, 697, Trivandrum Road. ✆: 2502626, 2502633
• Venus Cabs, 75, Madurai Road, ✆ 2331931
• Professional cabs, Madurai Road, Tirunelveli Jn. ✆ : 2331627

Where to stay?

Tirunelveli (STD : 0462)

- **Sri Janakiram Hotels,** 30, Madurai Road, ℂ 2331941
- **Pleasant Stay Hotels P. Ltd.,** 11-K, Thomas Road, ℂ 2577855
- **Hotel Tamil Nadu,** Collectorate Complex, Kokkirakulam, ℂ 2582200
- **Hotel Sakunthala International,** 5C/3, Trivandrum Road, Vannarpet. ℂ 2580769
- **Hotel Seethalakshmi,** A1, St. Thomas Road, Maharaja Nagar, ℂ 2572740
- **Syed Tourist Home,** 108, Madurai Road, ℂ 2333304
- **Gomathi Mills Rest House,** 18th Cross Street, Maharaja Nagar, ℂ 2577993

Important Silk Emporiums

R.M.K.V. Cloth Merchants, North Car Street, Tirunelveli Town. ℂ : 2333105

Pothy's Cloth Merchants, North Car Street, Tirunelveli Town.

Nalli Silk House, S.N.High Rd., Tirunelveli Town.

Ganthimathi Co-optex, Raja Building, Near bus stand, Tirunelveli Junction.

D.Arumugampillai Cloth Merchants, East Great Cotton Road, Thoothukudi.

Abirami Textiles, East Great Cotton Road, Near Sivan Koil, Thoothukudi.

Seematti Textiles, East Great Cotton Road, Thoothukudi.

Important Festivals in Thoothukudi and Tirunelveli Districts

JANUARY: Pongal Tourist Festival.

FEBRUARY: R.C. Church Car Festival at Uvari.

APRIL: Papanasam Chitthirai Vishu Festival.

MAY: Veerapandia Kattabomman Vizha - Panchalamkurichi.

JUNE: Lord Murugan Temple Car Festival at Tiruchendur, Kazhugumalai and Thirumalaiappan pozhil.

JULY: Saaral Thiruvizha, Courtallam.

Nellaiyappar Ganthimathi Car Festival - Tirunelveli.

Adi Thapasu Festival - Sankarankoil.

Govt. Exhibition at Tirunelveli.

AUGUST: Adi Amavasai Festival at Papanasam.

SEPTEMBER: World Tourism Day at Tirunelveli.

Pottal Pudur - Mask Sandanakoodu Festival.

OCTOBER: Tiruchendur Lord Muruga Temple Kandasashti Festival.

Aathankarai Pallivasal Mask Sandhanakoodu Festival.

NOVEMBER: Kulasekarappattinam Dhasara Vizha.

DECEMBER: Kurukkuthurai - Tirunelveli Junction Karthigai Deepa Thiru Vizha.

Important Hospitals

- **Tirunelveli Medical College Hospital,** High Ground Road, Palayamkottai. ℂ 2572911/733
- **Melapalayam Govt. Hospital,** Melapalayam, ℂ 2352514.
- **Tirunelveli Corporation Hospital - Women & Children,** Kandyaperi. ℂ 2333326.
- **Pushpalatha Hospital,** Palayamkottai, ℂ 2580237.
- **Little Flower Health Care,** Palayamkottai, ℂ 2577675.
- **Rose Children Hospital,** Tisayanvillai. ℂ 2272962.
- **Sundaram Arulraj Hospitals,** Perumalpuram. ℂ 2322661.

Clubs

Rotary Club, High Ground Road, Palayamkottai.

Lions Club, S.N. High Road, Tirunelveli Jn.

Innerwheel (Ladies Club), Ganapathi Mills Compound, Vannarapettai, Palayamkottai.

District Club, High Ground Road, Palayamkottai.

Important Money Changers

State Bank of India and other nationalised and scheduled banks are transacting foreign exchange.

Note : Foreigners are advised to get their currency forms endorsed by the money changers at the time of exchanging their currency.

Important Banks

- State Bank of India, S.N. High Road, Tirunelveli Junction.
- Canara Bank, Raja Buildings, New Bus Stand, Tirunelveli Junction.
- Indian Bank, Near Bus Stand, Madurai Road, Tirunelveli Junction.
- State Bank of Travancore, S.N.High Road, Tirunelveli Junction.
- Union Bank of India, S.N. High Road, Tirunelveli Junction.
- Indian Overseas Bank, Near Super Market Building, Madurai Road, Tirunelveli Junction.
- Central Co-operative Bank, Vannarapettai, Palayamkottai.

Posts & Telegraphs

● Head Post Office and Telegraph Office, S.N. High Road, Tirunelveli Jn.
● R.M.S. Post Office, Railway Station, Tirunelveli.

Important Auditoriums and Marriage Halls

● Sangeetha Sabha, Kailasapuram, Tirunelveli Junction.
● Municipal Kalyana Mandapam, Near Palayamkottai Bus Stand.
● Rose Mahal Marriage Hall, Near Science Centre, Kokkirakulam.
● Raj Mahal Marriage Hall.

Kanyakumari

(The Confluence of A Sea, An Ocean and A Bay)

Kanyakumari is the land's end and at the confluence of the Bay of Bengal, Indian Ocean and the Arabian Sea. On full moon days, one could see the moonrise and sunset at the same hour. The full moon day in the month of Chitthirai (April-May) is the best time, since on that day the sunset and moon-rise take place when the sun and moon are face to face in a straight line along the horizon. It is the tip of the Indian peninsula and its antiquity goes to pre-Himalayan days. Actually, it is the residual part of the lost Lemuria which extended up to Africa and Australia. So, the rocks are geologically the oldest of their kind. It was ruled by the Pandyas and later, parts of it were in Kerala and after the reorganisation of the states, all the Tamil speaking areas were seceded and the district was formed in 1956. Natural vegetation abounds on the western side and the eastern side is a fertile plain. It has 68 km length of sandy seashore rich in atomic minerals. The sands of the beach are of different hues due to the mineral content. It is the meeting place of Tamil and Malayalam and

even Tamil is spoken differently, like Malayalam with nasalized accent. As it is surrounded on three sides by sea, it enjoys a temperate climate. Besides, it is a major pilgrim centre with a heavy floating population.

How to get there?

Kanyakumari is connected with Tirunelveli, Chennai, Thiruvananthapuram and Coimbatore by broad gauge railway. Tirunelveli (83 km) is connected to Chennai, Madurai etc.

It is well connected to almost all the towns in India by road. The nearest airport is Thiruvananthapuram (87 km) from where flights are available to Coimbatore, Madurai, Bengalooru, Chennai and Mumbai. Local buses are available to all the places of tourist attraction in the district.

In Kanyakumari

Kanyakumari Amman Temple: This temple is associated with the Goddess Parvathi doing a penance for the arrival of Her consort Siva to claim Her hand in marriage. She is doing the penance daily and at the same time guarding the country. There is another legend on the diamond nose stud of the Goddess which misguided many a ship with its lustre resulting in a tragedy with the ships hitting the submerged rocks. Hence, the door on the side facing the sea has been closed for ever. This Devi in Her fiercest aspect killed Banasura and in the Tamil month of Purattasi (September-October) during the festival, a drama of this event is enacted. The virgin Goddess Kanyakumari is standing with a rosary in Her hand bestowing benediction.

Gandhi Memorial : There is a memorial mandapam to the Father of the Nation, Mahatma Gandhi, erected on the place where his ashes were kept for public homage before being immersed at the confluence of the

3 seas. There is an architectural brilliance in the construction that it has been so designed that the rays of the sun fall on the same spot where the urn was kept exactly, on the 2nd of October every year i.e. on the birthday of Mahatma.

Thiruvalluvar Statue : The 133 feet tall stone sculpture of the Tamil saint and poet Tiruvalluvar is located atop a small island near the town of Kanyakumari, where the three oceans, the Bay of Bengal, the Indian Ocean and the Arabic Sea meet.

Kamaraj Manimandapam : The memorial of K.Kamarajar, former chief minister of Tamil Nadu is situated on the seashore, where the ashes of the late leader was immersed. The memorial contains the photographs narrating the life and services of the great leader.

Vivekananda Memorial : The Vivekananda Memorial has been built on the Vivekananda Rock, so called because Vivekananda used to swim to the rock and meditate there hours together during his sojourn at Kanyakumari. It is one of the two rocks jutting out of the ocean and providing the visitors a view of the land's end of India.

The memorial is a blend of all the styles of the Indian architecture and was completed in 1970. A statue of Swami Vivekananda is installed. Ferry services are available to go to the memorial from 7 a.m. to 11 a.m. and from 2 p.m. to 5 p.m.

Close to it is another rock called *Sripadaparai* with the footprint of the Goddess who guards India from the southern tip. Both these rocks offer a good view of the land's end.

On this rock, a memorial to Thiruvalluvar, the unmatched poet-saint who gave to the world his immortal work, Thirukkural, which shows a right path for leading a good life, has been erected. The statue is made of a titanesque size rising 133 ft. which is a world wonder of this millennium. The statue was unveiled on January 1, 2000 A.D.

Guganathaswami Temple : This temple built by Rajaraja Chola I is about 1000 years old. The Siva Lingam at the sanctum sanctorum of this temple is 1.4 metre high. It is near the railway station.

Vivekananda Kendra : It sprang up after the Vivekananda Memorial in a spacious area of over 100 acres. Its aim is to give a practical shape to Swami Vivekananda's message of service. The headquarters is named Vivekanandapuram. It is a spiritual retreat and a centre of service to humanity.

Government Museum : The Government Museum is near the Transit Office, Beach Road. It contains bronzes, tribal articles, wood carvings and zoological and botanical specimens. The Samythoppu temple car is also exhibited. A whale's bone obtained from Manavalakurichi is another attraction.

Timings : 9.30 a.m. to 5.00 p.m.

Holiday : Fridays & Second Saturdays.

Entrance fee : Re.1 for Adults, 0.50 N.P. for Children and 0.25 N.P. for School Children.

Around Kanyakumari

Suchindram : It is 13 km from Kanyakumari. The famous Thanu-Mal - Ayan (Siva, Vishnu, Brahma) temple is located here. The temple has a 7 tier gopuram, from the top of it the cape is clearly visible. There is a musical pillar inside the temple. The temple corridors are second only to Rameswaram in magnificence. Inscriptions belonging to 9th century A.D. could be seen in the temple. Two chief attractions are the giant size Statue of Hanuman (Monkey God)

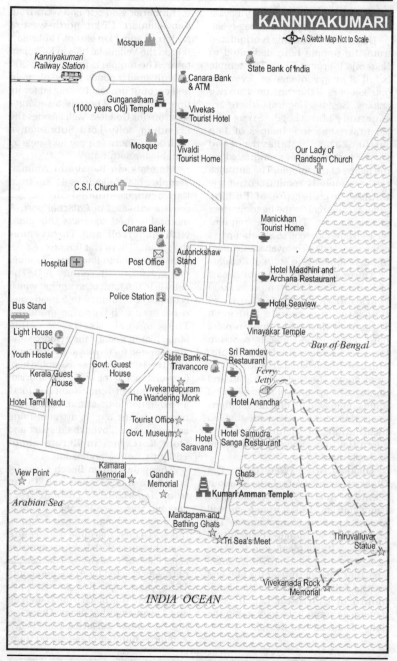

KANNIYAKUMARI

A Sketch Map Not to Scale

Mosque

Kannniyakumari
Railway Station

Gunganatham
(1000 years Old) Temple

Mosque

C.S.I. Church

Canara Bank

Hospital

Post Office

Police Station

Bus Stand

Light House

TTDC
Youth Hostel

Kerala Guest
House

Hotel Tamil Nadu

Govt. Guest
House

State Bank of
Travancore

Vivekandapuram
The Wandering Monk

Tourist Office

Govt. Museum

Hotel
Saravana

Kamaraj
Memorial

View Point

Gandhi
Memorial

Arabian Sea

State Bank of India

Canara Bank
& ATM

Vivekas
Tourist Hotel

Vivaldi
Tourist Home

Our Lady of
Randsom Church

Manickhan
Tourist Home

Autorickshaw
Stand

Hotel Maadhini and
Archana Restaurant

Hotel Seaview

Vinayakar Temple

Bay of Bengal

Sri Ramdev
Restaurant

Ferry
Jetty

Hotel Anandha

Hotel Samudra.
Sanga Restaurant

Ghata

Kumari Amman Temple

Mandapam and
Bathing Ghats

Tri Sea's Meet

Thiruvalluvar
Statue

Vivekanada Rock
Memorial

INDIA OCEAN

rising 25 ft. and the statue of Vinayaki (female form of Vinayaka) as bas-relief.

Nagercoil : The name is originated from the temple here dedicated to Nagaraja (Serpent God). The temple is full of images of snakes. Even the gate keepers of the sanctums are two snakes. Besides Nagaraja, there are sanctums for Lord Siva and Anantakrishna too. Images of Jain Tirthankaras, Mahavira and Parswanatha are seen engraved on the pillars of the temple. The entrance to the temple is reminiscent of the Chinese architecture of Buddha Vihara. Nagercoil is the headquarters of the district. There are frequent buses from Nagercoil to all other parts of the state and to Thiruvananthapuram in the neighbouring state of Kerala.

Thirupathisaram : It is north-east of Nagercoil and the temple is 5000 years old. King Kulasekara has renovated this temple and even Thirumalai Nayak has done repairs here. There is no separate sanctum for the Goddess in this temple. Thiruvazhimarpan (Vishnu) is the chief deity. The idol is 9 ft. tall and made of a special element called Kadusamagayogam and no ablutions are performed to it. Dasavathara (Ten incarnations of Vishnu) paintings adorn the Indra Kalyana Mandapam of this temple.

Olakkay Aruvi (Waterfalls): The Olakkay Aruvi Waterfalls is about 8 kms north of Azhagiya Pandyapuram, 14 km from Nagercoil and 35 km from Kanyakumari. The waterfalls is surrounded by beautiful sceneries. It is a picnic and trekking spot attracting good crowd. A small Agasthiyar temple is near the falls and on the full moon day in the Tamil month of Chitthirai (April-May) devotees throng here to worship the deity after a bath in the falls.

Kumarak Koil : It is 34 km from Kanyakumari, 15 km north-west of Nagercoil and 3 km east of Thukkalay. It is on the Vellimalai hills in Kalkulam taluk. The temple is on a hillock 200 ft. high amidst paddy fields, plantain and coconut groves. It is noted for its fine sculptures. There is a separate sanctum for Goddess Valli besides the presiding deity Lord Subramanya (Muruga). There is a big lake nearby suitable for bathing.

Mandaikadu Bagavathi Amman Temple : Mandaikadu is 41 km from Kanyakumari situated on the sea coast north-east of Colachel port. A motorable road connects this place with Nagercoil and Thiruvanan-thapuram. There is a famous temple here dedicated to Bagavathi Amman dating back to 7th century A.D. The deity is in the form of an ant hill which is about 12 ft. high with 5 heads and is believed to be growing gradually. The annual festival called Mandaikadu Kodai, falls in March and is celebrated for ten days. At that time, over two lakhs of people assemble here for worshipping the deity. The Tourism Department of Tamil Nadu conducts an exhibition at that time. Though the temple is not big, it attracts huge crowds from all over the district and from Kottayam in Kerala about 160 kms from Mandaikadu.

Thengaipattinam Beach : It is 54 kms from Kanyakumari and 35 km from Nagercoil. As coconut trees abound, this place is called Thengai (coconut) Pattinam. In ancient times, this was a busy maritime trade centre doing business with foreign countries especially with the Arabs. The mosque here was erected by Arab merchants 1200 years ago. Bus services are available to this place from Nagercoil and Thiruvananthapuram. There is a fine backwater and an excellent beach and large number of people go there for relaxation and fun. Seabathing and boating are specialities of this place. It is a fine picnic spot.

Agastheeswaram : Located in Puzhichchalur the presiding deity in this temple is Agastheeswarar. The shrine is said to have been visited by sage Agastya. Traditionally, it is said that all the shrines visited by the sage are known as Agastheeswaram. The shrine for Sani in this temple is considered to be next to Tirunallar.

St. Xavier Church, Kottar (Nagercoil) : It is 15 km from Kanyakumari. An old church dating back to 15th century A.D. is built here. A ten day festival from 24th November to 3rd December attracts hugh crowd.

Curusadi St. Antony's Church: This church near Nagercoil is said to be 400 years old. Once a Hindu Nadar found a stone with a cross embossed on it. He had dreams and received orders from a form of light to build a church. Worship began in a humble manner and the place came to be called *Curusadi* (Curusu–'cross'in Tamil). Later on after 21 years of construction, a new church came into being in 1911. It has two beautiful towers rising high. People from far and near visit this church with faith. St. Antony being a miracle saint has worked wonders among the devotees fulfilling their desires.

Pechipparai Dam : The dam is 75 km from Kanyakumari. It is a popular picnic site. There is a park and boating facilities are also made here. Buses ply from Kanyakumari to the dam. Dormitory accommodations are available.

Udayagiri Fort : This fort built by king Marthanda Varma (1729-1788 A.D) is about 34km from Kanyakumari. The fort was popularly known as a foundry for casting guns. The grave of De Lennoy, the Dutch General, one of the most trusted generals, of the king lies within the fort.

Padmanabhapuram : This was the capital of Travancore till 1333. It is 45 kms from Kanyakumari. There is a palace inside a fort covering over 6 acres. There is also a temple inside. The palace is an art museum with mural paintings and exquisite wood carvings. Many objects including an armour of the royal family are exhibited. A clock made 400 years ago and a cot made of herbal wood used by the Maharaja to sleep on, can also be seen. The Ramasamy Temple inside has beautiful wood carvings depicting scenes from Ramayana, like Sita's wedding, Ravana's end etc. In the Neelakantaswamy temple, the image of a fierce Nataraja – the only one of its kind – is seen.

Thirupparappu Waterfalls : It is 60 km from Kanyakumari. An ancient temple dedicated to Mahadeva is located here. It is a picnic spot. People throng in large numbers to bathe in the waterfalls.

Thiruvattar : The place is 60 km from Kanyakumari. The Thiruvattar temple is one of the 13 Divyadesams (holy country) of Vishnu in Malai Nadu. Chaitanya of the Bhakti Cult movement has visited this place. The temple is in picturesque setting surrounded on three sides by 3 rivers (Kottaiyar, Paraliyar and Thamirabarani). The Lord is lying on His snake couch and has to be viewed through three doors. Deepalakshmis are many but none resembles the other. The Otraikkal Mandapam (Single Stone Hall) made of single stone 3 ft. thick is a marvel. Oorthuva Thandavam, Venugopala, Rathi, Manmatha, Lakshmana and Indrajit are excellently carved. The temple is also renowned for its murals.

Thirunandikarai : This place is near Thiruvattar. There is a rock-cut temple here. Once in 12 years, the Lingam is anointed with ghee on the Mahasivarathri day (March-April). The sanctum is circular with a conical dome in the typical Kerala style with the roof copper plated.

Thirucharanathumalai (Chitharal) : Thirucharanathumalai is located in Chitharal village 6 kms from Kuzhithurai and 55 kms from Kanyakumari. It is a hillock. On the top of the hill under a path that seems naturally hanging there is a temple with mandapam, corridor and Balipeetam with a Madappalli (Kitchen). There are 3 sanctums housing Mahavira, Parswanatha and Padmavathi Devi. The idol of Bagavathi was installed instead of Padmavathi Devi by Sri Moolam Thirunal, King of Travancore in 1913 A.D. Above the hanging path, there is a dilapidated tower on a rock on the northern side. Bas-relief sculptures of all the 29 Tirthankaras are found. Some inscriptions belonging to the 9th century A.D. are also found here. It was a Jain training centre for both men and women in those days.

Government Fruit Farm : This farm is located 2 kms from Kanyakumari on the road to Suchindram. All kinds of plants and rare species can be seen here. Tourists are allowed to go around the farm.

Muttam : Muttam is 32 kms from Kanyakumari. A beautiful beach with fine rocky backdrop near the shore and a lighthouse make it a fine picnic spot. The place is a favourite haunt for cine technicians to shoot films.

Tourist Information

Govt. of Tamil Nadu Tourist Office, Beach Road. ✆ 04652-246276

Information Centre, Vivekananda Rock Memorial, Beach Road. ✆ 04652-246250

SHOPPING

Souvenirs and handicraft articles made from sea shells, and palm leaf articles are the main items to buy at Kanyakumari. Trinklets and packets of coloured sea sand for children can also be bought here. There are several shops selling these articles. Prices vary depending upon your bargaining power.

Other Information

Communications : Post/Telegraph/STD/ISD/Telex/Fax etc. –Available

Banks/Money Changers : State Bank of India, Canara Bank, State Bank of Travancore.

Medical Facilities : Hospitals, Chemists - Available.

Yoga : Classes are organised at Vivekanandapuram.

For details, please contact : The Secretary, Vivekananda Kendra at Vivekanandapuram, Kanyakumari.

Where to Stay?
Kanyakumari (STD : 04652)
- Hotel Seaview, East Car Street, Kanyakumari - 629 709. ✆ 247841, Fax: 247203
- Indien Heritage, Kumariyur Marungoo, Kanyakumari - 629402 ✆ 293501/293502 Email : indienhermitage@yahoo.co.in
- Hotel Maadhini, East Car Street, Kanyakumari - 629 709 ✆ 246787/ 246757 Fax : 246657
- Hotel Sangam, Main Road, Kanyakumari - 629 702. ✆ 246351, 246352 Fax : 246627
- Hotel Shivas Residency, 2/77A, South Car Street, Kanyakumari - 629 702. ✆ 246929, 246150
- Sivamurugan Lodging, 2/93, North Car Street, Kanyakumari - 629 702 ✆ 246862 / 246872 Fax : 246882
- Hotel Park, Colachel, Kanyakumari - 629251. ✆ 04651 - 225800 / 225801 Fax : 227787

At Nagercoil (STD : 04652)
- Hotel Ganga, ✆ 232999
- Parvathi International, ✆ 233020
- Hotel Pioneer Paradise, Tower Junction, Nagercoil - 629 001. ✆ 238451 Fax : 04652 - 238544
- Harris Residency, Ramavarmapuram, Nagercoil - 629 001. ✆ 278681, 278917

❖❖❖

Train Timings

in major cities/towns of Tamil Nadu

The days of operations given within brackets below the Train Nos. are with regard to the ORIGINATING stations whereas the Arrival and Departure correspond to the RESPECTIVE stations.

All the trains are express trains unless otherwise mentioned.

Abbreviations

1.	Ahm	- Ahmadabad	38.	Krk	- Karaikal
2.	Alp	- Alappuzha	39.	Knr	- Kannur
3.	Ark	- Arakonam	40.	Krb	- Korba
4.	Bbr	- Bhubaneshwar	41.	Lkn	- Lucknow
5.	Bkr	- Bokaro Steel City	42.	LmT	- Lokmanya Tilak
6.	Blp	- Bilaspur	43.	Mdu	- Madurai
7.	Blr	- Bangalore	44.	Mmb	- Mumbai
8.	Brn	- Barauni	45.	Mnd	- Manmad
9.	Cbe	- Coimbatore	46.	Mng	- Mangalore
10.	Chn	- Chennai	47.	Mpr	- Muzzaffarpur
11.	Cpr	- Chhapra	48.	Msr	- Mysore
12.	Dbd	- Dhanbad	49.	Mtp	- Mettupalayam
13.	Ddn	- Dehradun	50.	Myl	- Mayiladuthurai
14.	Ddr	- Dadar	51.	Ngc	- Nagercoil
15.	Del	- Delhi	52.	Ngr	- Nagore
16.	Dgh	- Dibrugarh	53.	Pdr	- Podanur
17.	Enk	- Ernakulam	54.	Ptn	- Patna
18.	Erd	- Erode	55.	Qui	- Quilon
19.	Gkp	- Gorakhpur	56.	Rjk	- Rajkot
20.	Gnd	- Ghandhidham	57.	Rnt	- Rajendra Nagar Terminus
21.	Grv	- Guruvayur			
22.	Gwt	- Guwahati	58.	Rms	- Rameswaram
23.	Hbl	- Hubli	59.	Sam	- Salem
24.	HNm	- Hazrat Nizamuddin	60.	Sec	- Secunderabad
25.	Hta	- Hatia	61.	Slm	- Shalimar
26.	Hwr	- Howrah	62.	Tks	- Tenkasi
27.	Hyd	- Hyderabad	63.	Tmb	- Tambaram
28.	Inr	- Indore	64.	Tnj	- Thanjavur
29.	Jlp	- Jolarpettai	65.	Tnv	- Tirunelveli
30.	Jmt	- Jammu Tawi	66.	Tpt	- Tirupati
31.	Jdp	- Jodhpur	67.	Trc	- Thiruchirappalli
32.	Jpr	- Jaipur	68.	Ttn	- Tuticorin
33.	Kbk	- Kumbakonam	69.	Tvm	- Thiruvananthapuram
34.	Kch	- Kochi	70.	Var	- Varanasi
35.	Kkd	- Karaikkudi	71.	Vas	- Vasco-da-Gama
36.	Kkn	- Kakinada	72.	Vdr	- Virudunagar
37.	Knk	- Kanniyakumari	73.	Vjd	- Vijayawada
			74.	Ypr	- Yesvantpur

B.H. - Brief Halt	Ex - Except	

Chennai Central

Train No.	Train Name	Arr.	Dep.	Train No.	Train Name	Arr.	Dep.
11028 (Daily)	Chn - Mmb (Mumbai Mail)	-	22.50	12609 (Daily)	Chn - Blr (Bangalore)	-	13.35
11027 (Daily)	Mmb - Chn (Chennai Mail)	04.55	-	12610 (Daily)	Blr - Chn (Chennai Exp.)	14.30	-
11042 (Daily)	Chn - Mmb (CST Exp.)	-	11.55	12611 (Sat)	Chn - HNm (Garib Rath)	-	06.10
11041 (Daily)	Mmb - Chn (CST Exp.)	16.45	-	12612 (Tue)	HNm - Chn (Garib Rath)	20.15	-
12007 (Ex. Wed)	Chn - Msr (Shatabdi Exp.)	-	06.00	12615 (Daily)	Chn - Del (Grand Trunk)	-	19.15
12008 (Ex. Wed)	Msr - Chn (Shatabdi Exp.)	21.25	-	12616 (Daily)	Del - Chn (Grand Trunk)	06.15	-
12027 (Ex. Tue)	Chn - Blr (Shatabdi Exp.)	-	17.30	12621 (Daily)	Chn - Del (Tamilnadu)	-	22.00
12028 (Ex. Tue)	Blr - Chn (Shatabdi Exp.)	11.00	-	12622 (Daily)	Del - Chn (Tamilnadu)	07.15	-
12077 (Ex. Tue)	Chn - Vjd (Jan Shatabdi)	-	07.00	12623 (Daily)	Chn - Tvm (Trivandrum)	-	19.45
12078 (Ex. Tue)	Vjd - Chn (Jan Shatabdi)	21.10	-	12624 (Daily)	Tvm - Chn (Chennai Mail)	06.55	-
12269 (Mon,Fri)	Chn - Nzm (Duronto Exp.)	-	06.40	12639 (Daily)	Chn - Blr (Brindavan)	-	07.15
12270 (Wed,Sun)	Nzm - Chn (Duronto Exp.)	20.10	-	12640 (Daily)	Blr - Chn (Brindavan)	20.25	-
12291 (Sat)	Ypr - Chn (Yesvantpur)	05.15	-	12656 (Daily)	Chn - Ahm (Navajivan)	-	09.35
12292 (Sat)	Chn - Ypr (Yesvantpur)	-	22.45	12655 (Daily)	Ahm - Chn (Navajivan)	16.05	-
12433 (Fri,Sun)	Chn - HNm (Rajdhani Exp.)	-	06.10	12657 (Daily)	Chn - Blr (Bangalore Mail)	-	23.15
12434 (Thu,Sat)	HNm - Chn (Rajdhani Exp.)	20.15	-	12658 (Daily)	Blr - Chn (Chennai Mail)	04.40	-
12601 (Daily)	Chn - Mng (Mangalore Mail)	-	20.25	12669 (Mon,Sat)	Chn - Cpr (Ganga Kaveri)	-	17.35
12602 (Daily)	Mng - Chn (Chennai Mail)	05.25	-	12670 (Wed,Fri)	Cpr - Chn (Ganga Kaveri)	14.25	-
12603 (Daily)	Chn - Hyd (Hyderabad)	-	16.45	12671 (Daily)	Chn - Mtp (Nilgiri Exp.)	-	21.00
12604 (Daily)	Hyd - Chn (Chennai Exp.)	05.55	-	12672 (Daily)	Mtp - Chn (Nilgiri Exp.)	05.05	-
12607 (Daily)	Chn - Blr (Lalbagh Exp.)	-	15.35	12673 (Daily)	Chn - Cbe (Cheran Exp.)	-	22.10
12608 (Daily)	Blr - Chn (Lalbagh Exp.)	12.15	-	12674 (Daily)	Cbe - Chn (Cheran Exp.)	06.35	-

Train No.	Train Name	Arr.	Dep.	Train No.	Train Name	Arr.	Dep.
12675 (Daily)	Chn - Cbe (Kovai Exp.)	-	06.15	12830 (Fri)	Bbr - Chn (BBS Chennai)	08.55	-
12676 (Daily)	Cbe - Chn (Kovai Exp.)	21.40	-	12839 (Daily)	Hwr - Chn (Howrah Mail)	03.50	-
12679 (Daily)	Chn - Cbe (Coimbatore Exp.)	-	14.30	12840 (Daily)	Chn - Hwr (Howrah Mail)	-	23.40
12680 (Daily)	Cbe - Chn (Coimbatore Exp.)	13.50	-	12841 (Daily)	Hwr - Chn (Coramandel)	17.15	-
12681 (Sat)	Chn - Cbe (Weekly Exp.)	-	22.30	12842 (Daily)	Chn - Hwr (Coramandel)	-	08.45
12682 (Sat)	Cbe - Chn (Weekly Exp.)	07.45	-	12851 (Mon)	Blp - Chn (Bilaspur Exp.)	08.55	-
12685 (Ex.Wed)	Chn - Mng (Mangalore)	-	17.00	12852 (Mon)	Chn - Blp (Bilaspur Exp.)	-	21.10
12686 (Ex.Tue)	Mng - Chn (Mangalore)	08.00	-	12967 (Tue,Sun)	Chn - Jpr (Jaipur Exp.)	-	17.35
12687 (Thu)	Chn - Ddn (Dehradun)	-	09.45	12968 (Tue,Sun)	Jpr - Chn (Jp Chn Exp.)	09.45	-
12688 (Wed)	Ddn - Chn (Dehradun)	02.15	-	16031 (W,Th,Su)	Chn - Jmt (Andaman)	-	05.15
12689 (Fri)	Chn - Ngc (Nagercoil)	-	18.15	16032 (M,Tu,Fr)	Jmt - Chn (Andaman)	10.10	-
12690 (Mon)	Ngc - Chn (Nagercoil)	12.25	-	16041 (Daily)	Chn - Alp (Alleppey Exp.)	-	21.15
12691 (Fri)	Chn - Blr (Bangalore)	-	23.30	16042 (Daily)	Alp - Chn (Chennai Exp.)	06.05	-
12692 (Mon)	Blr - Chn (Chennai Exp.)	05.15	-	16053 (Daily)	Chn - Tpt (Tirupati Exp.)	-	13.50
12695 (Daily)	Chn - Tvm (Trivandrum S.F.)	-	15.25	16054 (Daily)	Tpt - Chn (Chennai Exp.)	13.15	-
12696 (Daily)	Tvm - Chn (Trivandrum S.F.)	09.50	-	16057 (Daily)	Chn - Tpt (Saptagiri Exp.)	-	06.25
12697 (Sun)	Chn - Tvm (Trivandrum)	-	15.15	16058 (Daily)	Tpt - Chn (Saptagiri Exp.)	20.35	-
12698 (Sun)	Tvm - Chn (S.F. Weekly)	12.25	-	16093 (Tue,Sat)	Chn - Lkn (Lucknow Exp.)	-	05.15
12711 (Daily)	Vjd - Chn (Pinakini Exp.)	-	14.05	16094 (Wed,Sat)	Lkn - Chn (Lucknow Exp.)	10.10	-
12712 (Daily)	Chn - Vjd (Pinakini Exp.)	13.00	-	16203 (Daily)	Chn - Tpt (Tirupati Exp.)	-	16.35
12759 (Daily)	Chn - Hyd (Charminar)	-	18.10	16204 (Daily)	Chn - Tpt (Tirupati Exp.)	10.30	-
12760 (Daily)	Hyd - Chn (Charminar)	08.15	-	16221 (Daily)	Msr - Chn (Chennai Exp.)	07.25	-
12829 (Fri)	Chn - Bbr (Bhubaneswar)	-	21.10	16222 (Daily)	Chn - Msr (Mysore Exp.)	-	21.30

Train No.	Train Name	Arr.	Dep.	Train No.	Train Name	Arr.	Dep.
16627 (Daily)	Chn - Mng (West Coast)	-	11.30	17311 (Fri)	Chn - Vas (Chn Vasco)	-	14.10
16628 (Daily)	Mng - Chn (West Coast)	15.15	-	17312 (Fri)	Vas - Chn (Vasco Chn)	11.55	-
16669 (Daily)	Chn - Erd (Yercaud Exp.)	-	22.40	17313 (Sun)	Chn - Hbl (Chh Hubli)	-	14.10
16670 (Daily)	Erd - Chn (Yercaud Exp.)	04.30	-	17314 (Sun)	Hbl - Chn (Hbl Chennai)	11.55	-

Trains Passing through Chennai Central

Train No.	Train Name	Arr.	Dep.	Train No.	Train Name	Arr.	Dep.
12295 (Daily)	Blr - Ptn (Sangamitra Exp.)	15.05	15.40	12969 (Fri)	Cbe - Jpr (Cbe Jaipur)	17.10	17.35
12296 (Daily)	Ptn - Blr (Sangamitra Exp.)	13.35	14.00	12970 (Thu)	Jpr - Cbe (Jpr Cbe Sup.)	09.45	10.10
12507 (Wed)	Enk - Gwt (Guwahati)	09.30	09.55	13351 (Daily)	Bkr - Alp (Dhn Alp Exp.)	03.00	03.25
12508 (Sun)	Gwt - Enk (Ghy Ers Exp.)	04.15	04.40	13352 (Daily)	Alp - Dbd (Dbd/Tatanagr)	22.15	23.00
12509 (Th,F,Sa)	Blr - Gwt (Guwahati)	05.40	06.20	15227 (Thu)	Ypr - Mpr (Muzaffarpur)	09.30	09.55
12510 (Tu,W,Th)	Gwt - Blr (Guwahati)	04.15	04.40	15228 (Wed)	Mpr - Ypr (Mfp Ypr Exp.)	03.55	04.15
12511 (M,Fr,Sa)	Gpr - Tvm (Raptisagar)	23.20	23.45	16309 (Tue,Wed)	Enk - Ptn (Patna Exp.)	05.40	06.20
12512 (Tu,W,Su)	Tvm - Gpr (Raptisagar)	23.05	23.25	16310 (Sat,Sun)	Ptn - Enk (Patna Exp.)	03.55	04.15
12515 (Mon)	Tvm - Gwt (Guwahati)	05.40	06.20	16323 (Fri,Sun)	Tvm - Slm (Shalimar Exp.)	09.35	09.55
12516 (Fri)	Gwt - Tvm (Guwahati)	04.15	04.40	16324 (Tue,Thu)	Slm - Tvm (Shalimar Exp.)	03.55	04.15
12521 (Wed)	Brn - Enk (Barauni)	23.20	23.45	16325 (Tue)	Inr - Tvm (Ahilyanagri Exp.)	23.20	23.45
12522 (Fri)	Enk - Brn (Barauni)	23.05	23.25	16326 (Sat)	Tvm - Inr (Ahilyanagri Exp.)	23.05	23.25
12577 (Thu)	Dbg - Blr (Bagmathi Exp.)	14.20	14.45	16327 (Thu,Sun)	Krb - Tvm (Korba Exp.)	23.20	23.45
12578 (Sat)	Blr - Dbg (Bagmathi Exp.)	15.50	16.15	16328 (Mon,Thu)	Tvm - Krb (Korba Exp.)	23.05	23.25

Chennai Egmore

Train No.	Train Name	Arr.	Dep.	Train No.	Train Name	Arr.	Dep.
11063 (Daily)	Chn - Sam (Salem Exp.)	-	23.00	12389 (Mon)	Gaya - Chn (Gaya Chn Exp.)	20.45	-
11064 (Daily)	Sam - Chn (Chennai Exp.)	04.50	-	12390 (Tue)	Chn - Gaya (Chn Gaya Exp.)	-	07.30
12163 (Daily)	Ddr - Chn (Dadar Exp.)	19.45	-	12605 (Daily)	Chn - Trc (Pallavan Exp.)	-	15.45
12164 (Daily)	Chn - Ddr (Chennai Exp.)	-	06.50	12606 (Daily)	Trc - Chn (Pallavan Exp.)	12.15	-

Train No.	Train Name	Arr.	Dep.	Train No.	Train Name	Arr.	Dep.
12631 (Daily)	Chn - Tnv (Nellai Exp.)	-	21.15	16107 (Daily)	Chn - Mng. (Mangalore Exp.)	-	22.15
12632 (Daily)	Tnv - Chn (Nellai Exp.)	06.40	-	16108 (Daily)	Mng - Chn (Chennai Exp.)	05.05	-
12633 (Daily)	Chn - Knk (Kanyakumari)	-	17.30	16125 (Sat)	Chn - Jdp (Jodhpur Exp.)	-	15.15
12634 (Daily)	Knk - Chn (Kanyakumari)	06.50	-	16126 (Wed)	Jdp - Chn (Jodhpur Exp.)	16.55	-
12635 (Daily)	Chn - Mdu (Vaigai Exp.)	-	12.45	16127 (Daily)	Chn - Grv (Guruvayur Exp.)	-	07.40
12636 (Daily)	Mdu - Chn (Vaigai Exp.)	14.35	-	16128 (Daily)	Grv - Chn (Guruvayur Exp.)	21.15	-
12637 (Daily)	Chn - Mdu (Pandian Exp.)	-	21.15	16175 (Daily)	Chn - Ngr (Karaikal Exp.)	-	23.15
12638 (Daily)	Mdu - Chn (Pandian Exp.)	05.35	-	16176 (Daily)	Ngr - Chn (Karaikal Exp.)	05.25	-
12661 (Daily)	Chn - Sct (Pothigai Exp.)	-	20.05	16177 (Daily)	Chn - Kbk (Rockfort Exp.)	-	22.30
12662 (Daily)	Sct - Chn (Pothigai Exp.)	07.05	-	16178 (Daily)	Kbk - Chn (Rockfort Exp.)	05.15	-
12667 (Thu)	Chn - Ngc (Nagercoil Exp.)	-	18.50	16713 (Daily)	Chn - Rms (Rameswaram)	-	17.00
12668 (Sat)	Ngc - Chn (Nagercoil Exp.)	06.00	-	16714 (Daily)	Rms - Chn (Rameswaram)	08.20	-
12693 (Daily)	Chn - Ttn (Pearl City Exp.)	-	19.35	16723 (Daily)	Chn - Tvm (Ananthapuri)	-	19.15
12694 (Daily)	Ttn - Chn (Pearl City Exp.)	07.40	-	16724 (Daily)	Tvm - Chn (Ananthapuri)	08.40	-
12793 (Fri,Sun)	Chn - Mdu (Madurai Exp.) (Via Myladuthurai)	-	22.45	16735 (Daily)	Chn - Tiru (Tiruchendur)	-	16.05
12794 (Fri,Sun)	Mdu - Chn (Chennai Exp.) (Via Myladuthurai)	07.20	-	16736 (Daily)	Tiru - Chn (Tiruchendur)	11.40	-
15629 (Mon)	Chn - Gwt (Guwahati Exp.)	-	22.30	16853 (Daily)	Chn - Trc (Tiruchirappalli)	-	08.20
15630 (Sun)	Gwt - Chn (Guwahati Exp.)	20.15	-	16854 (Daily)	Trc - Chn (Tiruchirappalli)	17.45	-
15929 (Thu)	Chn - Dgh (Dibrugarh Exp.)	-	22.30	17643 (Daily)	Chn - Kkn (Circar Exp.)	-	17.20
15930 (Wed)	Dgh - Chn (Dibrugarh Exp.)	20.15	-	17644 (Daily)	Kkn - Chn (Circar Exp.)	06.30	-
				17651 (Daily)	Chn - Kch (Kacheguda Exp.)	-	17.00
				17652 (Daily)	Kch - Chn (Kacheguda Exp.)	07.15	-

Train No.	Train Name	Arr.	Dep.		Train No.	Train Name	Arr.	Dep.
	## Trains Passing through Chennai Egmore							

Train No.	Train Name	Arr.	Dep.	Train No.	Train Name	Arr.	Dep.
12641 (Thu)	Knk - Nzm (Tirukkural Exp.)	08.50	09.05	12666 (Sat)	Knk - Hwr (Howrah Exp.)	22.10	22.30
12642 (Sun)	Nzm - Knk (Tirukkural Exp.)	18.05	18.30	12897 (Wed)	Pdy - Bbr (Pdy Bbs Exp.)	22.10	22.30
12651 (Sun, Tue)	Mdu - Nzm (Sampark Kranti)	08.50	09.05	12898 (Wed)	Bbr - Pdy (Bbs Pdy Exp.)	09.00	09.20
12652 (Wed, Fri)	Nzm - Mdu (Sampark Kranti)	18.05	18.30	14259 (Thu)	Rms - Var (Varanasi Exp.)	13.00	13.15
12663 (Fri, Mon)	Hwr - Trc (Hwh Tpj Exp.)	20.00	20.20	14260 (Tue)	Var - Rms (Varanasi Exp.)	10.35	10.50
12664 (Tue, Fri)	Trc - Hwr (Howrah Exp.)	22.10	22.30	18495 (Sun)	Rms - Bbr (Bhubaneswar)	22.10	22.30
12665 (Tue)	Hwr - Knk (Howrah Exp.)	20.00	20.20	18496 (Sun)	Bbr - Rms (Bhubaneswar)	09.00	09.20

Coimbatore

Train No.	Train Name	Arr.	Dep.	Train No.	Train Name	Arr.	Dep.
11013 (Daily)	LmT - Cbe (Coimbatore)	06.30	-	12675 (Daily)	Chn - Cbe (Kovai Exp.)	13.55	-
11014 (Daily)	Cbe - LmT (Lokamanya TT)	-	08.00	12676 (Daily)	Cbe - Chn (Kovai Exp.)	-	14.20
12625 (Daily)	Tvm - Del (Kerala Exp.)	19.55	20.00	12677 (Daily)	Blr - Enk (Ernakulam)	13.05	13.10
12626 (Daily)	Del - Tvm (Kerala Exp.)	05.10	05.15	12678 (Daily)	Enk - Blr (Bangalore)	12.45	12.50
12643 (Tue)	Tvm - HNm (Nizamuddin)	23.35	23.45	12679 (Daily)	Chn - Cbe (Coimbatore)	22.15	-
12644 (Sat)	HNm - Tvm (Swarna Jayanti)	01.15	01.20	12680 (Daily)	Cbe - Chn (Chennai Exp.)	-	06.15
12645 (Sat)	Enk - HNm (Nizamuddin)	23.35	23.45	12681 (Sun)	Chn - Cbe (Coimbatore)	06.50	-
12646 (Thu)	HNm - Enk (Millenium Exp.)	01.15	01.20	12682 (Fri)	Cbe - Chn (Chennai Exp.)	-	23.45
12647 (Sun)	Cbe - HNm (Kongu Exp.)	-	15.15	12695 (Daily)	Chn - Tvm (Trivandrum)	23.05	23.10
12648 (Fri)	HNm - Cbe (Kongu Exp.)	09.30	-	12696 (Daily)	Tvm - Chn (Tvm Chennai)	02.05	02.10
12671 (Daily)	Chn - Mtp (Nilgiri Exp.)	04.50	05.15	13351 (Daily)	Dbd - Alp (Dhanbad Exp.)	12.05	12.10
12672 (Daily)	Mtp - Chn (Nilgiri Exp.)	20.30	20.55	13352 (Daily)	Alp - Dbd (Dhanbad Exp.)	11.55	12.00
12673 (Daily)	Chn - Cbe (Cheran Exp.)	06.10	-	16107 (Daily)	Chn - Mng (Mangalore Ex.)	10.40	10.45
12674 (Daily)	Cbe - Chn (Cheran Exp.)	-	22.20	16108 (Daily)	Mng - Chn (Chennai Exp.)	15.45	15.50

Train No.	Train Name	Arr.	Dep.	Train No.	Train Name	Arr.	Dep.
16309 (Mon,Tue)	Enk - Ptn (Patna Exp.)	21.30	21.35	16360 (Thu)	Ptn - Enk (Patna Exp.)	18.25	18.30
16310 (Sat,Sun)	Ptn - Enk (Patna Exp.)	12.35	12.40	16525 (Daily)	Knk - Blr (Bangalore)	22.50	22.55
16317 (Sat)	Knk - Jmt (Himsagar Exp.)	00.55	01.00	16526 (Daily)	Blr - Knk (Kanyakumari)	05.25	05.30
16318 (Thu)	Jmt - Knk (Himsagar Exp.)	10.00	10.05	16613 (Mon)	Rjk - Cbe (Coimbatore)	02.00	-
16321 (Fri)	Blr - Tvm (Trivandrum)	01.55	02.00	16614 (Thu)	Cbe - Rjk (Rajkot Exp.)	-	23.45
16322 (Thu)	Tvm - Blr (Bangalore)	00.55	01.00	16627 (Daily)	Chn - Mng (West Coast)	19.55	20.00
16323 (Fri,Sun)	Tvm - Slm (Shalimar Exp.)	01.25	01.30	16628 (Daily)	Mng - Chn (West Coast)	06.20	06.25
16324 (Thu,Tue)	Slm - Tvm (Shalimar Exp.)	12.35	12.40	16687 (Tue)	Mng - Jmt (Navyug Exp.)	00.55	01.00
16325 (Wed)	Inr - Tvm (Ahilyanagari)	07.55	08.00	16688 (Sun)	Jmt - Mng (Navyug Exp.)	10.00	10.05
16326 (Sat)	Tvm - Inr (Ahilyanagari)	15.15	15.20	16865 (Daily)	Ngr - Enk (Ernakulam Ex)	00.55	01.00
16327 (Fri,Mon)	Krb - Tvm (Korba Exp.)	07.55	08.00	16866 (Daily)	Enk - Ngr (Nagore Exp.)	02.55	03.10
16328 (Mon,Thu)	Tvm - Krb (Korba Exp.)	15.15	15.20	17229 (Daily)	Tvm - Hyd (Sabari Exp.)	16.30	16.35
16359 (Sun)	Enk - Ptn (Patna Exp.)	03.10	03.15	17230 (Daily)	Hyd - Tvm (Sabari Exp.)	08.30	08.35

Erode

Train No.	Train Name	Arr.	Dep.	Train No.	Train Name	Arr.	Dep.
11013 (Daily)	LmT - Cbe (Coimbatore)	04.05	04.10	12645 (Sun)	Enk - HNm (Nizamuddin)	01.15	01.20
11014 (Daily)	Cbe - LmT (Lokmanya TT)	09.30	09.35	12646 (Wed)	HNm - Enk (Millenium)	23.20	23.25
12623 (Daily)	Chn - Tvm (Trivandrum Mail)	01.05	01.10	12647 (Sun)	Cbe - HNm (Kongu Exp.)	16.45	16.50
12624 (Daily)	Tvm - Chn (Chennai Mail)	00.45	00.50	12648 (Fri)	HNm - Cbe (Kongu Exp.)	07.10	07.15
12625 (Daily)	Tvm - Del (Kerala Exp.)	21.55	22.00	12671 (Daily)	Chn - Mtp (Nilgiri Exp.)	02.30	02.35
12626 (Daily)	Del - Tvm (Kerala Exp.)	3.25	3.30	12672 (Daily)	Mtp - Chn (Nilgiri Exp.)	22.25	22.30
12601 (Daily)	Chn - Mng (Mangalore Mail)	02.05	02.10	12673 (Daily)	Chn - Cbe (Cheran Exp.)	03.50	03.55
12602 (Daily)	Mng - Chn (Chennai Mail)	23.05	23.10	12674 (Daily)	Cbe - Chn (Cheran Exp.)	00.01	00.05
12643 (Wed)	Tvm - HNm (Nizamuddin)	01.15	01.20	12675 (Daily)	Chn - Cbe (Kovai Exp.)	11.55	12.00
12644 (Sat)	HNm - Tvm (Swarna Jayanthi)	23.20	23.25	12676 (Daily)	Cbe - Chn (Kovai Exp.)	15.40	15.45

Train No.	Train Name	Arr.	Dep.	Train No.	Train Name	Arr.	Dep.
12677 (Daily)	Blr - Enk (Ernakulam Exp.)	11.25	11.30	(Tue) 16332 (Sat)	(Trivandram) Tvm - Mmb (Mumbai Exp.)	15.00	15.10
12678 (Daily)	Enk - Blr (Bangalore Exp.)	14.25	14.35	16339 (Thu,Fri, Sat,Mon)	Mmb - Ngc (Nagarcoil Exp.)	17.00	17.10
12679 (Daily)	Chn - Cbe (Coimbatore Exp.)	20.20	20.25	16340 (Mon,Tue,	Ngc - Mmb (Mumbai Exp.)	15.45	15.55
12680 (Daily)	Cbe - Chn (Chennai Exp.)	07.40	07.45	Wed,Fri)			
12685 (Ex.Tue)	Chn - Mng (Mangalore)	22.40	22.45	16359 (Sun)	Enk - Ptn (Patna Exp.)	05.00	05.05
12686 (Ex.Tue)	Mng - Chn (Mangalore)	01.40	01.45	16360 (Thu)	Ptn - Enk (Patna Exp.)	16.40	16.50
12695 (Daily)	Chn - Tvm (Trivandrum S.F.)	21.20	21.25	16525 (Daily)	Knk - Blr (Bangalore)	00.30	00.35
12696 (Daily)	Tvm - Chn (Trivandrum S.F.)	03.40	03.45	16526 (Daily)	Blr - Knk (Kanyakumari)	03.40	03.45
12697 (Sun)	Chn - Tvm (Trivandrum)	20.45	20.50	16527 (Daily)	Ypr - Knr (Yesvanpur Exp.)	01.40	01.45
12698 (Sun)	Tvm - Chn (Chennai Exp.)	05.55	06.00	16528 (Daily)	Knr - Ypr (Yesvanpur Exp.)	01.00	01.05
13351 (Daily)	Dbd - Alp (Dhanbad Exp.)	10.15	10.25	16613 (Mon)	Rjk - Cbe (Coimbatore)	23.40	23.45
13352 (Daily)	Alp - Dbd (Dhanbad Exp.)	13.50	14.00	16614 (Fri)	Cbe - Rjk (Rajkot Exp.)	01.15	01.20
16041 (Daily)	Chn - Alp (Alleppey Exp.)	02.50	02.55	16627 (Daily)	Chn - Mng (West Coast)	18.00	18.10
16042 (Daily)	Alp - Chn (Chennai Exp.)	23.30	23.35	16628 (Daily)	Mng - Chn (West Coast)	08.25	08.30
16309 (Mon,Tue)	Enk - Ptn (Patna Exp.)	23.20	23.25	16669 (Daily)	Chn - Erd (Yercaud Exp.)	06.25	-
16310 (Sat,Sun)	Ptn - Enk (Patna Exp.)	10.35	10.45	16670 (Daily)	Erd - Chn (Yercaud Exp.)	-	21.00
16317 (Sat)	Knk - Jmt (Himsagar Exp.)	02.45	03.05	16687 (Tue)	Mng - Jmt (Navyug Exp.)	02.45	03.05
16318 (Thu)	Jmt - Knk (Himsagar Exp.)	07.50	08.20	16688 (Sun)	Jmt - Mng (Navyug)	07.50	08.20
16321 (Fri)	Blr - Tvm (Trivandram)	00.05	00.10	16731 (Daily)	Ttn - Msr (Mysore Exp.)	00.05	00.15
16322 (Thu)	Tvm - Blr (Bangalore Exp.)	02.35	02.40	16732 (Daily)	Msr - Ttn (Tuticorin Exp.)	03.15	03.25
16323 (Fri,Sun)	Tvm - Slm (Shalimar Exp.)	03.00	03.05	16733 (Sat)	Rms - Okha (Rmm Okha Exp.)	04.55	05.05
16324 (Thu,Tue)	Slm - Tvm (Shalimar Exp.)	10.35	10.45	16734 (Thu)	Okha - Rms (Rameswaram)	12.20	12.30
16325 (Wed)	Inr - Tvm (Ahilyanagari)	06.05	06.15	16865 (Daily)	Ngr - Enk (Nagore Exp.)	23.00	23.05
16326 (Sat)	Tvm - Inr (Ahilyanagari)	17.00	17.10	16866 (Daily)	Enk - Ngr (Nagore Exp.)	04.35	04.40
16327 (Fri,Mon)	Krb - Tvm (Korba Exp.)	06.05	06.15	17229 (Daily)	Tvm - Hyd (Sabari Exp.)	18.20	18.30
16328 (Mon,Thu)	Tvm - Krb (Korba Exp.)	17.00	17.10	17230 (Daily)	Hyd - Tvm (Sabari Exp.)	06.35	06.45
16331	Mmb - Tvm	17.00	17.10				

Salem

Train No.	Train Name	Arr.	Dep.	Train No.	Train Name	Arr.	Dep.
11013 (Daily)	LmT - Cbe (Coimbatore)	02.55	03.00	12686 (Ex.Tue)	Mng - Chn (Mangalore)	02.40	02.45
11014 (Daily)	Cbe - LmT (Lokmanya TT)	10.35	10.40	12695 (Daily)	Chn - Tvm (Trivandrum S.F.)	20.05	20.10
12601 (Daily)	Chn-Mng (Mangalore Mail)	01.05	01.10	12696 (Daily)	Tvm - Chn (Trivandrum S.F.)	04.40	04.45
12602 (Daily)	Mng - Chn (Chennai Mail)	00.05	00.10	12697 (Sun)	Chn - Tvm (Trivandrum)	19.45	19.50
12623 (Daily)	Chn - Tvm (Trivandram Mail)	00.05	00.10	12698 (Sun)	Tvm - Chn (Chennai Exp.)	06.50	06.55
12624 (Daily)	Tvm - Chn (Chennai Mail)	01.40	01.45	13351 (Daily)	Dbd - Alp (Dhanbad Exp.)	09.00	09.05
12625 (Daily)	Tvm - Del (Kerala Exp.)	22.55	23.00	13352 (Daily)	Alp - Dbd (Dhanbad Exp.)	15.00	15.05
12626 (Daily)	Del - Tvm (Kerala Exp.)	02.10	02.15	16041 (Daily)	Chn - Alp (Alleppey Exp.)	01.45	01.50
12643 (Wed)	Tvm - HNm (Nizamuddin)	02.15	02.20	16042 (Daily)	Alp - Chn (Chennai Exp.)	00.30	00.35
12644 (Sat)	HNm - Tvm (Swarna Jayanti)	22.05	22.10	16309 (Tue,Wed)	Enk - Ptn (Patna Exp.)	00.20	00.25
12645 (Sun)	Enk - HNm (Nizamuddin)	02.15	02.20	16310 (Sat,Sun)	Ptn - Enk (Patna Exp.)	09.15	09.20
12646 (Wed)	HNm - Enk (Millennium)	22.05	22.10	16317 (Sat)	Knk - Jmt (Himsagar)	04.00	04.05
12647 (Sun)	Cbe - HNm (Kongu Exp.)	17.50	17.55	16318 (Thu)	Jmt - Knk (Himsagar)	06.35	06.40
12648 (Fri)	HNm - Cbe (Kongu Exp.)	06.05	06.10	16321 (Thu)	Blr - Tvm (Trivandram)	23.05	23.10
12671 (Daily)	Chn - Mtp (Nilgiri Exp.)	01.30	01.35	16322 (Thu)	Tvm - Blr (Bangalore)	03.35	03.40
12672 (Daily)	Mtp - Chn (Nilgiri Exp.)	23.25	23.30	16323 (Fri,Sun)	Tvm - Slm (Shalimar Exp.)	04.00	04.05
12673 (Daily)	Chn - Cbe (Cheran Exp.)	02.45	02.50	16324 (Thu,Tue)	Slm - Tvm (Trivandram)	09.15	09.20
12674 (Daily)	Cbe - Chn (Cheran Exp.)	00.55	01.00	16325 (Wed)	Inr - Tvm (Ahilyanagari)	04.45	04.50
12675 (Daily)	Chn - Cbe (Kovai Exp.)	10.55	11.00	16326 (Sat)	Tvm - Inr (Ahilyanagari)	18.05	18.10
12676 (Daily)	Cbe - Chn (Kovai Exp.)	16.36	16.40	16327 (Fri,Mon)	Krb - Tvm (Korba Exp.)	04.45	04.50
12677 (Daily)	Blr - Enk (Ernakulam)	10.02	10.05	16328 (Mon,Thu)	Tvm - Krb (Korba Exp.)	18.05	18.10
12678 (Daily)	Enk - Blr (Bangalore)	15.31	15.35	16331 (Tue)	Mmb - Tvm (Trivandram)	15.45	15.50
12679 (Daily)	Chn - Cbe (Coimbatore)	19.17	19.20	16332 (Sat)	Tvm - Mmb (Mumbai Exp.)	16.00	16.05
12680 (Daily)	Cbe - Chn (Chennai Exp.)	08.37	08.40	16339 (Thu,Fri, Sat, Mon)	Mmb - Ngc (Nagarcoil Exp.)	15.45	15.50
12681	Chn - Cbe (Coimbatore)	03.10	03.15	16340 (Mon,Tue, Wed,Fri)	Ngc - Mmb (Mumbai Exp.)	16.45	16.50
12685 (Ex.Tue)	Chn - Mng (Mangalore)	21.35	21.40				

Train No.	Train Name	Arr.	Dep.	Train No.	Train Name	Arr.	Dep.
16359 (Sun)	Enk - Ptn (Patna Exp.)	06.00	06.05	16669 (Daily)	Chn - Erd (Yercaud Exp.)	04.55	05.00
16360 (Thu)	Ptn - Enk (Patna Exp.)	15.25	15.30	16670 (Daily)	Erd - Chn (Yercaud)	21.55	22.00
16525 (Daily)	Knk - Blr (Bangalore)	01.25	01.30	16687 (Tue)	Mng - Jmt (Navyug Exp.)	04.00	04.05
16526 (Daily)	Blr - Knk (Kanayakumari)	02.25	02.30	16688 (Sun)	Jmt - Mng (Navyug Exp.)	06.35	06.40
16527 (Daily)	Ypr - Knr (Yesvantpur)	00.40	00.45	16731 (Daily)	Ttn - Msr (Mysore Exp.)	01.10	01.15
16528 (Daily)	Knr - Ypr (Yesvantpur)	01.55	02.00	16732 (Daily)	Msr - Ttn (Tuticorin Exp.)	02.00	02.05
16613 (Mon)	Rjk - Cbe (Coimbatore)	22.35	22.40	16733 (Sat)	Rms - Okha (Rmm Okha Exp.)	06.00	06.05
16614 (Fri)	Cbe - Rjk (Rajcot Exp.)	02.15	02.20	16734 (Thu)	Okha - Rms (Rameswaram)	11.15	11.20
16627 (Daily)	Chn - Mng (West Coast)	16.40	16.45	17229 (Daily)	Tvm - Hyd (Sabari Exp.)	19.25	19.30
16628 (Daily)	Mng - Chn (West Coast)	09.35	09.40	17230 (Daily)	Hyd - Tvm (Sabari Exp.)	05.25	05.30

Jolarpettai

Train No.	Train Name	Arr.	Dep.	Train No.	Train Name	Arr.	Dep.
12601 (Daily)	Chn - Mng (Mangalore Mail)	23.30	23.32	12680 (Daily)	Cbe - Chn (Chennai Exp.)	10.18	10.20
12602 (Daily)	Mng - Chn (Chennai Mail)	01.53	01.55	12695 (Daily)	Chn - Tvm (Trivandrum)	18.38	18.40
12609 (Daily)	Chn - Blr (Bangalore)	17.06	17.08	12696 (Daily)	Tvm - Chn (Chennai Exp.)	06.18	06.20
12610 (Daily)	Blr - Chn (Chennai Exp.)	10.28	10.30	12697 (Sun)	Chn - Tvm (Trivandrum)	18.18	18.20
12625 (Daily)	Tvm - Del (Kerala Exp.)	00.40	00.45	12698 (Sun)	Tvm - Chn (Chennai Exp.)	08.48	08.50
12626 (Daily)	Del - Tvm (Kerala Exp.)	00.40	00.45	16041 (Daily)	Chn - Alp (Alleppey Exp.)	00.18	00.20
12639 (Daily)	Chn - Blr (Brindavan)	10.30	10.32	16042 (Daily)	Alp - Chn (Chennai Exp.)	02.23	02.25
12640 (Daily)	Blr - Chn (Brindavan)	16.43	16.45	16627 (Daily)	Chn - Mng (West Coast)	14.48	14.50
12657 (Daily)	Chn - Blr (Bangalore Mail)	02.23	02.25	16628 (Daily)	Mng - Chn (West Coast)	11.38	11.40
12658 (Daily)	Blr - Chn (Chennai Mail)	01.03	01.05	16733 (Sat)	Rms - Okha (Rmm Okha Exp.)	07.50	07.55
12673 (Daily)	Chn - Cbe (Cheran Exp.)	01.18	01.20	16734 (Thu)	Okha - Rms (Rameswaram)	09.38	09.40
12674 (Daily)	Cbe - Chn (Cheran Exp.)	02.48	02.50	16669 (Daily)	Chn - Erd (Yercaud Exp.)	02.58	03.00
12675 (Daily)	Chn - Cbe (Kovai Exp.)	09.18	09.20	16670 (Daily)	Erd - Chn (Yercaud Exp.)	00.13	00.15
12676 (Daily)	Cbe - Chn (Kovai Exp.)	18.23	18.25	17229 (Daily)	Tvm - Hyd (Sabari Exp.)	21.20	21.25
12679 (Daily)	Chn - Cbe (Coimbatore)	17.33	17.35	17230 (Daily)	Hyd - Tvm (Sabari Exp.)	03.48	03.50

Train No.	Train Name	Arr.	Dep.	Train No.	Train Name	Arr.	Dep.
				Katpadi			
12623 (Daily)	Chn - Tvm (Trivandrum)	21.28	21.30	15227 (Thu)	Ypr - Mpr (Muzaffarpur)	06.30	07.05
12624 (Daily)	Tvm - Chn (Chennai Mail)	04.33	04.35	15228 (Wed)	Mpr - Ypr (Muzaffarpur)	06.23	06.25
12625 (Daily)	Tvm - Del (Kerala Exp.)	02.00	02.05	12601 (Daily)	Chn - Mng (Mangalore Mail)	22.23	22.25
12626 (Daily)	Del - Tvm (Kerala Exp.)	23.25	23.30	12602 (Daily)	Mng - Chn (Chennai Mail)	03.00	03.05
12639 (Daily)	Chn - Blr (Brindavan Exp.)	09.13	09.15	16041 (Daily)	Chn - Alp (Alleppey Exp.)	23.03	23.05
12640 (Daily)	Blr - Chn (Brindavan Exp.)	17.58	18.00	16042 (Daily)	Alp - Chn (Chennai Exp.)	03.33	03.35
12643 (Wed)	Tvm - HNm (Nizamuddin)	05.28	05.30	16221 (Daily)	Msr - Chn (Chennai Exp.)	04.05	04.10
12644 (Sat)	HNm - Tvm (Swarna Jayanti)	19.33	19.35	16222 (Daily)	Chn - Msr (Mysore Exp.)	23.43	23.45
12645 (Sun)	Enk - HNm (Nizamuddin)	05.28	05.30	16309 (Tue,Wed)	Enk - Ptn (Patna Exp.)	03.18	03.20
12646 (Wed)	HNm - Enk (Millennium)	19.33	19.35	16310 (Sat,Sun)	Ptn - Enk (Patna Exp.)	06.23	06.25
12657 (Daily)	Chn - Blr (Bangalore Mail)	01.08	01.10	16317 (Sat)	Knk - Jmt (Himsagar)	07.08	07.10
12658 (Daily)	Blr - Chn (Chennai Mail)	02.08	02.10	16318 (Thu)	Jmt - Knk (Himsagar)	03.48	03.50
12671 (Daily)	Chn - Mtp (Nilgiri Exp.)	22.48	22.50	16323 (Fri,Sun)	Tvm - Slm (Shalimar Exp.)	07.00	07.05
12672 (Daily)	Mtp - Chn (Nilgiri Exp.)	02.23	02.25	16324 (Thu,Tue)	Slm - Tvm (Shalimar Exp.)	06.23	06.25
12675 (Daily)	Chn - Cbe (Kovai Exp.)	08.10	08.12	16325 (Wed)	Inr - Tvm (Ahilyanagari)	01.45	01.50
12676 (Daily)	Cbe - Chn (Kovai Exp.)	19.33	19.35	16326 (Sat)	Tvm - Inr (Ahilyanagari)	20.53	20.55
12679 (Daily)	Chn - Cbe (Coimbatore)	16.18	16.20	16359 (Sun)	Enk - Ptn (Patna Exp.)	09.30	09.35
12680 (Daily)	Cbe - Chn (Chennai Exp.)	11.28	11.30	16360 (Thu)	Ptn - Enk (Patna Exp.)	12.35	12.40
12695 (Daily)	Chn - Tvm (Trivandrum S.F.)	17.18	17.20	16669 (Daily)	Chn - Erd (Yercaud Exp.)	00.53	00.55
12696 (Daily)	Tvm - Chn (Trivandrum S.F.)	07.28	07.30	16670 (Daily)	Erd - Chn (Yercaud Exp.)	01.35	01.40
12697 (Sun)	Chn - Tvm (Trivandrum)	17.03	17.05	16687 (Sun)	Mng - Jmt (Navyug Exp.)	07.08	07.10
12698 (Sun)	Tvm - Chn (S.F. Weekly)	09.58	10.00	16688 (Sun)	Jmt - Mng (Navyug Exp.)	03.48	03.50
13351 (Daily)	Dbd - Alp (Dhanbad Exp.)	05.50	05.55	17209 (Daily)	Blr - Kkn Port (Sheshadri Exp.)	17.50	17.55
13352 (Daily)	Alp - Dbd (Dhanbad Exp.)	18.25	18.30	17210 (Daily)	Kkn port - Blr (Sheshadri Exp.)	07.58	08.00

Train No.	Train Name	Arr.	Dep.	Train No.	Train Name	Arr.	Dep.
17229 (Daily)	Tvm - Hyd (Sabari Exp.)	22.45	22.47	17311 (Fri)	Chn - Vas (Vasco Exp.)	16.08	16.10
17230 (Daily)	Hyd - Tvm (Sabari Exp.)	02.38	02.40	17312 (Fri)	Vas - Chn (Vasco Exp.)	09.28	09.30

Thanjavur

Train No.	Train Name	Arr.	Dep.	Train No.	Train Name	Arr.	Dep.
16177 (Daily)	Chn - Kbk (Rockfort)	06.15	06.20	12084 (Ex.Tu)	Cbe - Kbk (Jan Shatabdi)	11.43	11.45
16178 (Daily)	Kbk - Chn (Rockfort)	20.25	20.30	16231 (Daily)	Myl - Msr (Mysore Exp.)	19.10	19.15
12083 (Ex.Tu)	Kbk - Cbe (Jan Shatabdi)	15.38	15.40	16232 (Daily)	Msr - Myl (Mayiladuturai)	05.03	05.05

Thiruchirappalli

Train No.	Train Name	Arr.	Dep.	Train No.	Train Name	Arr.	Dep.
11043 (Sat)	LmT - Mdu (Madurai Exp.)	08.45	08.50	12652 (Thu,Sat)	Hnm - Mdu (Sampark Kranti)	00.35	00.40
1044 (Sat)	Mdu - LmT (Lokamanya TT)	20.45	20.50	12661 (Daily)	Chn - Tks (Pothigai Exp.)	01.35	01.40
12605 (Daily)	Chn - Trc (Pallavan Exp.)	21.20	-	12662 (Daily)	Tks - Chn (Pothigai Exp.)	01.10	01.15
12606 (Daily)	Trc - Chn (Pallavan Exp.)	-	06.30	12693 (Daily)	Chn - Ttn (Pearl City Exp.)	01.25	01.30
12631 (Daily)	Chn - Tnv (Nellai Exp.)	02.30	02.35	12694 (Daily)	Ttn - Chn (Pearl City Exp.)	01.25	01.30
12632 (Daily)	Tnv - Chn (Nellai Exp.)	00.20	00.25	16127 (Daily)	Chn - Grv (Guruvayur)	13.05	13.15
12633 (Daily)	Chn - Knk (Kanyakumari)	23.00	23.05	16128 (Daily)	Grv - Chn (Guruvayur)	14.05	14.10
12634 (Daily)	Knk - Chn (Kanyakumari)	00.30	00.35	16177 (Daily)	Chn - Kbk (Rockfort Exp.)	05.30	05.40
12635 (Daily)	Mdu - Chn (Vaigai Exp.)	18.05	18.15	16178 (Daily)	Kbk - Chn (Rockfort Exp.)	21.55	22.20
12636 (Daily)	Mdu - Chn (Vaigai Exp.)	08.45	08.50	16351 (Wed,Sun)	Mmb - Ngc (Nagercoil Exp.)	20.40	20.45
12637 (Daily)	Chn - Mdu (Pandian Exp.)	03.00	03.05	16352 (Thu,Sun)	Ngc - Mmb (Mumbai Exp.)	12.25	12.30
12638 (Daily)	Mdu - Chn (Pandian Exp.)	23.10	23.15	16723 (Daily)	Chn - Tvm (Ananthapuri)	01.10	01.20
12641 (Thu)	Knk - Niz (Thirukural Exp.)	02.55	03.00	16724 (Daily)	Chn - Tvm (Ananthapuri)	02.10	02.15
12642 (Mon)	Niz - Knk (Thirukural Exp.)	00.35	00.40	16865 (Daily)	Krk - Enk (Ernakulam)	20.00	20.10
12651 (Tue,Sun)	Hnm - Mdu (Sampark Kranti)	02.55	03.00	16866 (Daily)	Krk - Ngr (Karaikal Exp.)	07.40	07.50

Train No.	Train Name	Arr.	Dep.	Train No.	Train Name	Arr.	Dep.

Madurai

Train No.	Train Name	Arr.	Dep.	Train No.	Train Name	Arr.	Dep.
11043 (Sat)	Lmt - Mdu (Madurai Exp.)	12.30	-	12662 (Daily)	Tks - Chn (Pothigai Exp.)	22.05	22.10
11044 (Sat)	Mdu - Lmt (Lokamanya TT)	-	18.00	12693 (Daily)	Chn - Ttn (Pearl City Exp.)	04.15	04.20
12631 (Daily)	Chn - Tnv (Nellai Exp.)	05.25	05.30	12694 (Daily)	Ttn - Chn (Pearl City Exp.)	22.45	22.50
12632 (Daily)	Tnv - Chn (Nellai Exp.)	21.25	21.30	16127 (Daily)	Chn - Grv (Guruvayur)	16.35	16.40
12633 (Daily)	Chn - Knk (Kanyakumari)	01.55	02.00	16128 (Daily)	Grv - Chn (Guruvayur)	11.00	11.10
12634 (Daily)	Knk - Chn (Kanyakumari)	21.45	21.50	16339 (Thu,Fri, Sat,Mon)	Mmb - Ngc (Nagercoil Exp.)	21.15	21.20
12635 (Daily)	Chn - Mdu (Vaigai Exp.)	20.50	-	16340 (Mon,Tue, Wed,Fri)	Ngc - Mmb (Mumbai Exp.)	11.45	11.50
12636 (Daily)	Mdu - Chn (Vaigai Exp.)	-	06.45	16351 (Thu,Mon)	Mmb - Ngc (Nagercoil Exp.)	00.35	00.40
12637 (Daily)	Chn - Mdu (Pandian Exp.)	06.15	-	16352 (Thu,Sun)	Ngc - Mmb (Mumbai Exp.)	09.45	09.50
12638 (Daily)	Mdu - Chn (Pandian Exp.)	-	20.35	16723 (Daily)	Chn - Tvm (Ananthapuri)	03.50	03.55
12641 (Wed)	Knk - Niz (Thirukural Exp.)	23.45	23.50	16724 (Daily)	Chn - Tvm (Ananthapuri)	23.00	23.05
12642 (Mon)	Niz - Knk (Thirukural Exp.)	03.25	03.30	16731 (Daily)	Ttn - Msr (Mysore Exp.)	19.45	19.50
12651 (Mon,Sat)	Mdu - Hnm (Sampark Kranti)	-	23.55	16732 (Daily)	Msr - Ttn (Tuticorin Exp.)	07.20	07.25
12652 (Thu,Sat)	Hnm - Mdu (Sampark Kranti)	03.45	-				
12661 (Daily)	Chn - Tks (Pothigai Exp.)	04.40	04.45				

Tirunelveli

Train No.	Train Name	Arr.	Dep.	Train No.	Train Name	Arr.	Dep.
12631 (Daily)	Chn - Tnv (Nellai Exp.)	08.30	-	16339 (Fri,Sat, Sun,Tue)	Mmb - Ngc (Nagercoil Exp.)	01.15	01.20
12632 (Daily)	Tnv - Chn (Nellai Exp.)	-	18.35	16340 (Mon,Tue Wed,Fri)	Ngc - Mmb (Mumbai Exp.)	08.30	08.40
12633 (Daily)	Chn - Knk (Kanyakumari)	04.45	04.50	16351 (Thu,Mon)	Mmb - Ngc (Nagercoil Exp.)	03.40	03.45
12634 (Daily)	Knk - Chn (Kanyakumari)	18.55	19.00	16352 (Thu,Sun)	Ngc - Mmb (Nagercoil Exp.)	06.15	06.20
12641 (Wed)	Knk - Niz (Thirukural Exp.)	20.50	20.55	16723 (Daily)	Chn - Tvm (Ananthapuri)	06.55	07.00
12642 (Mon)	Niz - Knk (Thirukural Exp.)	06.25	06.30	16724 (Daily)	Chn - Tvm (Ananthapuri)	19.40	19.50
16127 (Daily)	Chn - Grv (Guruvayur)	19.25	19.30				
16128 (Daily)	Grv - Chn (Guruvayur)	07.40	07.50				

Train No.	Train Name	Arr.	Dep.	Train No.	Train Name	Arr.	Dep.

Nagercoil Jn.

Train No.	Train Name	Arr.	Dep.	Train No.	Train Name	Arr.	Dep.
12633 (Daily)	Chn - Knk (Kanyakumari)	06.10	06.15	16339 (Fri,Sat, Sun,Tue)	Mmb - Ngc (Nagercoil Exp.)	03.15	-
12634 (Daily)	Knk - Chn (Kanyakumari)	17.35	17.40	16340 (Mon,Tue Wed,Fri)	Ngc - Mmb (Mumbai Exp.)	-	06.55
12641 (Wed)	Knk - Niz (Thirukural Exp.)	19.35	19.40	16351 (Thu,Mon)	Mmb - Ngc (Nagercoil Exp.)	05.35	-
12642 (Mon)	Niz - Knk (Thirukural Exp.)	08.10	08.15	16352 (Thu,Sun)	Ngc - Tpt (Mumbai Exp.)	-	04.40
16127 (Daily)	Chn - Grv (Guruvayur)	21.25	21.40	16525 (Daily)	Knk - Blr (Bangalore)	10.50	10.55
16128 (Daily)	Grv - Chn (Guruvayur)	05.30	05.45	16526 (Daily)	Blr - Knk (Kanyakumari)	17.25	17.35
16317 (Fri)	Knk - Jmt (Himsagar)	14.20	14.25	16723 (Daily)	Chn - Tvm (Ananthapuri)	09.00	09.10
16318 (Thu)	Jmt - Knk (Himsagar)	21.10	21.15	16724 (Daily)	Chn - Tvm (Ananthapuri)	17.40	17.55
16335 (Sun)	Gnd - Ngc (Nagercoil)	04.45	-				
16336 (Tue)	Ngc - Gnd (Gandhidham)	-	13.30				

Tuticorin Jn.

Train No.	Train Name	Arr.	Dep.	Train No.	Train Name	Arr.	Dep.
12693 (Daily)	Chn - Ttn (Pearl City Exp.)	07.30	-	16731 (Daily)	Ttn - Msr (Mysore Exp.)	-	16.35
12694 (Daily)	Ttn - Chn (Pearl City Exp.)	-	19.45	16732 (Daily)	Msr - Ttn (Tuticorin Exp.)	11.00	-

Kanyakumari

Train No.	Train Name	Arr.	Dep.	Train No.	Train Name	Arr.	Dep.
12633 (Daily)	Chn - Knk (Kanyakumari)	06.50	-	16317 (Fri)	Knk - Jmt (Himsagar Exp.)	-	14.00
12634 (Daily)	Knk - Chn (Kanyakumari)	-	17.20	16318 (Thu)	Jmt - Hwr (Himsagar Exp.)	22.00	-
12641 (Wed)	Knk - Niz (Thirukural Exp.)	-	19.15	16525 (Daily)	Knk - Blr (Banglore)	-	10.30
12642 (Mon)	Niz - Knk (Thirukural Exp.)	08.45	-	16526 (Daily)	Blr - Knk (Kanyakumari)	19.00	-

Census - 2011 (Tamil Nadu)

	Population			Population Growth during last decade (2001-2011)	Literacy Rate (in %)			Density (per sq. km.)	Sex Ratio (per 1000 Male)
	Male	Female	Total		Male	Female	Total		
Tamil Nadu	36,158,871	35,980,087	72,138,958	15.60	86.81	73.86	80.33	555	995
Ariyalur	3,73,319	3,79,162	7,52,481	81.19	82.06	62.22	71.99	387	1016
Chennai	23,57,633	23,23,454	46,81,087	7.77	93.47	87.16	90.33	26,903	986
Coimbatore	17,35,362	17,37,216	34,72,578	19.06	89.49	79.16	84.31	748	1001
Cuddalore	13,11,151	12,89,729	26,00,880	13.80	86.84	71.20	79.04	702	984
Dharmapuri	7,72,490	7,30,410	15,02,900	16.04	69.16	60.03	64.71	332	946
Dindigul	10,81,934	10,79,433	21,61,367	12.39	84.91	68.82	76.85	357	998
Erode	11,34,191	11,25,417	22,59,608	12.05	80.81	65.07	72.96	397	992
Kancheepuram	20,10,309	19,80,588	39,90,897	38.69	90.34	80.17	85.29	927	986
Kanniyakumari	9,26,800	9,36,374	18,63,174	11.17	93.86	90.45	92.14	1106	1010
Karur	5,34,392	5,42,196	10,76,588	15.06	84.86	67.05	75.86	371	1015
Krishnagiri	9,63,152	9,20,579	18,83,731	20.67	79.65	64.86	72.41	370	956
Madurai	15,28,308	15,12,730	30,41,038	17.95	86.55	76.74	81.66	823	990
Nagapattinam	7,97,214	8,16,855	16,14,069	8.41	90.38	78.00	84.09	568	1025
Namakkal	8,66,740	8,54,439	17,21,179	15.25	83.09	66.68	74.92	506	986
Perambalur	2,81,436	2,83,075	5,64,511	14.36	83.39	66.11	74.68	323	1006
Pudukottai	8,03,337	8,15,388	16,18,725	10.90	86.19	69.51	77.76	348	1015

Census - 2011 (Tamil Nadu)

	Population			Population Growth during last decade (1991-2011)	Literacy Rate (in %)			Density (per sq. km.)	Sex Ratio (per 1000 Male)
	Male	Female	Total		Male	Female	Total		
Ramanathapuram	6,76,574	6,60,986	13,37,560	12.63	87.89	74.93	81.48	320	977
Salem	17,80,569	16,99,439	34,80,008	15.37	80.70	65.43	73.23	663	954
Sivagangai	6,70,597	6,70,653	13,41,250	16.09	88.61	72.33	80.46	324	1000
Thanjavur	11,83,112	12,19,669	24,02,781	8.42	89.06	76.61	82.72	691	1031
The Nilgiris	3,60,170	3,74,901	7,35,071	-3.55	92.15	79.44	85.65	288	1041
Theni	6,24,922	6,18,762	12,43,684	13.69	85.48	69.72	77.62	433	990
Thiruchirappalli	13,47,863	13,65,995	27,13,858	12.22	90.00	77.24	83.56	602	1013
Thiruvallur	18,78,559	18,47,138	37,25,697	35.25	89.18	78.39	83.82	1049	983
Thiruvannamalai	12,38,688	12,30,277	24,68,965	12.94	83.73	65.71	74.72	399	993
Thiruvarur	6,27,616	6,40,478	12,68,094	8.43	89.65	77.02	83.26	533	1020
Tirunelveli	15,18,595	15,54,285	30,72,880	13.66	89.66	76.38	82.92	458	1024
Thoothukkudi	8,58,919	8,79,457	17,38,376	9.14	91.42	81.77	86.52	378	1024
Vellore	19,59,676	19,68,430	39,28,106	12.96	86.96	72.43	79.65	646	1004
Viluppuram	17,44,832	17,18,452	34,63,284	16.99	80.58	63.51	72.08	482	985
Virudunagar	9,67,437	9,75,872	19,43,309	10.96	88.46	73.14	80.75	454	1009